Renewable Energy Technologies
in Africa

African Energy Policy Research Series

African Energy: Issues in Planning and Practice
AFREPREN (1990)

Energy Management in Africa
M. R. Bhagavan and S. Karekezi (eds)
(1992)

Rural Electrification in Africa
V. Ranganathan (ed.)
(1992)

Energy Options for Africa: Environmentally Sustainable Alternatives
S. Karekezi and Gordon Mackenzie (eds)
(in association with the UNEP Collaborating Centre on Energy and
Environment)
(1994)

Biomass Energy and Coal in Africa
D. O. Hall and Y. S. Mao (eds)
(1994)

Energy Utilities and Institutions in Africa
M. R. Bhagavan (ed.)
(1996)

Transport and Energy in Africa
M. R. Bhagavan (ed.)
(1996)

Renewable Energy Technologies in Africa
S. Karekezi and T. Ranja
(1997)

Biomass Energy Policy in Africa
D. O. Hall (ed.)
(1997)

Renewable Energy Technologies in Africa

Stephen Karekezi and Timothy Ranja

Zed Books Ltd
LONDON & NEW JERSEY

in association with

African Energy Policy Research Network
(Afrepren)

and

The Stockholm Environment Institute (SEI)

Renewable Energy Technologies in Africa
was first published by
Zed Books Ltd, 7 Cynthia Street, London N1 9JF, UK and
165 First Avenue, Atlantic Highlands, New Jersey 07716, USA
in association with
the African Energy Policy Research Network (AFREPREN),
PO Box 30979, Nairobi, Kenya
and
the Stockholm Environment Institute (SEI),
PO Box 2142, S-103 14, Stockholm, Sweden,
in 1997.

Copyright © African Energy Policy Research Network (AFREPREN), 1997
Cover design by Andrew Corbett.
Laserset by Longhouse Publishing Services,
Cumbria, UK
Printed and bound in the United Kingdom
by Biddles Ltd., Guildford and King's Lynn

A catalogue record for this book
is available from the British Library

Library of Congress Cataloging-in-Publication Data
Karekezi, Stephen.
 Renewable energy technologies in Africa / by Stephen Karekezi
and Timothy Ranja.
  p. cm.
 Includes bibliographical references and index.
 ISBN 1-85649-089-0 (hd.) -- ISBN 1-85649-090-4 (pb)
 1. Renewable energy sources--Africa. I. Ranja, Timothy, 1972-
  II. African Energy Policy Research Network. III. Stockholm
Environment Institute. IV. Title.
TJ807.9.A35K37 1997
 333.79'4'096--dc21   97-5701
                                                              CIP

ISBN   Hb 1 85649 089 0
        Pb 1 85649 090 4

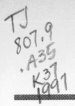

TJ
807.9
.A35
K37
1991

Contents

List of figures

List of tables

List of boxes

List of appendices

List of Abbreviations

ACFC	Agro-Chemical and Food Corporation (Kenya)
ACTS	African Centre for Technological Studies (Kenya)
ADB	Agricultural Development Bank
ADF	African Development Foundation
AFREPREN	African Energy Policy Research Network
ARCSE	African Regional Centre for Solar Energy (Burundi)
ARDA	Agricultural Rural Development Authority (Zimbabwe)
ATC	Appropriate Technology Centre (Kenya)
ATS	Appropriate Technology Section (Lesotho)
BHEL	Bob Harries Engineering Limited
BIG/STIG	Biomass-Integrated Gasifier/Steam-Injected Turbine
BIG/GT	Biomass-Integrated Gasifier/Gas Turbine
BOOT	Build, Own, Operate, Transfer
BRET	Botswana Renewable Energy Technology Project
BTC	Botswana Technology Centre.
BTI	Butwal Technical Institute (Nepal)
BUN	Biomass Users Network
CAMARTEC	Centre for Agricultural Mechanization and Rural Technology (Tanzania)
CEB	Central Electricity Board
CEBEA	Centre for Alternative Energy (Burundi)
CEST	Condensing-Extraction Steam Turbine
COMESA	Common Market of Eastern and Southern Africa
CRT	Centre for Rural Technology
CRUEA	University Research Center for Utilization of Alternative Energy (Burundi)
CSC	Commonwealth Science Council
DANIDA	Danish International Development Association
DC	Direct current
DENROI	Developpement des Energies Nouvelles et Renouvelables dans l'Ocean Indien
DOE	Department of Energy
DTC	Development Technology Centre (Zimbabwe)
DUB	Bujumbura Urban Development (Burundi)
EIA	Energy Initiatives for Africa
EDF	European Development Fund
EDI	Energy/Development International (US)
EDRC	Energy for Development Research Centre (South Africa)
EEC	European Economic Community

EFTA	European Free Trade Association
EIC	Energy Information Centre
ERC	Energy Research Council (Kenya)
ESCOM	Electricity Supply Commission of Malawi
ESKOM	Electricity Supply Commission (South Africa)
ESMAP	Energy Sector Management Assistance Programme
ETHCO	Ethanol Company Limited (Malawi)
EU	European Union
FAO	Food and Agricultural Organization
FINESSE	Financing Energy Services for Small-Scale Energy Users
FOREX	Foreign Exchange
FUEL	Flacq United Estate Limited
FWD	Foundation for Woodstove Dissemination
GDP	Gross Domestic Product
GEF	Global Environment Facility
GHG	Greenhouse Gases
GTZ	Deutsche Gesellschaft Fur Technische Zusammenarbeit (German Technical Cooperation Organization)
HAWT	Horizontal Axis Wind Turbine
HRSG	Heat Recovery Steam Generator
IBRD	International Bank of Reconstruction and Development
IEE	Initial Environmental Examination (Madagascar)
IFSC	International Forest Science Consultancy
IGADD	Inter-Governmental Agency for Drought and Desertification
IIED	International Institute for Environment and Development
ISERST	National Science and Technology Institute (Djibouti)
ISES	International Solar Energy Society
ITDG	Intermediate Technology Development Group (UK)
IUCN	International Union for the Conservation of Nature
JEEP	Joint Energy and Environment Project (Uganda)
JIRAMA	Jiro Sy Rano Malagasy (national electricity and water utility, Madagascar)
KCFC	Kisumu Chemical and Food Corporation (Kenya)
KCJ	Kenya Ceramic Jiko
KENGO	Kenya Energy and Environment Organization
KPLC	Kenya Power and Lighting Company Limited
KREDP	Kenya Renewable Energy Development Project
LEC	Lesotho Electricity Company
LPG	Liquid Petroleum Gas
NCCK	National Council of Churches of Kenya
NEC	National Energy Council (Zambia)
NGO	Non-Governmental Organization
NMH	Northern Mini Hydro Corporation (Australia)
NORAD	Norwegian Agency for Research and Development
NRA	National Range Agency (Somalia)
NRI	National Resources Institute
NRSE	New and Renewable Sources of Energy
ODA	Overseas Development Agency
ONATEL	Office Nationale de la Tourbe (Burundi)
PV	Photovoltaic

RAPS	Remote Area Power Supplies (South Africa)
REDPU	Renewable Energy Development Project Unit
REF	Rural Electrification Fund (Zambia)
REFAD	Renewable Energy for African Development
RENEL	Romanian Electric Authority
RET	Renewable Energy Technology
RIIC	Rural Industries Innovations Centre (Botswana)
RRA	Rapid Rural Appraisal
RTE	Rural Technologies Enterprises
RWEPA	Regional Wood Energy Programme for Africa
SADC	Southern Africa Development Community
SADCC	Southern African Development Coordination Conference
SAPP	Southern African Power Pool
SAREC	Swedish Agency for Research Cooperation with Developing Countries
SEI	Stockholm Environment Institute
SEIA	Solar Energy Industrial Association
SEP	Special Energy Programme (Kenya)
SERI	Solar Energy Research Institute (US)
SHEP	Stove and Household Energy Programme
SHP	Small Hydro Power
SIDA	Swedish International Development Cooperation Agency
SIF	Seychelles Islands Foundation
SREP	Sudan Renewable Energy Project
SSA	Sub-Saharan Africa
SWH	Solar Water Heater
TANESCO	Tanzanian Electricity Supply Commission
TDAU	Technology Development and Advisory Unit (Zambia)
TWICO	Tanzanian Wood Industry Corporation
UEB	Ugandan Electricity Board
UMN	United Mission to Nepal
UNDP	United Nations Development Programme
UNDTCP	United Nations Department of Technical Cooperation for Development
UNEP	United Nations Environmental Programme
UNESCO	United Nations Education, Scientific and Cultural Organization
UNICEF	United Nations Children's Fund
UNIDO	United Nations Industrial Development Organization
UNSO	United Nations Sudano-Sahelian Office
USAID	United States Agency for International Development
USSIA	Uganda Small-Scale Industries Association
VAWT	Vertical Axis Wind Turbine
VITA	Volunteers in Technical Assistance (USA)
WEC	World Energy Council (UK)
WEP	Women and Energy Project
WHO	World Health Organization
YWCA	Young Women's Christian Association
ZEEP	Zambian Environment Education Programme
ZESCO	Zambian Electricity Supply Corporation

List of Units

CO	Carbon monoxide
CO_2	Carbon dioxide
CH_4	Methane
C_2H_5OH	Ethyl alcohol
DM	Deutschmark
GW	Gigawatts
GWh	gigawatt hours
GW/yr	Gigawatts per year
H_2S	Hydrogen sulphide
K	Kwacha (Zambian currency)
kg	kilograms
kgoe	kilograms oil equivalent
km	kilometres
km^2	square kilometres
Ksh	Kenya shillings
KV	Kilovolt
KW	Kilowatts
KWh	Kilowatt hours
KWp	Kilowatts peak
l/s	litres per second
m^3	cubic metres
m/s	metres per second
MJ	Megajoules
MW	Megawatts
MWp	Megawatts peak
P	Pula (Botswana's currency)
rpm	rotations per minute
tc	tonne of cane
t/yr	tonnes per year
TJ	Terajoules
TWh	Terawatt hours
TWh/yr	Terawatt hours per year
US$	United States dollars
Wp	Watts peak

Acknowledgements

The authors gratefully acknowledge the support for the preparation of this publication provided by SIDA-SAREC (Swedish International Development Co-operation Agency), and the Stockholm Environment Institute (SEI).

We would also like to thank the following for taking their time to review the drafts of this report and providing extremely useful comments: Dr. Jenny Gregory, Intermediate Technology Power Ltd., U.K.; Dr. Monica Gullberg, Stockholm Environment Institute; Professor Bjorn Kjellstrom, Stockholm Environment Institute; Dr. Niels Juhl Thomsen, Riso National Laboratory Research Unit; Mr. Abeeku Brew-Hammond University of Sussex, Science Policy Research Unit, UK; Dr. Keith Kozloff, World Resource Institute; Dr. Steve Meyers, Lawrence Berkerly Laboratory, USA; Thomas Theisohn, Germany; Dr. John Aluma, National Agricultural Research Organization (NARO), Uganda; and Dr. Joy Dunkerly, USA.

In addition the authors wish to acknowledge the support of Lugard Majoro, Alex Tibwitta, Raphael Owino and Esther Ewagata in providing invaluable comments and assistance in editing this report. Other researchers and research assistants who provided valuable assistance include Patience Turyareeba, John Kimani, Mary Muthoni, Ottieno Francis, Ann Njoroge, J.K. Onyango-Abuje, Stanley Bii, Crispin Musumba, Kyalo Kibua, Eunice Gichangi, Pauline Kiraithe, Anne Kinyanjui, Wanjiru Mbuthia and Albert Waudo.

Relevant background information and data for this paper was sourced from, among other documents, research papers of the African Energy Policy Research Network (AFREPREN), particularly the early drafts of a regional study on renewable energy technologies by S. Karekezi and P. Turyareeba, and the 6 country case study reports namely; Botswana (M. Mosimanyane), Kenya (S. Karekezi and E. Ewagata), Lesotho (T. Phuroe), Seychelles (M. Razanajatovo), Uganda (G. Turyahikayo), and Zambia (R. Sampa). Their reports constituted an invaluable source of reference.

About the Authors

Stephen Karekezi is Director of the African Energy Policy Research Network (AFREPREN) as well as Executive Secretary of the Foundation for Woodstove Dissemination (FWD), Nairobi, Kenya. In 1995, he was appointed a member of the Scientific and Technical Advisory Panel (STAP) of the Global Environment Facility (GEF) co-managed by the World Bank, UNDP and UNEP. Stephen Karekezi is an engineer with post-graduate qualifications in management and economics. He has written, co-authored and edited some 87 publications, journal articles, papers and reports on energy and sustainable development. In 1990, he received the Development Association Award in Stockholm, Sweden in recognition of his work on the development and dissemination of the Kenyan Ceramic Jiko energy-efficient cooking stove.

Timothy Ranja is a natural scientist with specialized training in geography and education. He has wide experience in energy policy research with special emphasis on renewable energy technologies. He has worked with the AFREPREN/FWD Secretariat in Nairobi, Kenya for the past four years in various capacities and is currently involved in the coordination of two major energy policy study programmes that bring together senior researchers and policy makers from Botswana, Ethiopia, Kenya, Malawi, Tanzania and Zambia. Mr Ranja has travelled widely in Eastern and Southern Africa and participated in renewable energy expert missions and meetings in Kenya, Swaziland and Zimbabwe.

1

About AFREPREN, SEI and FWD

About AFREPREN
The African Energy Policy Research Network, or AFREPREN, was created in 1989 with the aim of promoting research relating to the formulation and implementation of appropriate policy in the field of energy in countries of East, Central and Southern Africa. It also seeks to strengthen research capability within the region. Currently, under its sponsorship, over 90 African energy professionals from ten countries are engaged in research on six themes – institutions; management and efficiency; capacity building and technology; financing and markets; local and regional environment; and climate change. The Network is coordinated and administered by a professional secretariat based in Nairobi. AFREPREN is funded by the Swedish International Development Co-operation Agency (Sida) and the Norwegian Agency for Development Cooperation (NORAD).

About the Foundation for Woodstove Dissemination (FWD)
The Foundation for Woodstove Dissemination (FWD) is a not-for-profit voluntary agency established to support agencies working on household energy and related biomass energy issues. The FWD offers information and assistance aimed at helping regional and national agencies and networks carry out their improved bio-energy technologies dissemination activities more effectively. The structure of the FWD is decentralized with a strong emphasis on enhancing the institutional, management and technical capability of its network members.

About the Stockholm Environment Institute (SEI)
The Stockholm Environment Institute (SEI) is an international research institute focusing on local, regional and global energy and environmental issues. The scientific and administrative work of the Institute is co-ordinated by the SEI's headquarters in Stockholm, Sweden, with centres in Boston, USA, York, UK and Tallinn, Estonia. The SEI has an international network of independent scientists and research institutes located in many parts of the world, working on a wide range of energy and environmental issues.

Introduction

Africa has substantial new and renewable energy resources, with more than 3,140Twh of exploitable technical hydro-power potential, more than 9,000 megawatts of geothermal potential, abundant biomass potential, substantial solar potential and, in some countries, significant wind potential. In contrast to fossil fuel reserves, which are potentially major sources of harmful local and global emissions and tend to be concentrated in a few countries, renewable sources of energy are not only environmentally benign but are better distributed throughout the region. In addition, the prospects of a major increase in fossil fuel supply are constrained by the unequal distribution of reserves, which entails large investments in distribution.

Although reliable region-wide energy statistics are not readily available, existing estimates of energy use in Africa indicate a significant and persistent dependence on traditional biomass energy technologies and limited use of modern renewable energy technologies. The consumption of biomass in its traditional and unprocessed form entails significant losses and inefficient end use. A more cost-effective use of biomass resources in the region would require conversion to more modern and valuable gaseous and liquid fuels and electricity.

A wide range of renewable energy technologies (RETs) have been introduced in sub-Saharan Africa. Although there has been no widespread success, in an increasing number of instances substantial numbers of RETs have been disseminated in African countries. RETs that have registered encouraging results include:

- Bio-energy technologies;
- Solar energy technologies;
- Wind energy technologies for water pumping; and
- Small hydro-power technologies.

This report reviews the prospects of these RETs in Africa by examining their current status and the barriers that limit their wide-scale use, and drawing lessons for ongoing and future efforts to engineer large-scale dissemination of RETs in Africa, with special emphasis on Eastern and Southern African countries.

1

Bio-energy

Regional awareness of large-scale modern biomass energy systems is limited. Large-scale biomass utilization encompasses direct combustion for process heat; ethanol production; gasification; co-generation; biogas production; and large-scale briquetting. The best-known proven systems in the region are co-generation using biomass as fuel stock and the production of ethanol as a substitute for petroleum fuel. The prospects for large-scale use of biomass energy in the region are promising. A recent study suggests that biomass energy plantations on existing unused, deforested or degraded land in the region, coupled with modern conversion technologies, could meet two-fifths of the region's primary energy demand by the year 2025.

Biomass energy is an important fuel for many small-scale and medium-scale industries in Eastern and Southern Africa. Examples include brick manufacture, lime production, fish smoking, tobacco curing, beer brewing and coffee and tea drying. Many of these operate in rural or peri-urban areas, sectors which are poorly covered in official statistics. Consequently, information on this important biomass energy consumption sub-sector is inadequate. In the past 20 years, substantial efforts have been directed towards the modernization of small-scale biomass energy systems. Two of the most sustained efforts have been the development of an energy-efficient charcoal kiln and an environmentally sound, improved cookstove for rural and urban households in sub-Saharan Africa.

A number of energy-efficient charcoal kilns made of brick, metal, or a combination of the two have been developed. Improved stove programmes now number in the hundreds in the region. Such programmes, particularly those targeting urban households, are increasingly becoming an established component of national energy programmes. Other small-scale biomass energy technologies that have attracted considerable attention over the past three decades in the region include small-scale briquetting and household biogas.

Solar energy

In the foreseeable future, few rural African communities are likely to be connected to the national electric grid because of the difficult and distant terrain that has to be traversed by mains grid distribution networks. This is compounded by low population density, with people living in scattered homesteads. Solar energy technologies have a significant role in filling this lacuna. The rapid reduction in the cost of photovoltaic (PV) systems realized in the last three decades, the lowered cost of related systems, and innovative financing schemes are beginning to make PV systems affordable to many rural households and communities. The reliability of PV systems has also continued to improve, even in remote rural areas of the region with limited access to qualified maintenance support.

Wind

Largely as a result of low wind speeds, the bulk of wind machines found in Eastern and Southern Africa are used for water pumping rather than electricity generation. The development of wind energy continues to be hampered by the absence of adequate measurements of wind speeds and potential, especially at the micro level. In remote areas with high wind potential, wind pumps make economic sense for large agricultural live-stock farms as they are more reliable than diesel pumps, which often face fuel supply problems.

Small hydro

With the exception of Djibouti, all the countries in the region have hydro-power potential, and attempts have been made to harness this potential through smal hydro projects. Small hydro developed remarkably after the first oil crises and as a result of greater concern over the harmful environmental effects of fossil fuels. Unfortunately, past attempts at promoting hydro-power technologies have often focused on large-scale applications for generating electricity. The dominant paradigm was extended to small hydro development which inevitably led to high costs and inappropriate institutional structures. Consequently, potentially attractive opportunities for small hydro systems have not been fully exploited.

There is a growing consensus among policy makers that past efforts to disseminate RETs in Africa have fallen short of expectations. While it is recognized that RETs cannot solve all Africa's energy problems, RETs are still seen as having a significant unexploited potential to enable African countries to meet their growing energy requirements. Renewable energy is already the dominant source of energy for the household sub-sector. If properly harnessed, it could meet a significant proportion of energy demand from the industrial, agricultural, transport and commercial sub-sectors.

Despite recognition that they are an important source of energy for sub-Saharan Africa, RETs have attracted neither the requisite level of investment nor tangible policy commitment. Although national and international resources allocated to developing, adapting and disseminating RETs in the last two decades may appear substantial, the total amount is still insignificant compared to that allocated to fossil fuels.

In its analysis of RET dissemination in the region, the study indicates that success has been limited by a combination of factors which include:

1 Poor institutional framework and infrastructure;

2 Inadequate RET planning policies;

3 Lack of coordination and linkage in RET programmes;

4 Pricing distortions which have placed renewable energy at a disadvantage compared with conventional fossil fuels;

5 High initial investment costs coupled with the absence of supporting financial instruments;

6 Weak dissemination strategies and excessive emphasis on the service and welfare functions, rather than on production and the entrepreneurial approach;

7 Lack of skilled manpower;

8 Poor baseline information;

9 Inadequate technological bases for the large-scale manufacture and distribution of RETS; and

10 Weak maintenance service and infrastructure.

In spite of the above barriers, the prospects for RET development in Africa are good. Although there has been limited success, in a growing number of instances substantial numbers of RETs have been disseminated in Eastern and Southern African countries. Notable successful cases include the Kenyan ceramic *jiko* (KCJ), an improved charcoal stove; solar water heaters in Botswana; PV systems in Kenya, Botswana and Zimbabwe; ethanol in Zimbabwe; and biogas in Tanzania. Measures that would encourage the large-scale dissemination of RETs in the region include the following:

1 From the outset, renewable energy programmes should be aggressive, long-term, policy-oriented and aimed at senior decision makers in both government and the private sector. All the institutions and agencies involved in RETs should work more closely in the development and promotion of the programmes. The energy policy programme of AFREPREN and the Foundation for Woodstove Development (FWD) provides a model that needs to be expanded and replicated in the region.

2 Innovative and sustainable financing programmes for RETs should be instituted. Of particular interest are financing programmes that mobilize local resources and facilitate the bundling of discrete small credit schemes into major financing opportunities for large multilateral and bilateral financing agencies.

3 All sources of energy should account for the social and environmental cost they incur, to ensure a level playing field for renewable and conventional energy technologies.

4 New RET dissemination strategies that have demonstrated encouraging signs of success should be more widely applied. Many of these strategies revolve around participation, income generation and small-

scale enterprise development. Existing systems of production, marketing and information dissemination should be utilized to the maximum to reduce cost and ensure sustainability (piggy-back principle).

5 Long-term renewable energy training programmes designed to develop a critical mass of locally trained personnel with the requisite technical, economic and socio-cultural skills should be initiated. There should be maximum use of local researchers and consultants.

6 Greater emphasis should be placed on quality control and regular and preventive maintenance. Technical and maintenance skills should be developed.

7 Countries should carry out studies to document as accurately as possible the types, location and quantities of the various forms of renewable energy sources. This information should be made readily available and regularly updated.

8 Initiation of technology assessment and applied research engineering programmes that identify and disseminate mature and new RETs that are suitable for wide-scale dissemination in Africa.

Part I

The Background

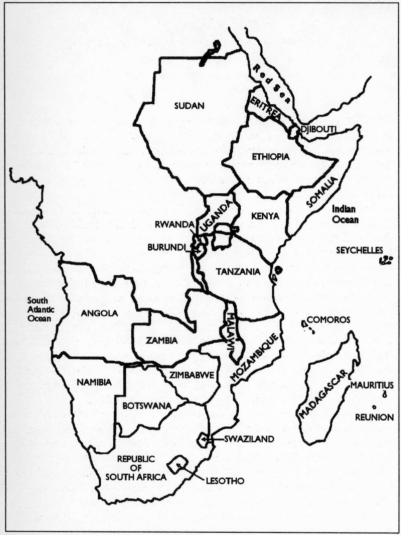

Note: Islands not to scale (enlarged to enhance visibility)

Figure 1.1 Eastern and Southern Africa

1

The Energy Sector in its
Geo-political and Socio-Economic Setting

The Eastern and Southern African region lies between 10°E and 60°E longitude, and between the Tropic of Cancer (23°N) and 35°S latitude, with the Indian Ocean to the east, the Atlantic Ocean to the west and the Sahara desert to the north, as shown in Figure 1.1. There are 25 countries in Eastern and Southern Africa, with very divergent geo-political and socio-economic characteristics.

The largest country in the region is the Sudan, with a total land area of 2,510,000 square kilometres (UNDP, 1994), while the smallest country is the Seychelles, with a total land area of 454 square kilometres, although this translates to 1.37 million square kilometres if the part of the Indian Ocean that falls under its jurisdiction is included. (Razanajatovo *et al.,* 1994). There are five island states in the region, namely Reunion, the Seychelles, Mauritius, Madagascar and the Comoros, and ten landlocked countries which consider the importation of fuels to be an issue of national security. The problem land-locked countries face in obtaining imported energy such as petroleum products is not simply physical and logistical. They also have to ensure good political relations with neighbouring countries which have coastal areas. During the war in Mozambique, the pipeline from Beira in Mozambique to Mutare in Zimbabwe was often guarded by Zimbabwean personnel.

The region has a diverse vegetative cover which includes tropical forests, mediterranean scrub, savannah woodlands, arid and semi-arid areas and mountain regions (Figure 1.2). Annual rainfall ranges from 25 mm in the arid areas of the Sudan and Namibia to 2,000 mm in the highlands of Madagascar and the islands of Lake Victoria. The highlands of Lesotho, Rwanda, Burundi and Kenya receive 1,600 mm/year (Chitauro, 1993). The widespread vegetative cover and relatively good rainfall pattern combine to bestow on the region a huge biomass potential. In addition, it is well endowed with both large and small rivers. Some of the major rivers include the Blue Nile, the White Nile, the Zambezi, the Limpopo and the Orange. All these rivers have large basins through which small rivers and streams flow. It is along these smaller tributary rivers that potential for small hydro-power (both mini- and micro) is found.

Wind speeds are generally low throughout the region, though speeds as high as 9.7 metres/second (m/s) have been recorded in South African coastal areas. Very low wind speeds (0.7 m/s) have been recorded in

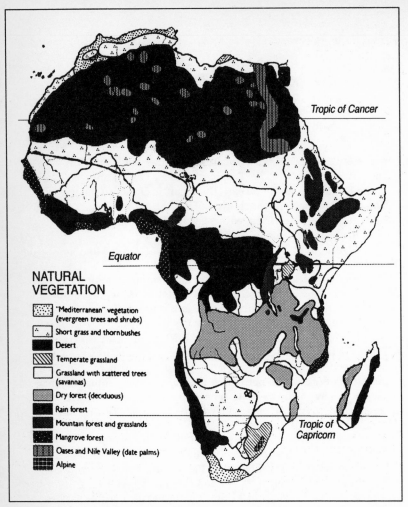

Figure 1.2 The vegetative cover of Africa
Source: Philips, 1995. *Philip's Atlas of the World.* George Philip Ltd, London.

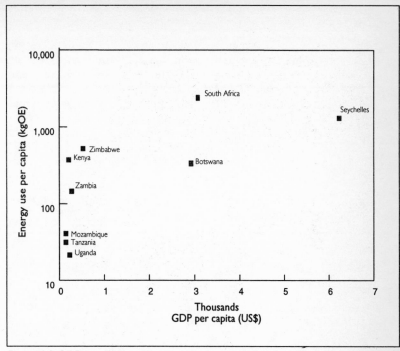

Figure 1.3 GDP *per capita* and energy use *per capita* in selected countries (1988)

Mozambique (Diab, 1988). Generally, the average wind speed in October is 2 to 4 m/s, with wind speeds of 6 m/s recorded on the north-western coast of Madagascar (Chitauro, 1993). This is an indication of poor to moderate wind energy potential. Average annual solar insolation ranges from 8,380 MJ/square metre in the Sudan to 6,688 MJ/square metre in other countries in the region (Le Houerou *et al.*, 1993): a clear indication of excellent solar energy potential.

The region's total population is 289.1 million, 68 per cent of whom live in rural areas (UNDP, 1994). Rwanda and Burundi (before the civil strife) had the highest percentage of rural population at 94 per cent and Djibouti the lowest at 14 per cent (UNDP, 1994). Population density ranges from 549 people per square kilometre in Mauritius to 2 people per square kilometre in Botswana (UNDP, 1994). Over half the population in the region live in rural areas, often in isolated homesteads which are difficult to supply with commercial energy. As a result, most countries have concentrated on supplying commercial energy to urban households and to commercial and industrial establishments. Rural energy infrastructure is almost without exception underdeveloped.

Economic issues

Generally, the real *per capita* gross domestic product (GDP) in the region is low, ranging from US$5,211 in Mauritius to US$370 in Ethiopia (UNDP, 1994). Some of the poorest countries in the world are in Eastern and Southern Africa, and some of these have not registered economic growth for more than two decades. This is reflected in the low energy consumption of the poorer nations. Figure 1.3 shows a correlation between GDP *per capita* and energy use *per capita*. As shown in Table 1.1, eight countries rely on agriculture while 12 rely mainly on services. Industry makes a major contribution in only three of the region's countries.

Table 1.1 Sectoral contribution to GDP as a percentage of total GDP in 1992

Country	Industry**	Manufacturing	Agriculture	Services
Angola*	23	3	46	31
Botswana	52	4	5	43
Burundi	20	15	54	26
Comoros*	14	4	36	50
Ethiopia	13	8	48	39
Kenya	19	12	27	54
Lesotho	45	17	11	45
Madagascar	14	–	33	53
Malawi	22	15	28	50
Mauritius	33	23	11	56
Mozambique	15	–	64	21
Namibia	26	6	12	62
Rwanda	22	16	41	37
Somalia	9	5	65	26
South Africa	42	25	4	54
Sudan	17	9	34	50
Swaziland*	30	20	24	46
Seychelles	18	9	6	76
Tanzania	12	5	61	26
Uganda	11	4	57	32
Zambia	47	36	16	37
Zimbabwe	35	30	22	43

* 1987 figures. ** Includes manufacturing

Sources: World Bank, 1989 and 1994.

In most countries in the region, the energy sector is responsible for a major portion of the national debt, incurred to establish large facilities for generating and distributing electricity. Total debt in the region was

US$69.1 billion in 1993, excluding Namibia, Somalia, Reunion and Eritrea (STARS World Tables, 1995). Between 10 and 30 per cent of total GDP is spent on the energy sector (Jhirad, 1990). Debt service ratios are very high. For example, the World Bank estimated that in 1992 Uganda spent 40.2 per cent of its export earnings on debt security (World Bank, 1994).

Access to adequate levels of energy services is a crucial prerequisite for the development of any country (Karekezi, 1994). For example, in Mauritius, energy consumption in the industrial and commercial sectors increased more than fourfold from 1970 to 1989, while GDP increased by a factor of 25. Thus the ratio of electricity demand per capita increased from 168KWh in 1970 to 568KWh in 1989 while GDP per capita increased from US$800 to US$1,865 respectively (Baguant, 1992). The decline in non-commercial use of biomass and increased commercial use is also viewed as an indication of socio-economic development (Zandbergen and Moreira, 1993). When compared to developed countries, the per capita commercial energy consumption for Sub-Saharan Africa was 135 kilogrammes of oil equivalent (kgoe) in 1991, which is still very low (Karekezi, 1994d). The comparative figure for Latin America and the Caribbean, and the Middle East and North Africa was 1,051 kgoe and 1,185 kgoe respectively (ibid.). Generally, most countries (except Mozambique) have had small increases in energy consumption, but some countries registered decreases between 1960 and 1991, notably the Sudan, Uganda, Zambia, Kenya and Tanzania (UNDP, 1994).

The energy sector

Energy supply
Although the Eastern and Southern African region has substantial conventional energy resources, these resources are not available in all countries in the region, as shown in Figure 1.4. Fifteen out of 25 countries have proven conventional energy reserves. There are 132,116 million metric tonnes of proven coal reserves in place distributed in 9 countries. Uranium is found in four countries, with a total of 453,550 metric tonnes of proven reserves. Proven reserves of crude oil amounting to 291 million metric tonnes are found in two countries (World Resources Institute, 1994: 336).

Renewable energy resources are better distributed. Biomass is available in almost all countries in the region. Hydro-electricity is available in most countries except Djibouti. Solar energy is available in all countries in the region and wind energy, exploitable at 3 m/s, is available in most countries. Geothermal energy, with exploitable potential estimated at 8,975 MW, is distributed in 15 countries (Musa, 1993).

Energy demand
Biomass has continued to dominate the energy sector in Eastern and Southern Africa, as shown in Figure 1.5. In 1990, biomass supplied 54 per cent of the total energy demand in sub-Saharan Africa (World Energy

Figure 1.4 Fossil fuel resources in Eastern and Southern Africa
Source: WEC, 1994. Session 3 – 'Supply of Energy; Rapporteurs Report', World Energy Council Regional Energy Forum for Southern and East African Countries, Cape Town, South Africa, 13–14 October 1994.

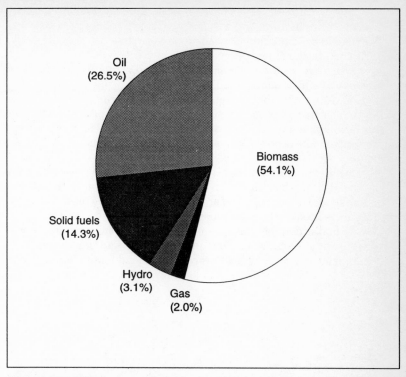

Figure 1.5 Total primary energy demand in 1990 for sub-Saharan Africa (including South Africa)

Source: World Energy Council, 1992

Table 1.2 Household energy consumption as a percentage of total biomass consumption in selected countries

Country	Biomass energy consumption (% of total energy consumption)	Household energy consumption (% of total biomass energy)
Burundi	94	78.5
Ethiopia	86	97
Kenya	70	93
Somalia	87	92
Sudan	84	90
Uganda	95	78.6

Source: FWD, 1992

Council, 1992). Currently the household sector dominates energy demand in most countries in the region, as shown in Table 1.2, but this is expected to change as economic growth leads to greater demand from industry, transport and the commercial sector.

The transport sector has continued to grow rapidly, particularly between 1973 and 1980, a period of low economic growth in the region (Davidson, 1993). Distribution networks are also growing to meet growing demand. The transport sector is, therefore, a major priority sector for energy development. Production of biomass-based liquid fuels can replace 20 per cent or more of petroleum requirements, as experience in Zimbabwe has shown.

Agricultural production mainly depends on animated power which is always available if the human and animal population is healthy and has sufficient food. Increasing use of arable land may require mechanization, leading to the increased use of modern energy. Currently, agro-processing activities such as crop-growing rely mainly on direct solar and traditional biomass energy. Deployment of more efficient agro-processing technologies on a larger scale will also increase demand for modern energy.

Part 2

The Development and Role
of Renewable Energy Technologies
in Africa

An Introductory Note to Part 2

With the exception of biomass, renewable energy is presently a minor contributor to the energy supply of Eastern and Southern Africa, accounting for less than 2 per cent of the total supply (Karekezi, 1994d). However, its potential vis-a-vis the decentralized energy needs of the rural population and its environmentally benign nature makes it an attractive option for meeting the future energy needs of the region. Increased consumption of non-renewable forms of energy, particularly fossil fuels, not only has adverse effects on the environment but further drains the region's limited reserves of convertible currencies.

Eastern and Southern Africa could eschew the traditional energy-intensive and environmentally harmful modernization path of the North and develop an ecologically sound path to sustainable development by investing in increased consumption of modern renewable energy (Karekezi, 1994d). While Sub-Saharan Africa (SSA) has significant unexploited reserves of fossil fuels, the prospects for major increases in fossil fuel supply are constrained by the unequal distribution of reserves which entails large investments in distribution. According to the BP Shell Statistical Review of World Energy (1992), known petroleum reserves in Africa at the end of 1991 amounted to 60.4 thousand million barrels with 40 per cent and 30 per cent of this reserve located in Libya and Nigeria respectively. In addition, it states that most of the natural gas reserves are also concentrated in two countries – namely Algeria which has 3,300 billion m^3 and Nigeria which had 2,800 billion m^3. As far as recoverable coal reserves are concerned, South Africa is stated to have had a share of 55,333 million tonnes while the whole of Africa had a total of 60,811 million tonnes. Renewable energy resources are, on the other hand, relatively well distributed in the region and would not require major investments in energy distribution networks.

The modular nature of renewable energy technologies would allow even the poorest countries in the region to begin a phased energy investment programme that would not strain its national financial resources or draw funds away from other pressing basic needs such as nutrition, health, shelter and education needs (Karekezi, 1994d).

A wide range of RETs has been developed and introduced in the region. This section addresses four key mature RETs, namely biomass, solar, wind and small hydro energy technologies. Each section examines the fundamentals of the technology, global and regional dissemination status with case studies examined for each technology.

2

Bio-Energy

Bio-energy refers to energy derived from the combustion or transformation (into liquid or gaseous fuel) of biomass. Biomass is the organic material produced by photosynthesis, a process that converts solar energy into stored chemical energy (UNIDO, 1994). Fourteen per cent of the energy consumed in the world, and 35 per cent of consumption in developing countries, is obtained from biomass (Hall, 1993a). Biomass is used in the household and industrial sectors as well as in electricity generation. Bio-energy potential in Eastern and Southern Africa varies from high-potential areas with vast forests to low-potential desert and semi-desert areas, and depends on natural and artificial regeneration.

This chapter focuses on biomass energy in its modern, efficient and environmentally benign form, as opposed to its traditional form. The technologies discussed are those that enhance the most efficient utilization of biomass, whether on a large or a small scale. Large-scale commercial applications require substantial investment and a wide distribution network; they produce large amounts of energy and create employment for many people, both directly and indirectly. Small-scale commercial and subsistence applications, on the other hand, create a limited number of jobs per unit, but generate a large number at an aggregate level.

Large-scale biomass energy applications

The applications commonly included under large-scale biomass are co-generation, ethanol production, large-scale biogas production, large-scale briquetting, direct combustion for process heat, and gasification. These produce heat, electricity, liquid fuels, solid fuels and combustible gases.

Co-generation
Co-generation is the production of electricity and process heat from a single thermodynamic machine (Williams and Larson, 1993; Moreira and Poole, 1993). Biomass such as bagasse (sugarcane fibre) is used to fuel the thermodynamic machine that heats up steam which then drives a turbine to produce electricity. The steam that is raised from low to high pressure is not all used up in power generation but is also available for other processes within the plant. The sugar industry, for instance, makes use of

excess steam produced from sugar refining to generate electricity from steam turbines and also to pre-heat the steam (Beeharry and Baguant, 1995).

There are three principal mechanisms for increasing the efficiency of a co-generation cycle in the sugar industry:

- Increasing steam and power generation;

- Decreasing the amount of steam needed to operate a sugar factory (thus making more steam and/or bagasse available for power generation);

- Drying and densifying bagasse more efficiently.

Co-generation is applied by many agro-processing industries in order to meet their power requirements. Some of the industries involved include the paper and pulp, palm, wood and rice industries. Examples of co-generation systems are the condensing-extraction steam turbine (CEST), biomass-integrated gasifier/gas turbine (BIG/GT) and biomass-integrated gasifier/steam-injected gas turbine (BIG/STIG) (Williams and Larson, 1993).

Co-generation offers enormous opportunities for increasing electricity and/or heat energy supply without making huge investments, while avoiding the negative environmental effects of increased fossil fuel

Figure 2.1 Simple cycle gas turbine configured for co-generation applications

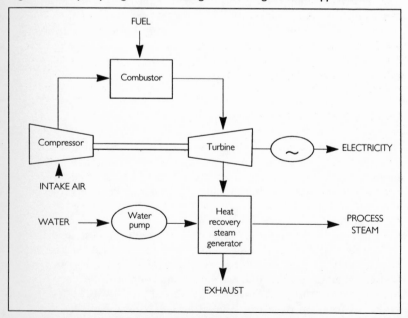

Source: Adapted from Beeharry and Baguant, 1995

combustion (Davidson and Karekezi, 1993). With co-generation, industries can be located in remote areas not connected to the grid for industry. Near the grid, the extra electricity generated can be made available to other users by interconnecting the co-generator with the utility grid. For industries close to the grid, sale of surplus electricity to the national utility would increase their income.

Co-generation plants can produce electricity only during the sugar cane harvesting period when bagasse is available. As a result, most sugar factories which produce electricity through co-generation have been unable to sell the excess electricity to the grid, since the utilities insist on buying electricity from sources that can supply power all year round. In Mauritius, however, the sugar industry uses coal when it runs out of bagasse to fuel the co-generators (Table 2.2).

Co-generation has been in existence for close to 100 years, but interest in the system was boosted by the oil crisis of the early 1970s and 1980s. The sugar industry realized that in bagasse it had an under-utilized and under-valued resource, and consequently changed its emphasis from self-sufficiency to maximum exploitation, producing surplus electricity for sale to other consumers.

A number of ethanol plants in Brazil generate enough electricity for their own consumption and sell the surplus (about 10 to 15 per cent) to the local power company (Goldemberg *et al.*, 1994). Co-generation plants have also been installed in wood and rice industries in Malaysia and Thailand. In Thailand, electricity generated by private producers from biomass is sold to the national grid or to third-party consumers (COGEN,

Table 2.1 Technical potential of biomass-based co-generation in developing countries (based on estimates for 1990)

	TWh	% of 1990 total
Total electricity generation	2,410	
Potential from sugar industry		
• Best available steam technology	100	4
• Best available steam technology and using tops and leaves	250	10
• Advanced gasification technology using tops and leaves.	600	25

Source: Karekezi, 1996

Table 2.2 Total electricity output in Mauritius

	Normal year (GWh/year)	Dry year (GWh/year)
CEB – Diesel/fuel oil	350.00	350.00
FUEL – Coal/bagasse	72.51	63.02
CEB – Gas turbine (Nicolay Road)	23.00	23.00
Total:	445.51	436.02

Source: Baguant, 1992

Table 2.3 Net electricity production potential with biomass-integrated/steam-injected turbines (BIG/STIG) in the sugar-cane industries of Eastern and Southern Africa countries

	Cane production (million tonnes per year)		Electricity production (TWh per year)		
	1987	2027	Potential from cane in 2027	Actual from all sources in 1987	E = C/D
	A	B	C	D	
Angola	0.32	1.10	0.7	0.81[a]	0.90
Ethiopia	1.65	5.69	3.8	0.81	4.66
Kenya	4.00	13.80	9.2	2.63	3.48
Madagascar	1.80	6.21	4.1	0.50	8.25
Malawi	1.60	5.52	3.7	0.58	6.32
Mauritius	6.23	21.50	14.3	0.49	29.13
Mozambique	0.67	2.31	1.5	0.50	3.07
Reunion	2.11	7.29	4.8	–	–
Somalia*	0.37	1.28	0.8	0.26	3.27
South Africa	20.00	69.00	45.8	122.30[b]	0.37
Sudan	5.00	17.25	11.5	1.06	10.81
Swaziland	4.00	13.80	9.2	–	–
Tanzania	1.08	3.71	2.5	0.87	2.83
Uganda	0.60	2.07	1.4	0.66	2.08
Zambia	1.25	4.31	2.9	8.48	0.34
Zimbabwe	3.80	13.11	8.7	7.01	1.24
TOTAL	54.48	187.95	124.9	146.96	76.75

[a] For 1986
[b] Public electricity production in 1989
* Somalia: civil war has probably led to complete interruption in sugar and centralized electricity production
Source: Adapted from Williams and Larson, 1993

1994b). In 1995, feasibility studies were being carried out by sugar industries in Indonesia and the Philippines to establish similar plants *(ibid.).* Table 2.1 shows the technical potential of biomass-based co-generation in developing countries based on estimates for 1990.

Sugar is produced in a number of Eastern and Southern African countries. It is a major agricultural export for Ethiopia, Malawi, Mozambique, Madagascar, Mauritius, Swaziland, Zambia and Zimbabwe. The potential for electricity production from bagasse is high (Table 2.3). Co-generation equipment is almost uniformly an integral component of sugar factory designs.

Potential for electricity generation from sugar cane wastes, estimated on the basis of 1985 sugar cane production, was 30×10^9 KWh per annum in Africa and over 13×10^9 KWh in the Eastern and Southern African region (Biomass Users Network, 1989). In sub-Saharan Africa, however, this potential is currently under-exploited.

Experience gained from co-generation in Mauritius demonstrates the viability of this technology. This application has been in use since the mid-1950s with bagasse as the main fuel. In the mid-1980s, the largest sugar company on the island, Flacq United Estate Limited (FUEL), designed and installed a dual furnace. The furnace uses both coal and bagasse, producing electricity from coal between January and May and from bagasse during the rest of the year (the sugar cane harvesting season). Weather conditions, however, affect the output of the coal/bagasse station.

Sixteen out of the 19 factories in Mauritius produce surplus electricity which meets about 10 per cent of the country's power needs, a figure that could rise to 26 per cent by the year 2010 (Davidson and Karekezi, 1993).

Ethanol Production

Ethyl alcohol (C_2H_5OH), better known as ethanol, is alcohol produced from the fermentation of biomass. It can also be produced by acid hydrolysis of hydrocarbons (petroleum or gas) (World Bank, 1980). Ethanol from biomass is a major renewable energy source that offers an alternative to fossil fuels. It is also used as an alcoholic beverage (vodka and gin, for example) and as an intermediate chemical in toiletries, cosmetics and pharmaceutical preparations *(ibid.).*

Ethanol can be produced from different kinds of biomass: the main categories are sugar, starch, and cellulosic biomass. Sugar biomass comprises sugar cane and sugar beet. Starch biomass includes cereals such as corn, wheat, sorghum and barley, and tubers such as potatoes and cassava. Cellulosic biomass includes wood and straw.

Sugar-bearing plants, unlike other feedstock, store carbohydrate as a simple sugar: no pre-treatment is required and ethanol production is therefore more economical (Heber *et al.*, 1985). Grain sorghum and corn have the highest yield, of 387 and 370 litres per ton respectively, but are uneconomical to use because of the high cost of pre-treatment.

When using sugar cane to produce ethanol (Figure 2.2), the mature

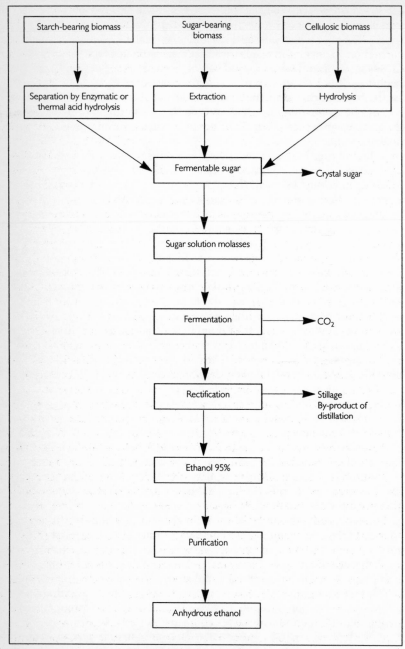

Figure 2.2 Flow diagram of production of ethanol

Source: Adapted from Heber et al, 1985

cane is washed and crushed to produce sugar containing juice and raw fibre (bagasse). This mixture is filtered so as to isolate the bagasse, which when dried can be used to fuel the ethanol plant. If production is being carried out at a sugar manufacturing plant, water is added to the sugar juice for concentration and evaporation purposes. The sugar crystallizes and is separated by centrifugation. The remaining substance (molasses) is concentrated and sterilized, then fermented with yeast as a catalyst.

Ethanol is separated from the fermentation products by distillation in the process of rectification. The ethanol obtained (crude ethyl alcohol; approximately 95 per cent pure) is purified further through dehydration to procure anhydrous ethanol (99.8 per cent pure). Anhydrous ethanol is also referred to as power alcohol. After ethanol has been extracted from the fermentation products, what remains is called stillage. It contains 2-3 per cent nutrients and can thus be used as fertilizer.

There are several advantages associated with the use of ethanol. It can be obtained from a variety of sources such as sugar cane, beet, corn, sorghum, potatoes and grapes. Because its production is labour-intensive, the benefits in terms of employment can be significant, especially in the rural areas. In Brazil, the ProAlcool ethanol programme is estimated to have generated 700,000 jobs directly and three to four times as many indirectly (Hall *et al.*, 1993).

Ethanol production is a technically feasible undertaking and the requisite technology is commercially viable. The technology can also be assembled using local labour, as in the case of Zimbabwe where 60 per cent of the plant was fabricated and constructed locally (Scurlock *et al.*, 1991b). The final cost of constructing the Zimbabwe plant (US$6.4 million) made it one of the cheapest plants of its capacity in the world and the cost per litre of ethanol was one of the lowest (Scurlock *et al.*, 1991b).

Research conducted by the ProAlcool programme in Brazil led to increased sugar cane productivity (Hall *et al.*, 1993) and in both Zimbabwe and Brazil the gains in sugar technology skills, biotechnology and fermentation are valuable for industrial development (Hall *et al.*, 1993).

By-products of ethanol production such as hydrolysed bagasse and dry yeast are very useful. Stillage and dry yeast are used as animal feeds (Johansson *et al.*, 1993), while bagasse can be used to generate electricity or for heating (Wood and Hall, 1993). In Zimbabwe, diluted stillage used to irrigate the sugar cane plantations increased the sugar cane crop yield by 7 per cent (Hall *et al.*, 1993). Some stillage was spread on the murram roads as a binding agent to reduce erosion and dust, thus curbing road accidents (Scurlock *et al.*, 1991b). As an octane booster, ethanol is a substitute for environmentally hazardous lead compounds in gasoline.

Compared with petroleum, power alcohol has lower emissions of carbon monoxide (CO), nitrogen oxides (NO_x) and hydrocarbons (HC). Figure 2.3 shows hypothetical emissions for different fuel engines in Brazil. The graph summarizes, in terms of relative emissions, a comparison between the baseline emissions in 1989 (when the fleet was

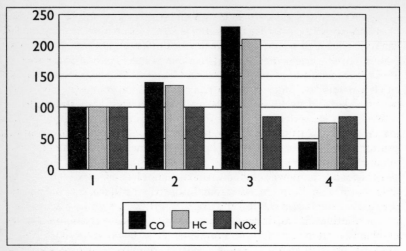

Figure 2.3 Hypothetical relative emissions – 1989
Source: Pranco and Szwarc, 1992.

almost equally divided between alcohol and gasohol vehicles) and three hypothetical fleet scenarios for same year: only gasohol vehicles (option 2 in the graph), only gasoline vehicles (option 3) and only ethanol vehicles (option 4).

Power alcohol has a research octane number (designation of anti-knock quality of gasoline) of 128 (Little, 1993). When used in gasohol, it increases the octane number of the gasoline blend. This allows the substitution of the environmentally harmful lead compounds in gasoline which are added to boost octane numbers. In addition, power alcohol can generate substantial energy savings in refinery operations since less processing is needed to produce a lower octane number gasoline (World Bank, 1980).

The search for energy security and independence is one of the major reasons why alcohol programmes are often implemented in countries without indigenous oil reserves. Some of the considerations taken into account include whether the country is landlocked, the political vulnerability of the supplier or conduit country, foreign exchange limitations and strategic priorities (Scurlock *et al.*, 1991b; Hall *et al.*, 1993).

Despite all the advantages associated with the production of ethanol, there are some shortcomings. Large amounts of water are required for alcohol rectification. About 200 cubic metres of water are needed for every cubic metre of ethanol produced. Most of this considerable volume of oxygen-depleted water is fed into rivers after use, causing ecological stress. Fortunately, recycling of the waste water is now being undertaken at some plants. Where there is no combustible material, such as bagasse in the case of sugar-bearing feedstock, a further disadvantage is that high energy inputs are required to fuel the plant (Heber *et al.*, 1985).

Alcohol production from biomass is not an entirely new concept; it can be traced back at least 2,000 years to the Egyptians, who produced ethanol as a beverage. At the turn of the century engines were built to use ethanol. Henry Ford, inventor of the well-known Ford vehicles, invented an engine that could use both ethanol and gasoline. A short while later, however, petroleum sources – relatively cheaper to extract and refine – were discovered. Renewed interest in ethanol developed in the wake of the 1970s and 1980s oil crises, as a result of major increases in petroleum prices, concern over future supplies and the need to depend on a locally available resource.

Ethanol is widely recognized as the best candidate for the rapid introduction of a new liquid fuel source, although to date its use is limited to the spark ignition engine (Hall and de Groot, 1987). A number of countries are currently embarking on alcohol research and development programmes, including the USA, Brazil, Sweden, Germany, France, New Zealand, the Philippines, Malawi, Kenya and Zimbabwe, all net oil importers. It is now mandatory in Europe to use fuels that are environmentally friendly, such as alcohol-blended fuels.

Worldwide, government expenditure on power alcohol schemes (grants, subsidies, loans, etc.) amounts to over US$2 billion each year (Hall and de Groot, 1987). The largest programme is in Brazil, where the government in 1987 spent over US$1 billion subsidizing the production of alcohol from sugar cane. Brazil is currently the world's leading producer of fermentation ethanol, which provides approximately 50 per cent of gasoline requirements in the country (Goldemberg *et al.*, 1994).

REGIONAL STATUS

Within Eastern and Southern Africa, ethanol has been exploited on a large scale in Zimbabwe, Malawi and Kenya. Zimbabwe, which is a landlocked country with no known petroleum reserves, has to import petroleum products by pipeline and rail through Mozambique or South Africa. The political vulnerability of these two countries, and sanctions imposed on the former Rhodesian government coupled with foreign exchange limitations, increased the need for an independent source of fuel (Scurlock *et al.*, 1991b; Hall *et al.*, 1993).

In November 1978, a sugar company located in north-eastern Zimbabwe, Triangle Ltd, built a distillery at the sugar mill. Production started in March 1980. Local technology was preferred to sophisticated imported equipment. As we have seen, the result was local fabrication of 60 per cent of the equipment (only specialized items were imported) and the total cost of the plant was US$6.4 million (1980 prices), the lowest capital/litre cost in the world (World Resources Institute, 1994). Ethanol production starts in April and ends in November, in tandem with the sugar cane crushing season. During this season, the plant is powered by bagasse. During the sugar cane growing season, the plant uses stored and imported molasses for ethanol production and is powered by coal. About 120,000 litres of anhydrous ethanol are produced each day. The maximum annual capacity is 40 million litres.

The Zimbabwean ethanol programme has made a substantial contribution to the economy by reducing annual gasoline imports by about 40 million litres (Scurlock et al., 1991b). Initially, Zimbabwe had a 15/85 ethanol/gasoline blend. Owing to increased fuel consumption, the blend now stands at about 12/88 (Scurlock et al., 1991b; Hall et al., 1993). The community around the plant has also benefited from employment created on the sugar plantation and in the ethanol plant. The incomes of about 150 local farmers and private companies, from whom the plant buys supplementary cane and molasses, have also been boosted (ibid.). In addition, neighbouring countries have found a ready market in Zimbabwe for their molasses, formerly a waste product.

A few problems have been experienced at the plant. At one time, abnormal corrosion of the fermentation tanks occurred. Re-welding and coating of the joints with epoxy paint helped in part to solve this problem (Wenmann, 1985). A stillage disposal problem was overcome by diluting the waste (1:200) with irrigation water. The mixture is finally applied as fertilizer to the plantation, increasing crop yields, as we have seen, by 7 per cent (Scurlock et al., 1991b; World Resources Institute, 1994).

Like Zimbabwe, Malawi is a landlocked country with no indigenous oil resources or refining capacity. In 1982, Malawi imported 100 per cent of its oil requirements in the form of refined petroleum, spending a large part of the country's foreign exchange in doing so. In 1991, the country spent 17 per cent of the returns from the country's largest foreign exchange earner, tobacco, on oil importation. This figure grew to 21 per cent in 1992. Unfortunately, tobacco prices remained stagnant for a while, then fell due to the global anti-tobacco campaign (Kafumba, 1994).

In 1982, a molasses-based ethanol plant was commissioned. The Ethanol Company Limited (ETHCO), is the sole producer and distributor of ethanol in Malawi. Molasses from two sugar mills is used. The distillery has a capacity of 60,000 litres/day, while the annual capacity is 17 million litres (Kafumba, 1994). Production averages 13 million litres per year. The target blend ratio with fuel was 20:80. In 1993, the ratio was 15:85 (Kafumba, 1994). This, unfortunately, was not maintained. There have been constant tussles between ETHCO and the oil industry, the main problem between the two parties being acceptable market shares and the pricing of ethanol in relation to imported gasoline.

Critics of the ethanol project also argue that the economic advantage of the plant no longer exists. The need for ethanol in the 1980s was due to the high oil prices, but since the Gulf war the trend has changed. This argument is further strengthened by the fact that part of the feedstock is imported. As a result, a number of critics have recommended that ethanol research and expansion plans be postponed or cancelled (Kafumba, 1994).

Available evidence, however, demonstrates that the plant helped to reduce foreign exchange spending by a substantial amount. The demand for petroleum has also been lowered by more than 10 per cent per annum. Another positive outcome is that the sugar industry can now recycle its wastes, which were previously a hazard to the environment (Gielink, 1991; Kafumba, 1994).

While the multinational oil companies remain unwilling to increase the ratio of ethanol in Malawi's gasohol, they deny the ethanol company a chance to attain full capacity utilization and expand its operations. This is unlike the Zimbabwean case: there it is mandatory for all the gasoline used in the country to be blended with ethanol.

Kenya's interest in ethanol was sparked off by the oil crisis in the early 1970s. Like other countries, Kenya was keen to exploit locally available sources of energy (Omondi, 1991). In the liquid fuel sector, ethanol was one of the attractive options. The Agro-Chemical and Food Corporation (ACFC) was established in 1978 with the main objective of utilizing the surplus molasses produced by the sugar mills. In 1988, 145,000 tonnes of molasses were produced, of which 30,000 tonnes were exported to Europe, while 20,000 tonnes were used as animal feed. The surplus, which was dumped in pits, posed a serious environmental threat, particularly to soil and water (Baraka, 1991; Muruli, 1992). The molasses was also used by the local people to make cheap, illicit liquor, which owing to crude distillation contained a large dose of methanol, hazardous to human health (Muruli, 1992).

The ACFC plant, sited in Muhoroni near the three sugar factories (Omondi, 1991), has an installed capacity of 60,000 litres per day with a daily average production of 45,000 litres. The planned alcohol/gasoline blend was set at 10:90. The plant has benefited both the economy and the community: it employs about 200 people and has generated additional indirect employment for about 1,000 more (Baraka, 1991). In addition, it has helped to reduce dependence on imported energy supplies, in line with government policy (Kyalo, 1992).

The plant has encountered several problems. Though ACFC was established in 1978 with the specific mission of developing a renewable source of energy, half-hearted commitment by the government and the absence of clear-cut production, blending and marketing policies led to the collapse of the programme (Okwatch, 1994). As a result, most of the ethanol is exported and little or no gasohol is available on the local market. In 1992 drought resulted in low sugar cane yields, affecting the operation of the plant. Poor infrastructure affected transportation of sugar cane to the mills and molasses to the ethanol plant, particularly during the rainy season.

Two other major plants (the Kenya Chemical and Food Corporation and the Awendo Company) that were planned faced the major constraints of inadequate government support and planning. The Awendo molasses plant never started operations owing to a supply shortage, while the

Box 2.1
Economic analysis of the viability of an ethanol programme (Kenya)
———————————— * ————————————

In Kenya a recent study undertook an economic analysis of the ethanol programme on the basis of the following scenarios:
*   If the import price of gasoline is greater than or equal to the economic cost of ethanol produced from molasses, then commercial viability of blending ethanol with gasoline should be tested and tariff and fiscal incentives considered.
*   Alternatively, if the netback value of exported ethanol is greater than production costs, then export of ethanol is economic.
*   If however, the export value is less than the production cost, then the production of ethanol should be suspended.

In 1993 the production cost per litre of ethanol was US$0.26–0.33, as shown below:

		Ksh/l	US$/l
1.	*Variable costs*		
	Molasses	9.1	0.13
	Other (power, chemicals, fuel)	4.2	0.06
	Sub-total:	13.3	0.19
2.	*Fixed costs* (wages, administration)	2.1	0.03
3.	*Asset renewal[1]*	2.1	0.03
4.	*Operating cost*/total production cost of wet ethanol	17.5	0.25
5.	Cost to dry ethanol	0.9	0.01
	Total production cost (anhydrous)	18.4	0.26

Replacement cost US$ 21.4,
Conversion factor 70 Ksh/US$
[1] 2.5% of replacement cost per year.

The cost of a litre of delivered ethanol in Kenya ranges from US$0.26 to US$0.28, almost twice the cost of a litre of delivered gasoline in Kenya (between US$0.16 and US$0.17). The netback value (price less freight charges) of ethanol is US$0.26 per litre, therefore ethanol exports should continue. Based on the above calculations, the ethanol firm clearly should continue producing ethanol for export only. Options do, however, exist that would make ethanol more economically viable not only for export but eventually for blending with gasoline. One of these options is the reduction of production cost of ethanol. Integration of ACFC with a sugar company would either eliminate the cost of molasses, if the company can provide the total molasses requirement, or significantly reduce expenditure on molasses, if the company has to purchase part of the molasses from other sugar mills. Secondly, as demonstrated by firms in Brazil, ethanol production costs can be reduced by about 6.4 per cent through efficiency in fermentation, distillation and energy use (Goldemberg et al., 1994). Measures that could be considered at ACFC include alternative sources of energy such as electricity from bagasse or biogas from slurry.

Source: Karekezi et al, 1995a.

Kenya Chemical and Food Corporation suffered from budget overruns and lack of financing (Baraka, 1991).

The need for ethanol plants in the region cannot be over-emphasized. Most countries in the region spend a large proportion of their foreign exchange on petroleum imports. Foreign exchange savings from substitution, in part or wholly, could be used profitably in other sub-sectors of the economy. Based on 1991, 1994 and 1995 figures, Table 2.4 below shows the cane produced in selected countries and the estimated annual ethanol yield, demonstrating the region's high potential for ethanol production. If a few more countries in the region produced ethanol, they could assist neighbouring countries by exporting surplus ethanol to them. The latter, in turn, could export their molasses to the ethanol-producing countries.

In the transport sector, the use of clean and renewable energy sources has been recognized as one of the alternatives that would help curb the emission of greenhouse gases. Consequently, funding instruments such as the Global Environment Facility (GEF), which supports environmentally benign projects, could consider ethanol production as a viable option.

Table 2..4 Estimated annual ethanol production capacity in selected countries

Country	Annual cane production	Annual ethanol production capacity
Zimbabwe	1.9 million tonnes	40 million litres
Kenya	–	16.4 million litres
Malawi	–	17 million litres

– Data not available
Source: Scurlock et al., 1991b; Karekezi, Ewagata et al., 1995 and Kafumba, C., 1994a.

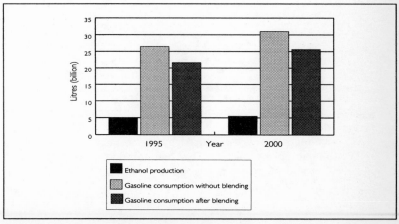

Figure 2.4 Projection of gasoline consumption in Eastern and Southern Africa, before and after blending with ethanol
(See Box 2.2 on p. 32 for explanations)

Box 2.2
Explanatory notes for the projection of gasoline consumption in Africa before and after blending with ethanol produced in Eastern and Southern Africa for the years 1995 and 200
——————————— * ———————————

1 Calculating the projected amount of ethanol produced in 1995 and 2000 respectively
   Calculate the estimated amount of cane to be produced in 1995
      $= 54.48 \times (1.031)^8$ million tonnes = 69.55 million tonnes.
   Amount of ethanol produced from the sugar cane
      $69.55 \times 70 \times 1000 = 4868500$ thousand litres
   For year 2000 would be :
      $= 54.48 \times (1.031)^{13}$ million tonnes = 81.02 million tonnes.
   Amount of ethanol produced from the sugar cane
      $= 81.02 \times 70 \times 1000 = 5671400$ thousand litres
2 Converting the amount of petroleum crude oil consumed from barrels per day to litres per year
   To convert barrels per day to tonnes per year: $= 1965 \times 49.8 \times 1000$
                                                         $= 97857$ thousand tonnes per year
   To convert tonnes per year to litres per year: $= 97857 \times 1164 \times 1000$
                                                         $= 113905548$ thousand litres
3 Calculating the amount of petrol consumed from the crude
      $= 113905548 \times 20\% = 22781109.6$ thousand litres
4 Calculate the amount of petroleum consumed in 1995 and in 2000 respectively
   Calculating estimated amount of petroleum consumed in 1995
      $= 22781109.6 \times (1.0325)^5 = 23521495.66$ thousand litres
   For 2000 petrol consumption would be 31367180.04 thousand litres
5 When all the ethanol is blended with petroleum
   The amount of petrol required to meet the same demand
      = the total amount of petroleum consumed – the amount of ethanol blended with the
      petroleum
   Therefore, Petrol requirement for 1995 would be
      $= 26731613.61 - 4868500 = 21863113.61$ thousand litres
   While for 2000 would be
      $= 31367180.04 - 5671400 = 2569780.04$ thousand litres

Notes:
1 The amount of petroleum consumed is for the whole African continent whereas the Ethanol production is for Eastern and Southern Africa. Though the two estimates are not of the same scope, the calculation is meant to clearly illustrate the effect of the use of ethanol on the amount of petroleum consumption. 2 Sugar cane production in 1987 amounted to 54.48 million tonnes (Karekezi et al, 1995) and all molasses are assumed to go into ethanol production. 3 One tonne of sugar cane produces 70 litres of ethanol. 4 The growth rate of sugar cane production is 3.1 per cent per year. 5 Petroleum crude oil consumption in Africa in 1990 was 1965 thousand barrels per day (BP, 1991). 6 Conversion factor from Barrels per day to Tonnes per year is 49.8 (BP, 1992). 7 Specific Gravity for crude oil given average API gravity as 33.5° (BP, 1992) for Arabian Light is 86. Hence the conversion factor used is 1164 litres per metric tonne (McGraw-Hill, 1984). 8 Assume that only 20% of crude oil is used as petrol since petrol consumption in the region could not be calculated due to lack of data. 9 Assume that the petrol consumed was primarily in the transport sector where ethanol can be used as a sustitute. 10 Oil consumption growth rate in Africa is 3.25% per annum
Source: Karakezi, Ewagata, et al., 1997; Williams and Larson, 1993; Kristoferson and Bokalders, 1987; African Technical Department, World Bank Database, 1992, and BP Statistical Review of World Energy, 1991.

Large-scale biogas production

Biogas is a combustible gas produced by the fermentation of organic material in the absence of oxygen. It is composed of about 60 per cent methane (CH_4) and 40 per cent carbon dioxide (CO_2). It has a faint, unpleasant smell. It burns with a hot blue flame, and can be used in gas lamps, to run refrigerators, to generate electricity (see Figure 2.5) and to power stationary diesel and petrol engines, among other applications (Hankins, 1987).

The production of biogas requires the use of carbohydrates, proteins and/or fats. The actual reactants, however, are soluble organic matter:

volatile fatty acids (mainly acetic acid), amino acids, long chain fatty acids, organic sulphur and ammonium compounds. These are found in food-processing effluent, in weeds, leaves and non-edible starch, and in sewage, municipal and other wastes (Dutt and Ravindranath, 1993).

The biogas production process occurs in digesters, which can be divided into two main groups: batch digesters and continuous flow digesters. Batch operation is the simplest method to adopt on a large scale. The plant is filled with substrate material and suitably inoculated to enable appropriate bacterial populations to predominate. At the completion of digestion (when gas falls to low levels) the material is removed and replaced with a new batch. Gas production varies and to achieve a constant gas production from this system, two or more digesters operating out of phase are required *(ibid.)*. After the biogas is obtained, slurry (digested material) remains and can be used as compost manure (Ellegard, 1990). Figure 2.5 illustrates the entire process from when the raw material is fed into the storage tank to the final stage when electricity is generated.

Biogas production can facilitate decentralized electricity generation in areas with no access to the grid. Its use precludes the formation of harmful intermediates and products formed during combustion of other fossil fuels such as polyaromatics, hydrocarbons, tar and soot *(ibid.)*. With biogas, less greenhouse gas emissions, particularly carbon monoxide, occur as

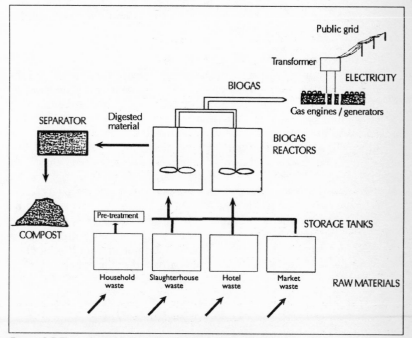

Figure 2.5 Flow sheet of a medium-large-scale biogas plant
Source: Adapted from Ahring, 1993

carbon is extracted from a substrate to form methane and carbon dioxide. Biogas facilitates low-cost, environmentally sound waste recycling. As well as polluting ground and surface water, wastes provide food and shelter to animals and insects that may spread infectious diseases (Moshi, 1993). All these problems can be curbed by using these wastes economically to produce biogas. The biological process of anaerobic digestion mineralizes organic material, which can then be used as fertilizer – a very important additional benefit for farmers. Biogas thus yields multiple benefits to users.

As with other combustible gases, the dangers of explosion exist. When replacement of worn-out biogas plant installations is not carried out promptly, gas pipes may burst. Another drawback is that the hydrogen sulphide (H_2S) produced is foul-smelling, poisonous and corrosive. Biogas slurry that is not properly handled can be environmentally harmful. In municipal and industrial waste composition, the slurry (containing minerals) should be monitored for the possible presence of harmful contents.

Biogas technology has been in use since the late 1940s, although its original purpose was not the production of fuel gas. Initially, biogas digesters were used for treating wastes and producing fertilizer, particularly in China and India where biogas technology is perceived to be an integral component of rural sanitation and agricultural systems *(ibid)*. In Denmark more than 15 large-scale plants, producing 2,000–15,000 cubic metres of biogas per day, had been built by 1993 and plans were under way to construct 100 more digesters (GEF, 1993).

REGIONAL STATUS
The development of large-scale biogas technology in Eastern and Southern Africa is still in its embryonic stage, but its potential is promising. In South Africa, research results indicate that major urban centres can produce about 120 MW from land fills and sewage. Many countries in the region, including Zimbabwe, Tanzania, and Zambia, have active country-specific biogas research and training activities (Hall, 1993).

In Tanzania, the use and development of biogas technology has been emphasized in the country's national energy policy. Municipal solid waste is a serious environmental problem that can be addressed by large-scale biogas technology. The GEF Project in Tanzania is expected to be one of the first in a series of projects to be conducted in Tanzania and Africa as a whole. The project – 'Electricity, Fuel and Fertilizer from Municipal and Industrial Organic Waste: A Demonstration Biogas Plant for Africa' – is designed to be economically self-sufficient through the sale of electricity, fuel and fertilizer. It aims at reducing methane emissions by adequately managing urban waste. It is to be connected to the national electricity grid by Tanzania Electricity Supply Commission (TANESCO) which will purchase the electricity at market rates. Income from the sale of electricity, fuel and fertilizer will cover operating costs.

The total cost of constructing the plant is estimated to be US$4 million

($2.5 million for the plant and $1.5 million for the training and capacity building elements) (GEF, 1993). At completion, the plant will have the capacity to treat 150 tonnes of organic waste per day, approximately 10 per cent of the total waste produced in Dar es Salaam. There will be organized waste handling and management. Eventually, about 90 per cent of Dar es Salaam's waste is to be treated, leading to a great reduction in methane emissions. Apart from waste management, benefits include a reduction in carbon dioxide emissions and the provision of an alternative fuel to replace diesel fuels. Reduced dependence on oil imports – which consume 40 per cent of export earnings – will also be realized, not to mention the alleviation of acute electricity shortages (Moshi, 1993; GEF, 1993). The project will also involve on-site training of Tanzanian nationals by Danish experts (GEF, 1993).

Box 2.3
Economic viability of a biogas plant
———————————————*———————————————

Revenue from a biogas project: the GEF project, Tanzania, annual expenditure versus income

Expenditure	US$	Income	US$
Total operating cost (including $60,000/year – salary of plant operator)	169,000	Fees for removing wastes from household and industries	53,000
		Sales of electricity to the public grid	361,350
Total	169,000	Total	414,350
		Net revenue (income – expenditure)	245,350

Adapted from GEF, 1993

From the third year and thereafter, the annual operating cost will reduce to US$109,000 (from US$169,000), so the expected annual revenue will increase to approximately US$300,000 (ibid.). The above project cost a total of US$3.9 million. This plant will have the capacity to treat about 60 tons of organic waste per day, or about 3 per cent of the waste produced daily in the city. The price of petrol is US$0.55/litre. Therefore, with the production of the equivalent of 30,000 litres of petrol a day, Tanzania can save US$16,500/day (US$6,022,500 /year) that would otherwise be spent on petrol (Rubindamayugi and Kivaisi, 1993).

Prospects for this technology in Eastern and Southern Africa will depend, to a certain extent, on the success or failure of the Tanzanian plant. The Eastern and Southern region faces municipal and industrial waste disposal problems which such projects will certainly help to curb, as well as generating employment. Income would also be earned by municipal councils from the sale of electricity, fuel and fertilizers.

Briquetting

Briquetting is the densification of loose granular material into compact and easily transportable fuel. Biomass suitable for briquetting includes residues and waste products from the wood industries, rubbish or garbage, charcoal residues and other combustible waste products. Large-scale industrial briquetting is usually motorized (Kristoferson and Bokalders, 1987).

Briquettes can be either carbonized or uncarbonized. For carbonized briquettes, the biomass is charred to form charcoal-like fuel, while in the uncarbonized process no charring is undertaken. Uncarbonized briquettes require a special stove which, unfortunately, few households would be able or willing to purchase (McChesney, 1989). They are suitable for large institutions and the industrial sector, but not for households (Boiling Point, 1991; Onaji and Siemons, 1993; KENGO, 1987). Carbonized briquettes, on the other hand, are affordable and are used as a substitute for wood charcoal, owing to their similar burning characteristics. It is also possible to make producer gas if carbonization is carried out at the briquetting plant. The gas can either be used to generate electricity for drying or can be heated to dry the briquettes.

There are two major technologies used in briquetting in the region, extrusion and pelletizing (see Figure 2.6). In the extrusion technology, a piston, conical screw or cylindrical press may be used. Briquettes prepared by extrusion at high temperature (about 250°C) and high pressure (approximately 1,000 bars) can be produced without the use of a binder (Brandt, 1989). A binder is the substance, such as tar, used to hold the loose material together.

Pelletizing technology, on the other hand, involves agglomerating and densifying the raw material in low-pressure eccentric pelletizers (Walubengo, 1990b; Bachou, 1990). The process involves enlargement by gluing powder particles together in a rotating piece of equipment. The rotation causes smooth rolling of the balls which grow larger in diameter until they are eventually pushed out of the agglomerator (Siemons *et al.*, 1989).

Briquetting residues expands their use in energy production by improving their calorific value and reducing the cost of transportation to urban areas. It may also improve the availability of fuel in rural areas (Kristoferson and Bokalders, 1987). The storage costs of fuel are also reduced (Brandt, 1989). Moreover, fuel briquettes have uniform properties and are an effective means of using loose agricultural residues, unsuitable for fodder or fertilizer and too difficult to transport, which otherwise would be discarded (Dutt and Ravindranath, 1993).

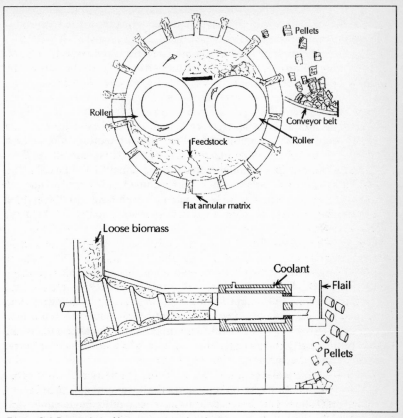

Figure 2.6 Principles of briquetting technologies
Source: Adapted from Kristoferson and Bokalders, 1987

Briquetting is an economical way for energy-processing industries to deal with wastes as well as producing fuel to meet their energy requirements. Briquette production can be economical if it is part of a disposal strategy in agro-industry (Gamser, 1987). Briquettes can be an important alternative for households, especially during periods of charcoal and fuelwood shortages (KENGO, 1987). They are also suitable for institutions as it is easier to keep records of fuel costs and one can easily notice changes in the fuel budget *(ibid.)*.

The price of briquettes is often higher than that of wood and charcoal, however, which can limit demand. The burning of briquettes (or pellets) produces a lot of smoke, especially during lighting (Young, 1987), and may cause technical problems requiring specialized equipment in certain applications: these factors also discourage wider use (Kristoferson and Bokalders, 1987). Briquettes are unlikely to become cheaper than traditional fuels and may find a niche only when the price of the latter has risen sharply (McChesney, 1989). Production and transportation costs can be reduced, however, if uncarbonized briquettes are made within the proximity of consumers such as large institutions and industries.

Briquetting technology has been in use since the nineteenth century to make solid fuel out of peat, animal feed and fertilizer. It was also in use in the US and Central Europe during the Second World War (Bachou, 1990). There are substantial briquetting activities in Nicaragua, Chile, Ecuador, Sweden and Mexico *(ibid.)*. Brazil and India are successfully producing briquette fuels for the industrial sector (Bennet, 1989). These two countries also manufacture briquette presses for local use and export *(ibid.)*. Other countries involved in the manufacture of briquetting machines are Germany and Thailand. A United Nations Sudano-Sahelian Office (UNSO)/ Danish International Development Association (DANIDA) project started in Gambia in 1987 is reported to be capable of producing 160,000 bags of briquettes weighing 47kg each in six months (Kristoferson and Bokalders, 1987).

REGIONAL STATUS

There are large-scale functional briquetting plants in Ethiopia, Kenya, Malawi, Uganda, Sudan, Zambia and Zimbabwe (Makau and Obura, 1991; Turyareeba, 1991a; Hassan, 1992). In Sudan, briquetting was developed within a decentralized carbonization and centralized briquetting strategy (Ali and Hood, 1992). This programme makes use of cotton stalks, traditionally burnt every year as a phyto-sanitary measure. Molasses from the sugar industry provide the binary agent for the carbonized cotton stalk briquettes. Production of alcohol is illegal in Sudan and therefore there is no investment in ethanol production (Walubengo, 1990b): molasses that otherwise would be used in the production of alcohol is thus available as a binding agent. The programme has generated significant employment and provided rural households with an additional income. A 0.5 tonne/hour press in Khartoum showed that substantial profits can be made with demand at centres as far as 500 km from the production centre (Bennet, 1989). One private briquetting firm produces spare parts for imported briquette presses *(ibid.)*.

Marketing of briquettes in Kenya (especially in the household sector) has been hampered by competition from charcoal and fuelwood which cost less. The management of briquetting plants has also been a major drawback as far as production and marketing is concerned (Makau and Obura, 1991). According to a survey conducted in Kenya, briquettes were considered to be more marketable as a fuel for industrial and institutional purposes than as a household fuel (Walubengo, 1990b). A paper manufacturing company in Kenya recorded annual savings of Ksh60,000 (approximately US$4,000) when using briquettes as a fuel in the mid-1980s (KENGO, 1987).

Three briquetting plants were established in Uganda but have faced significant operational problems. Two have been closed down while the third is operating below capacity. In one case, briquetting equipment which arrived in Uganda between 1986 and 1987 was not installed until December 1992 owing to a lack of trained operators. A study conducted in Malawi found that there is a market for carbonized briquettes in the household and industrial sectors. Plans are under way to invest in an 800 tonnes/year briquetting plant.

Direct combustion
Direct combustion is the burning of biomass in its natural state to produce process heat or steam (Ali, 1992). As the name of the application suggests, biomass is not converted into other forms such as liquid or gaseous fuels but is burnt directly. The actual burning process involves three main stages. These are drying; pyrolysis, when heat is added to the fuel; and oxidation, when heat is released (Kristoferson and Bokalders, 1987). Direct combustion is carried out in devices which range from very small domestic boilers, stoves and ovens to large-scale furnaces and multi-megawatt power plants (Pasztor and Kristoferson, 1990). A typical large-scale direct combustion system is illustrated inFigure 2.7. Process heat is used for large-scale purposes such as tobacco curing, beer brewing, fish smoking, brick burning, district heating and power generation (Strehler, 1990; Kaale, 1990).

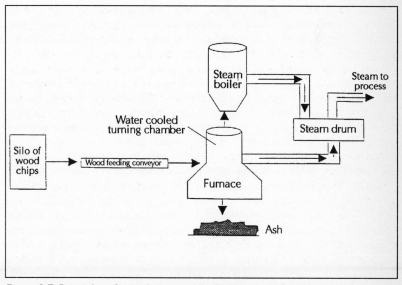

Figure 2.7 Principles of a modern wood-fuelled industrial combustion system
Source: Adapted from Kristoferson and Bokalders, 1987.

The most common feedstock for direct combustion systems – wood and agricultural residues – can usually be sourced locally. They are still comparatively cheaper than other fuels in most areas. With direct combustion, residues do not require pre-treatment. This application helps alleviate disposal problems and creates a useful by-product, ash, which can be used as a fertilizer owing to its mineral content (Ali, 1992). The technologies used for direct combustion are fairly simple and require basic operating skills. Planting trees in energy plantations for combustion diminishes soil erosion and adds aesthetic beauty, as well as providing energy. The sulphur content of biomass and SO_x emissions is insignificant. Direct combustion renewable systems are, therefore, an environmentally sound substitute for conventional fossil fuels, particularly coal and oil. An advantage of large-scale direct combustion over small domestic combustion is that fire can be managed much more effectively and pollution control equipment installed and operated more easily (Pasztor and Kristoferson, 1990).

If cooling of the combustion furnace is not possible by air or water flow, overheating and damage may occur. Most of the auxiliary equipment – required for mechanical fuel handling, combustion air and flue gas fans, process pumps and controls – requires a reliable supply of electricity, which is not available in all parts of the region. The risk of explosion also exists because of unburned combustible gases produced from the hot fuel bed. Another disadvantage is that the energy content of biomass is usually lower than that of coal: larger volumes are transported to the point of use *(ibid.)* which increases the cost of transportation. Cutting of logs may also be dangerous if care is not taken.

Direct combustion has been used extensively in human culture since time immemorial. Systems developed to accomplish biomass combustion have, in recent years, become highly sophisticated. This sophistication is a response to the rising prices of wood and crop-based fuels, the relatively high cost of fossil fuels, and the consequent need to make combustion more cost-effective (Tillman, 1987). Large furnaces are in use in Scandinavian countries, Austria, Switzerland, Canada, the USA and Germany, and in several developing countries where there are good sources of biomass for fuel. Fuels used include wood, straw and processing by-products such as rice hulls, bagasse and bark. In Sri Lanka, firewood represents an estimated 57 per cent of industrial energy demand while in Brazil it represents 21 per cent (Barnard, 1987). In Sweden, some demonstration plants (running district heating systems) are able to use wet fresh wood chips all year round. Denmark has demonstration district plants that use surplus agricultural straw. In Germany, there are three large wood chip furnaces with capacities ranging from 4 to 7 MW, installed in grass-drying units. In Italy (south and south-west of Milan), and in such typical rice-producing countries as India and the Philippines, rice hulls are used as fuel in steam and power generation. The range of power is typically from 0.5 MW to about 10 MW (Strehler, 1990).

REGIONAL STATUS

In 1990 it was estimated that direct combustion of biomass accounted for just under half of the industrial energy consumption in the Southern African Development Community (SADC) region (SADC, 1992). This is an important indicator of the potential role of this technology in the region's economy. In Uganda and Malawi the tobacco industry depends heavily on biomass to meet its energy needs. Kenya, another tobacco-growing country, uses significant amounts of fuelwood for tobacco curing and allied activities. The estimated total annual consumption of wood by the Kenyan tobacco industry is 89,000 cubic metres, of which 88 per cent is used as fuel for curing. This is approximately 0.3 per cent of all fuelwood used in Kenya (IFSC, 1986). The kind of furnace used deter-mines the amount of wood used in curing tobacco. It is estimated that the Malawian tobacco industry uses over 921,500 cubic metres of fuelwood, which represents 5.5 per cent of the total fuelwood used in the country. Tobacco curing consumes 88 per cent of the total fuelwood used in the industry. The rest is used in the construction of barns and in the manu-facture of cigarettes (IFSC, 1986). Zimbabwe also uses fuelwood for tobacco curing. It is estimated that the tobacco industry consumes 560,750 cubic metres of fuelwood every year. Nearly 126 million kilograms of tobacco are produced every year, with flue-cured tobacco contributing over 120 million kilograms *(ibid.)*. Agro-industries in Uganda consume nearly 457,000 cubic metres of wood every year (World Bank, 1986).

Gasification

Gasification is the conversion of biomass into a gaseous energy carrier known as producer gas, a process based on partial oxidation at high temperatures (Hos and Groeneveld, 1987). The gas produced is used mainly for heat production and electricity generation. It can also be used as a synthesis gas in the process industry to produce methanol or ammonia *(ibid.)*. The biomass converted into gaseous form is obtained mainly from wood and crop residues such as coconut, cotton, maize, rice and wheat residues. These can be acquired directly from energy plan-tations or from commercial and non-commercial biomass markets. Before it is gasified the biomass is treated, either physically by drying or cutting/chipping to reduce its size, or thermally by converting the material into charcoal. After this it is subjected to partial oxidation, then pyrolysis (heating to high temperatures in the absence of oxygen) in a machine known as a gasifier.

Different types of gasifiers are used for this purpose. The common types include:

• Updraught gasifier – gas and fuel flow in counter currents;
• Downdraught gasifier – gas and fuel flow in the same direction;
• Crossdraught gasifier – gas flows perpendicularly to fuel;

- Conventional fluidized bed gasifier – fuel particles are kept suspended in the upward gas flow;
- Circulating fluidized bed gasifier – fuel particles move upwards in the gasifier, are separated and then recirculated to the bottom of the fuel bed.

The gas generated consists of carbon monoxide, hydrogen, carbon dioxide, water vapour, methane, nitrogen and small amounts of condensable organic vapour. This gas can be burned directly in a furnace or boiler. In the case of combustion, no further treatment is required. It can also be used to generate electricity after it is cleaned and cooled further, as illustrated in Figure 2.8. Small-scale generation of electricity can be realized without the necessity of a steam cycle, simply by burning the gas in a reciprocating engine. Burning producer gas in boilers, kilns or furnaces can be very attractive. An advantage of producer gas over direct combustion is that it can be cleaned in relatively compact units prior to combustion (Hos and Groeneveld, 1987). Producer gas can be considered as one of the substitutes for petroleum fuels in engines and furnaces

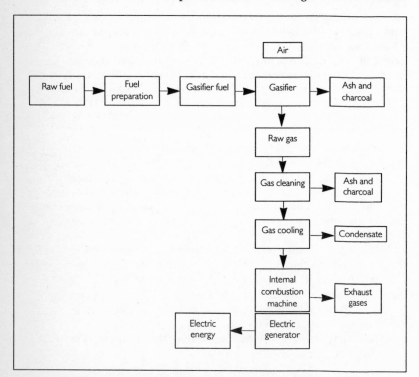

Figure 2.8 Principle schemes of gasifier plants for direct combustion and electric power generation

Source: Adapted from Kjellström, 1990

where either a 'clean fuel' or accurate temperature control is important. In this case, gasification can help in reducing dependence on and vulnerability to high energy prices or energy shortages. The process of gasification is also labour-intensive and therefore creates employment.

Table 2.5 Examples of producer gas plants operating in different parts of the world (1988)

Country	Producer gas plants for fuel gas generation to furnace or boiler	Producer gas plants for engine operation
Brazil	Lime kiln, Espera Feliz. Two down draught wood gasifiers, each 640 KW(t). Operating time each more than 19 000 hours.	A few hundred downdraught wood gasifiers of 30-120 KW reported to be operating. About 1000 crossdraught charcoal gasifiers installed on vehicles. Some also installed for operating stationery engines. Operating records covering up to 5200 hours available for one installation with 3 units.
Indonesia	Cacao dryer at Rajamandala, Java, downdraught wood gasifier of about 200 KW(t), over 2500 operating hours.	A few village power plants with engines operated by down-draught wood gasifiers; examples; Kebon Balong 14 KW(e), over 11000 hours, Jambi 35 KW(e), over 1800 hours.
Mali		Rice mill, Dogofiri, downdraught throatless rice husk gasifier of Chinese design for 160 KW(e) generator set. More than 55 000 operating hours.
Sweden	Three updraught wood gasifiers each about 5 MW(t) used for generation of fuel gas for boilers; operating record for each about 10 000 hours. Three circulating fluidized bed gasifiers of about 30 MW(t) each for generation of fuel gas to lime kilns in paper and pulp industry. Operating records from 15 000 to 5000 hours.	Two experimental installations, one with downdraught wood gasifier for engine of about 120 KW, one with circulating fluidized bed gasifier for engine of about 500 KW.

Source: Adapted from Kjellström, 1990

Gasification, however, has some important drawbacks. The technology is more complicated than direct combustion, requiring pre-treatment of the raw material. Gas-tight handling, gas cleaning, high temperature materials and safety have to meet requirements that are more stringent than for direct combustion equipment. The conversion of biomass into a fuel gas leads to decreased thermal efficiency caused by heat losses. As in the case of direct combustion systems, electricity is required to run motors and blowers. Maintenance and operation of a gasifier-boiler combination are complicated by comparison with a direct combustion system and usually require more operator attention *(ibid.)*. It can be dangerous if the operator violates the safety rules or neglects maintenance of the system.

Current technologies are still based on the designs of the mid-1940s. Only a few people have retained a practical knowledge of the design, material selection, operation and maintenance of the equipment. Gasifiers were extensively used for the generation of fuel gas from solid fuels at the beginning of this century. During the Second World War, many countries utilized gasifiers to enable vehicle engines to run on domestic solid fuels. When gasoline and diesel oil became available at reasonable prices after the war, the use of gasifiers was abandoned rapidly, but increasing petroleum prices during the 1970s brought a renewed interest in this technology as a means of reducing dependence on imported petroleum fuels (Kjellström, 1990).

The total number of operating producer gas installations to date is still fairly small, probably less than a few thousand world-wide. The current applications range from large industrial fuel gas generators of 30,000 KW (thermal) for lime kilns in the paper and pulp industry in Sweden and Finland, to small gasifier-operated engines of a few kilowatts for irrigation pumps used by individual farmers in rural areas in developing countries. Table 2.5 compares installations operating in different parts of the world (Kjellström, 1990).

REGIONAL STATUS
A plant to introduce, test and develop producer gas techniques for applications such as sawmilling, small-scale generation and vehicle usage was established by the Tanzanian Wood Industry Corporation (TWICO). Funding was provided by both the Tanzanian government and the Swedish International Development Cooperation Agency (SIDA). The plant has proved practical and economically feasible (Stockholm Environment Institute, 1990; Mwandosya, 1990). Sawmills, mainly concentrated around the mountain regions of Kilimanjaro and Meru, were initially powered by diesel engines as electricity was not available. In the 1980s, oil prices went up and, as a result, TWICO decided to test the operations of a sawmill run on charcoal gas with charcoal produced from the sawmill residue. This led to a reduction in dependence on oil. In 1987, a gasifier system was installed in Ethiopia about 140 km from Addis Ababa but this system is no longer in operation (Turyareeba, 1991a). Gasifier

systems were also installed in Sudan and Zimbabwe for sawmill operations and in Uganda to generate electricity for briquetting plants. Operation has been intermittent, however, and thus the briquetting plants have relied mainly on the national grid for electricity. Applied research is urgently needed into possibilities for the replication of gasifier technology in other industries (such as tobacco in Uganda, Kenya and Malawi) which rely on large amounts of biomass to meet energy needs (UNDP/World Bank, 1986; Bernard, 1990).

Small-scale biomass technologies

Small-scale biomass technologies encompass a wide range, including charcoal production, improved stoves, briquetting and household biogas.

Improved charcoal production technologies

Charcoal production is a process in which heat is applied to organic matter inside a relatively airtight container commonly referred to as a kiln. Hence, charcoal is wood charred in the absence of oxygen. Due to its lack of moisture and high carbon content, charcoal contains large amounts of energy. It has about twice the amount of energy as an equal amount of air-dry wood. Charcoal can be produced from many biomass materials such as wood, millet stems and corn cobs. Wood is one of the most suitable feedstocks, usually in the form of stems, branches and tops from softwoods (which produce soft, bulky charcoal), hardwoods (charcoal from these woods will burn longer) and palms. Residues from sawmills (off-cuts, but not sawdust and bark) can also be used. Its quality is normally good enough for domestic purposes (Roos and Rojczyk, 1984).

The process by which organic material becomes charcoal is called carbonization and can be broken into four distinct phases: combustion, dehydration, the exothermic phase and cooling. All of these phases may be going on in the kiln simultaneously, but each piece of wood must pass through the four-phase sequence.

1 The combustion phase is the only time during the carbonization process when large quantities of oxygen are required. In this phase, a fire is started in one part of the wood load (charge) until that section is burning well. During this stage, the kiln is heated from ambient temperature to over 500°C. After combustion is completed, the oxygen content is drastically reduced and the temperature of the kiln drops to as low as 120°C.

2 In the dehydration phase, the heat provided by combustion drives moisture out of the charge in the form of steam. As the charge dries, the temperature rises slowly to about 270°C. Dehydration continues until all the free moisture is driven off.

3   In the exothermic phase, once dehydration is completed, the wood itself starts to break down under the influence of heat, producing even more heat by exothermic reactions. The air is completely cut off at this point to prevent combustion. During the exothermic phase, the temperature rises to about 700°c. The remaining solid material is charcoal.

4   The cooling stage in the kiln allows the temperature of the charcoal to drop to a point where it can be extracted from the kiln.

Charcoal-making devices can be classified either as kilns – in which a portion of the wood load is burned to start the carbonization process – or as retorts – in which the heat needed to carbonize the wood load is applied from outside the shell of the device. Charcoal kilns can be further classified in two broad categories: improved and traditional charcoal production technologies. One main type of traditional charcoal production technology is the simple earth kiln, composed of a neatly stacked pile of wood which is then completely covered with green vegetation and earth (Fig 2.9).

There are a variety of improved technologies. The *Casamance kiln* (Fig 2.10) was developed from the earth kiln with several improvements. A platform is built to raise the wood load off the ground and a circumferential air chamber is extended all round the kiln. It has a single large chimney on one side to reverse the draught. This creates a sophisticated gas and heat circulation system which is easy to construct. The improvements achieve, with very little capital outlay, a dramatic yield increase

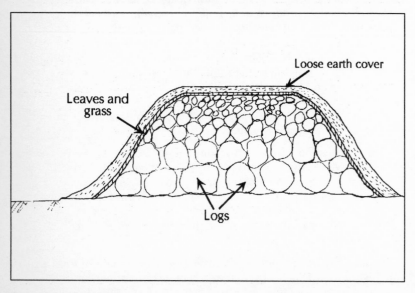

Figure 2.9 An earth kiln
Source: Adapted from Gate, 1984.

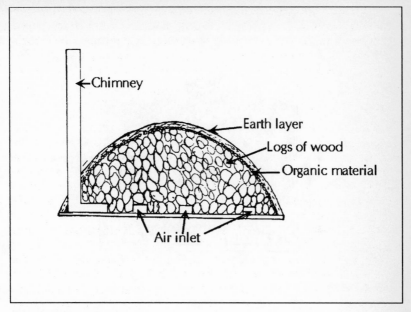

Figure 2.10 A Casamance kiln
Source: Adapted from Gate, 1984.

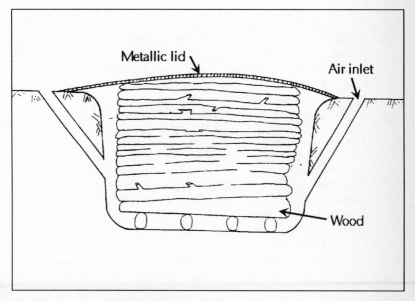

Figure 2.11 An improved pit kiln
Source: Adapted from Gate, 1984.

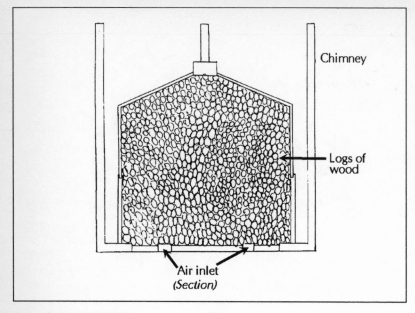

Figure 2.12 A Mark V kiln
Source: Adapted from Gate, 1984

and a shortened carbonization time. There is also the *improved pit kiln* (Fig 2.11): in its simplest form this is a hole in the ground in which a fire is started; then wood is added and the top is covered with vegetation and earth. Sometimes a metal cover is used to achieve a better air seal and reduce contamination. *Metal kilns* are constructed from metal either alone or in combination with other materials. The Mark V (Fig 2.12) is one of the best-known types. It has a main body of two cylinders joined with a slightly conical lid and top. This lid has a hole in the centre which is capped except during ignition. Joints between the 3 parts are sealed with sand. One of the best-known *cement kilns* is the Missouri kiln (Fig 2.13). This mammoth kiln takes up to 45 days to complete a carbonization cycle. It has alternate chimneys and vents along the sides and 4 lighting vents in the top. There are large metal doors in each end to facilitate mechanized loading and unloading (Gate, 1984).

Charcoal production has been practised for hundreds of years around the globe. In AD 500 it was used in the iron industry of Central Africa before the industrial revolution in Europe (Ackerman and de Almeida, 1990). In the late 1800s it was used to power steam boats on the Senegal river (Ribot, 1993). It is still used in Brazil for smelting iron because Brazil is not endowed with high-quality coal reserves (Ackerman and de Almeida, 1990). The charcoal is produced in large-scale systems using

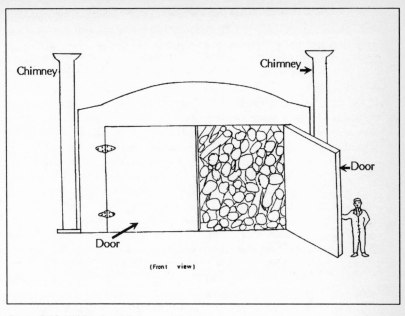

Figure 2.13 A Missouri kiln
Source: Adapted from Gate, 1984.

brick kilns, with dedicated forestry energy plantations as the source of raw material (Hollingdale *et al.*, 1991; Ackerman and de Almeida, 1990). Charcoal has also been produced in Japan for over 1,000 years: now it is produced there for purifying waste water, traditional heaters and special tea drinking ceremonies (Glow, 1990).

REGIONAL STATUS
Nearly all the charcoal used for household cooking in Eastern and Southern Africa is made by small producers in simple earth kilns or pit kilns near where the trees are felled. Charcoal is often produced sporadically when agricultural labour requirements are low or the producer needs extra cash. Usually, less than 5 cubic metres of wood are carbonized in one cycle. It has been argued that there is a substantial loss of useful energy in converting wood to charcoal and that the yield of charcoal from traditional kilns is 8–15 per cent of the weight of the wood consumed (O'Keefe *et al.*, 1984). There have been conflicting findings in various countries, however: in some countries, the introduction of improved charcoal production technologies was found to be unnecessary because the traditional methods compared well with improved methods in terms of efficiency, while other countries identified a need to introduce improved technologies.

In Zambia, charcoal is the most important household fuel, meeting the energy needs of about 83 per cent of urban households. With an urbanization level of 42 per cent, charcoal is the major source of energy for more than a third of the population. Charcoal production is thus an important Zambian industry, providing employment to a large number of people. Out of an estimated 45,000 in the whole industry (World Bank/ESMAP, 1990), 90 per cent are engaged in charcoal production and all of these workers are rurally based. The charcoal used in central Zambia is produced from Miombo woodland by the traditional earth kiln method. Until recently, this method was dismissed as being wasteful. This led to efforts to introduce what was considered a more efficient method, the use of a steel kiln. This type of kiln was not adopted by producers, however, partly due to its high costs and high demand on labour since the logs had to be cut into shorter billets to fit into the kiln. Meanwhile, the need to adopt improved techniques was disputed; it was found that the deforestation due to the use of Miombo woodland is a temporary problem, and that the regenerative capacity of the natural forest system is sufficient to withstand this degradation of the forest land. Further, the suggestion that the traditional method of production is less wasteful than previously assumed has been substantiated. A recent World Bank /ESMAP study (1990) showed that the traditional earth kiln technology is relatively efficient, with production efficiencies (calculated on a bone dry weight basis) ranging between 17 and 33 per cent (Hibajene, 1994).

In Somalia, as in Zambia and many other countries in the region, the major domestic fuel is charcoal. The most widely used charcoal production method there is the Bay method, which takes its name from the Bay region 300–350 km west of the capital, Mogadishu. This is a method in which the kiln is built by stacking timber upright on the soil floor. It is built into a circular mound two tiers high at the centre, with larger pieces making up the lower tier. It is packed as close as possible and the gaps are filled with smaller pieces of wood. The mound is then covered with metal sheets made from empty oil drums, overlapping at the edges. A 'skirt' of thorny branch wood is placed around the mound and then 5 cm of thick red soil is used to cover the mound, leaving about 125 cm from the ground level uncovered around the stack's circumference. To light the kiln, a worker must climb to the top and remove some of the soil and upper sheets until he has lit the timber. The sheets are then put back in place. Holes are made in the upper part of the kiln to allow air to enter and smoke to exit. The Bay method is widespread in the central and southern areas of the country and charcoal produced using this method used to account for about 80 per cent of the country's charcoal production.

Around half of the total land area of Somalia is covered with woodland and wooded brushland, the largest national resource for charcoal manufacture. Production of charcoal in the Bay region has been governed by strict regulations: only members of the Charcoal Producers Cooperative and their workers were allowed to manufacture the fuel and a licence had to be obtained from the National Range Agency (NRA). The charcoal producers remained in an area until the usable timber was exhausted – normally two years – before moving on to a new site. Researchers from the National Resources Institute (NRI), the Overseas Development Agency's (ODA's) scientific institute, examined the Bay method of charcoal production and compared it with a portable metal kiln of their own design which has been used widely in other developing countries. They discovered that the Bay method compares well with their own metal kiln. The method gives high yields, with over 40 per cent of the charcoal produced being of high quality (ODA, 1991).

In Tanzania, the most widely used method of charcoal production is the traditional earth kiln. At the Timber Utilization Research Centre at Moshi, tests were conducted on the performance of five different traditional earth kilns and the results obtained proved that the Casamance kiln is the most technically and economically viable method for charcoal production in the rural areas (BTC, 1992).

Improved stoves

In the last 35 years, substantial efforts have been directed towards the modernization of fuelwood production and end-use technologies. One of the most sustained efforts has been the development of environmentally sound and efficient improved stoves for rural and urban households and for institutions in developing countries.

The development of improved stoves has undergone three phases (Smith, 1989). The first phase started in the 1950s in countries such as India, where one of the early improved stoves designs, the *magan chula*, was developed (Krugmann, 1987). The objective of these early programmes was to uplift the living conditions of the poor majority in the developing world through self-sufficiency and general emancipation.

The second phase started in the early 1970s and it brought together two groups, technologists and energy specialists. The technologists were searching for a universally acceptable and super-efficient stove. The energy specialists were looking for a solution to the woodfuel crisis which was then said to be an important contributor to deforestation and desertification (Eckholm, 1975). Work in this phase was driven by a simple rationale which stated that the dissemination of millions of energy-efficient stoves would reduce woodfuel consumption and lead to fewer trees being cut down to provide cooking fuel. This was expected to slow down or possibly reverse deforestation and desertification.

The increasing concern over energy issues caused by the oil price hike in the early 1970s added more impetus to work on improved stoves – perceived then as one of the most important interventions in the household energy sector. The second phase was dominated by vigorous and extensive research and development and laboratory-based work. In this phase, technical and scientific concerns dominated the stove agenda. The socio-economic aspects of stove development and dissemination took a back seat.

The third phase, which began in the early 1980s, saw the dissolution of the scientific optimism that characterized the 1970s. While substantial progress on how to define, measure and improve the performance of the stove had been made (Prasad and Verhaart, 1983), the dissemination of millions of stoves had not taken place. Wide-scale dissemination proved to be a much more difficult undertaking than envisaged. For example, in Lesotho, a USAID project managed to disseminate only 139 stoves after spending close to US $150,000. This translates to over $1,000 per stove (Karekezi, 1988d). Long-term commitment of personnel and financial resources, together with substantial local participation, were clearly needed (Karekezi, 1990). There are important differences between stoves for rural and urban households and for institutions. Rural stoves often use various fuels ranging from wood to animal and agricultural residues. In many cases, the fuel is collected rather than bought from the market place (Karekezi and Walubengo, 1989). Urban stoves, on the other hand, are often single-fuel devices. In many urban areas of Asia and Africa, charcoal is an important urban fuel. In most cases, the fuel is purchased rather than collected. Agricultural residues are rarely used in urban areas. Institutional stoves are mainly used in remote hospitals, schools, restaurants and small hotels. The distinctive feature of institutional stoves is their large capacity to allow preparation of food for a large number of persons. Fuel for institutional stoves is almost invariably bought and this is often in large consignments which tends to facilitate the collection of the relevant fuel consumption data.

The improved stove saves fuel and money because heat loss is minimized by some form of insulation (e.g. air gap or ceramic liner and/or cement/vermiculite layer). The well insulated fire also burns hotter and more efficiently, resulting in greater heat output per mass of fuel. The insulated fire reduces accidental burn hazards, an important feature for families with children. The superior combustion rate reduces emissions of particulate and toxic fumes by 20 per cent. Many improved stoves are designed to provide greater stability.

On the other hand, improved stoves are generally more expensive than traditional stoves and, if poorly made, may not last long. To date, over 137 improved stove programmes have been implemented world-wide (Barnes, et al., 1993). Millions of stoves have been disseminated in developing countries, with countries such as China, Nepal and India accounting for large numbers. In Nepal, 35,000 stoves were disseminated between 1981 and 1987.

REGIONAL STATUS

In Eastern and Southern Africa, there are improved stove projects in almost all the countries. The projects range from small-scale grassroots initiatives by community-based organizations to large-scale national programmes which are usually supported by donor agencies (Karekezi, 1993b).

URBAN STOVES

One of the most successful charcoal stove projects in the region is the Kenyan Ceramic Jiko (KCJ) initiative. The KCJ is made up of metal cladding with a wide base and a ceramic liner which is held on to the metal by a thin layer of cement and vermiculite or cement mixed with diatomite where available. At least 25 per cent of the liner base is perforated with holes of 1.5 cm diameter to form the grate. The stove has three pot rests, two handles, three legs and a door. The door is used to control the air flow. The standard model weighs about 6 kg which means it can be carried around easily (KENGO, 1991).

The stove is suitable for cooking patterns where charcoal is used as a fuel; one pot is used at a time; power outputs are controllable; space heating is not a 'must'; and stove portability is essential *(ibid.)*. The KCJ helps to direct 25–40 per cent of the heat from the fire to the cooking pot. The traditional metal stove that the ceramic jiko replaces delivers only 10–20 per cent of the heat generated to the pot, whereas an open cooking fire yields efficiencies as low as 10 per cent (Kammen, 1995). The manufacturing of the KCJ is now a relatively mature cottage industry. As

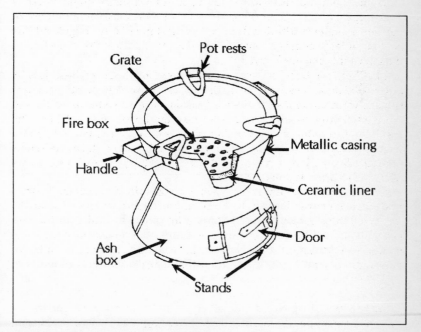

Figure 2.14 The Kenya Ceramic Jiko (KCJ)
Source: Adapted from KENGO, 1991.

expected, the level of specialization in the manufacture of the stove has increased as has the level of mechanization. There is now a discernible labour division. Shauri Moyo is the principal artisanal production centre in Nairobi, where there are artisans whose sole occupation is to purchase clay liners and metal claddings and to assemble and retail complete stoves to customers. There are two types of stove producers in Nairobi: mechanized manufacturers, like Jerri International and Waka Ceramics; and semi-mechanized producers like Sunrise Clayworks, Jiko Bora, Jerri/Miaki and Rural Enterprises. It is estimated that mechanized producers are manufacturing close to 3,200 liners a month. Semi-mechanized producers are now producing an estimated 10,600 liners per month. Thus, the total current production rate in Nairobi alone is in the region of 13,600 stoves a month. This yields an annual total of 163,200 stoves (Karekezi and Walubengo, 1989). As shown in Table 2.6, the number of KCJs disseminated in Kenya is now estimated to be over 700,000 (Kammen and Kammen, 1993; GTZ, 1994).

Box 2.4
Economic analysis of improved stoves

———————— ✱ ————————

In Kenya, average daily charcoal consumption with an improved stove fell to 0.39 kg per person per day from the 0.67 kg per person per day used by the traditional stove. This adds up to a total yearly saving of 613 kg per family, with a value of about 1,170 Kenya shillings (US$64.7). In Rwanda, the savings with improved charcoal stoves are great. There, consumption of charcoal dropped to 0.33 kg per person per day from 0.51 kg per person per day. This means that in a year, a family could save about 394 kg of charcoal worth 6,310 Rwanda Francs (US$84.1). Savings of this order are substantial for families in countries like Rwanda and Kenya where average incomes per person are only US$300–370 per year.

Sources: Kumar and Hotchkiss, 1988; ESMAP, 1991.

From the above information, the KCJ might be declared a success story, its further development assured for years to come. The future of this stove is not completely secure, however, because of several constraints. The overall penetration rate for Nairobi, for example, was found to be no higher than about 13 per cent, indicating that the dissemination of the KCJ is far from complete. Another source of concern is quality control, a question that has not been tackled adequately so far. As the attention given to the KCJ by NGOs and governments wanes, manufacturers are increasingly producing sub-standard stoves. Poor clay liners have begun to find their way on to the market.

The KCJ stove design has now been replicated successfully in Uganda,

Figure 2.15 The Black Power stove
Source: Otiti, 1991

Rwanda, Tanzania, Sudan, Ethiopia and Malawi. In Tanzania, the national stove project financed by the World Bank has disseminated over 50,000 KCJ-type Jiko Bora stoves (Otiti, 1991). In Uganda, there are two main improved charcoal stoves: the Usika Charcoal Stove and the Black Power stove (Fig 2.15). Both are KCJ adaptations made of mud-fired clay liners and metal claddings, differing only in shape. It is estimated that a total of about 52,000 of these stoves have been disseminated. Some producers make whole stoves, while others sub-contract part of the work. For instance, Usika Crafts Ltd produces liners and commissions traditional stove artisans to produce metal claddings. Most producers face market problems (Turyahikayo *et al.*, 1995). In 1993, Usika Crafts was producing 1,600 liners but could only sell 400 stoves each month; while Black Power, with a capacity of 700 stoves per month, could only sell about 200 (Turyareeba, 1993). There is no organized strategy for marketing household improved stoves. The commercial household stove producers do not carry out awareness programmes for customers, and there are no well-organized retail outlets. The producers depend on customers coming to them, despite stiff competition from the much cheaper traditional stoves. Improved stoves cost about US$8 while traditional stoves cost US$2–3.

Research and development work on the improved charcoal stove in Zambia was initiated in 1981 by Professor Yamba of the University of Zambia's Department of Engineering, who field tested both the traditional

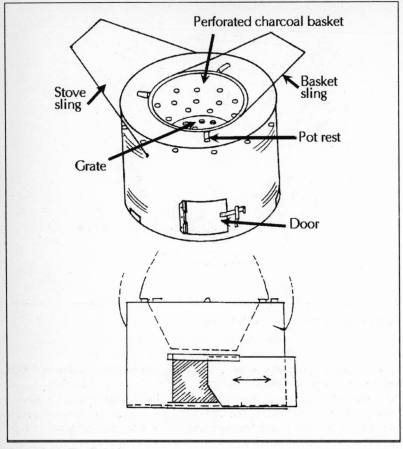

Figure 2.16 The Dub10
Source: Karekezi, 1987.

and improved charcoal stoves. The improved stove (Mbaula) differs from the traditional stove in that it does not have many holes punched into its walls. During these tests, it was established that the improved stove had an efficiency of 29–30 per cent as compared to the traditional stove's efficiency of 8 per cent. The project targeted local tinsmiths (artisans) and women's organizations working in programmes such as nutrition and community development. The aim of the project was to train the artisans to make the improved stoves and the women to use the improved stove properly. By 1989, over 340 tinsmiths in Lusaka alone and over 2,000 women had been trained since the project started. The project was publicized through T-shirts, posters, leaflets, radio, television, agricultural shows and trade fairs. At the 1988 Agricultural and Commercial Show in

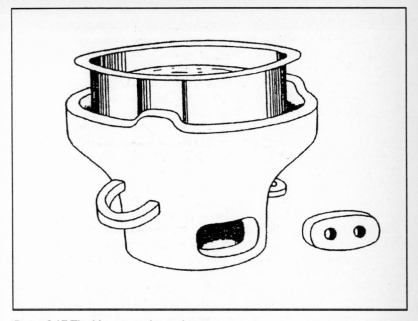

Figure 2.17 The Morogoro charcoal stove
Source: Otiti, 1991.

Lusaka, the project organized a successful exhibition and some 500 improved stoves were sold (Nachula, 1989). According to Sampa and Sichone (1995), however, the results of the dissemination have not been very positive of late. It is quite apparent, they assert, that the improved stove has not gained social acceptance and that the project has failed to commercialize the technology.

In Burundi, the Bujumbura Urban Development (DUB) household energy project developed about a dozen improved stove models with the help of World Bank consultants. DUB 10, shown in Figure 2.16, was eventually selected for wide-scale dissemination to replace the traditional Imbabura. To produce the improved stove, DUB procured all the necessary raw materials for its artisans and pays them 150 FBu (equivalent to US$1.20) per completed stove. DUB then sold the stoves for 250 FBu through its stalls at the four major markets of Bujumbura. There was no specialization in production; each artisan made his own stoves. The DUB workshop suffered high absenteeism and attrition rates which resulted directly from the low profit margins of the DUB 10 stoves (Karekezi, 1987).

In 1985 Tanzania's Morogoro Fuelwood Stove Project (MFSP) was launched with support from NORAD. One of the stoves developed under this project was the improved Morogoro charcoal stove (Fig 2.17) which uses up to 45 per cent less fuel than the traditional metal charcoal stove.

One major setback in the dissemination of this stove was the discovery that the all-ceramic Morogoro improved charcoal stoves crack when they are first used. The design was thus changed to incorporate a grate, which reduces the cracking rate to about 25 per cent. About 2,500 stoves have been sold, although not all are still in use. Experience gained by the MFSP indicates that people in Morogoro are generally not motivated to pay for or even use a stove if they can get firewood with relative ease and free of charge. Thus, the diffusion of these stoves has been fairly low. Another type of improved charcoal stove is the Kenyan double-walled stove designed by UNICEF. In Tanzania, the stove was christened the Jiko La Dodoma. This stove has a heat transfer efficiency of 36 per cent compared to 15–20 per cent for the traditional stove. Material production costs of the Jiko La Dodoma are four to five times higher than those of a traditional stove. Likewise, the labour input required is five times greater and the work needs a skilled artisan. The stove is both bulky and heavy and small pots tend to slide while food is being stirred. In spite of these drawbacks, the Dodoma stove has registered significant sales in Dodoma, Arusha, Tanga, Iringa and Dar es Salaam (Otiti, 1992).

A Dar es Salaam improved charcoal stove project has adopted the metal-ceramic design of the KCJ, which has been modified to suit prevailing Tanzanian production technology. The end result is the charcoal-burning Jiko Bora. This project was launched under the Renewable Energy Development Project Unit (REDPU) of the Ministry of Energy and Minerals. The project started by buying 200 KCJs from Kenya and giving them to households in and around Dar es Salaam. Residents were allowed to use the stoves for about one month. If they liked them, they paid for them; but if they found the stoves unsuitable, they were free to return them so that they could be given to other households to try. After one month, none of the households returned the stoves; instead, they asked for more stoves for their neighbours. Artisans were therefore trained to make this type of stove. About 300 stoves were made in Tanzania and laboratory-tested at the Institute of Production Innovation. The performance of the stoves was found to be acceptable. The future market of the Jiko Bora looks promising, with sales projected at over 60,000 units per year in the Dar es Salaam region alone and well over half a million annually country-wide (ibid.).

In Sudan both the traditional stove (wood and charcoal versions) and the improved charcoal stove are available. The recorded efficiency of the traditional charcoal stove is approximately 17 per cent. In 1983 the Energy Research Council (ERC) began to introduce, test and disseminate improved charcoal stoves in the Khartoum area. This work was funded by the Sudan Renewable Energy Project (SREP) and was limited to Khartoum. Two models have been used extensively: the Canun El Serour and the Thai bucket stove. It is estimated that at least 20,000 improved stoves have been disseminated in Khartoum since 1983 (ERC, 1990).

RURAL STOVES

The traditional firewood rural stove is free and requires no special skill or material to build. It is versatile, as it fits any size of pot, and is easily controlled by adding or removing fuel. It has few limitations on size and shape of fuel and it burns different kinds biomass (Turyareeba, 1990). It serves other purposes such as space heating and lighting and acts as a focus of social interaction. The fire also produces smoke which keeps away insects and preserves the thatch, timber, and food. It is, however, difficult to use during windy periods. The smoke produced poses a health danger (Karekezi, Turyareeba and Musumba, 1995, Hankins, 1987) and a lot of heat is lost by radiation and convection, reducing its efficiency (Hankins, 1987).

Improved rural woodstoves are designed to reduce heat loss, increase combustion efficiency and attain a higher heat transfer efficiency (Turyareeba, 1990). For example, enclosing the fire reduces heat loss by convection; insulating the firebox reduces heat loss by radiation; controlling flow of air through the fire and incorporating a grate in the firebox increases combustion efficiency (Turyareeba, 1990; Hankins, 1987). The materials used for the construction of improved rural stoves include sand and clay.

A large number of rural households buy neither fuel nor stoves. This has hindered the dissemination of improved woodstoves: it is difficult to

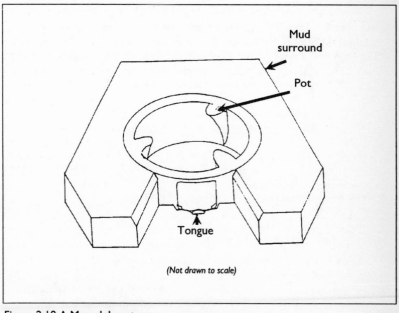

Figure 2.18 A Maendeleo stove
Source: Adapted from Walubengo, 1990a.

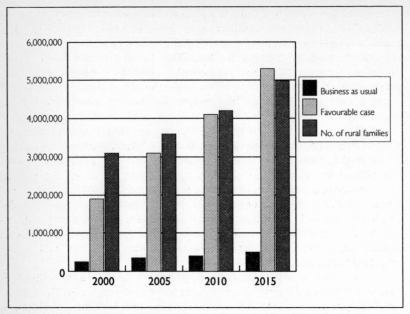

Figure 2.19 Projection for Maendeleo stove dissemination in Kenya
(See Box 2.5 for explanatory note.)

assess penetration without a major monitoring and evaluation exercise in the region. While Table 2.6 provides impressive figures in terms of the total number of stoves disseminated in urban areas, low penetration rates in rural areas appear to be the norm rather than the exception. The figures in Table 2.6 also need to be adjusted to reflect the number of stoves sold as replacements for worn-out ones. Some general assumptions made at the design stage which have hampered the dissemination of improved rural stoves include (Karekezi and Turyareeba, 1994):

- Traditional stoves are uniformly of low efficiency;
- Reduction of fuel consumption is the only way of increasing efficiency (disregarding the important role of improved cooking practices);
- Rural households do not require space heating;
- The open fire is used only for cooking;
- There is negligible use of agricultural residues for cooking;
- Households have pots of the same size.

In spite of these constraints, woodstove initiatives have continued to gather support in the region and encouraging results are beginning to emerge, among them the Maendeleo stove (Figs 2.18 and 2.19), produced and disseminated in Kenya. It is a one-pot, chimneyless wood-burning stove made as a fired ceramic liner and installed in a mud surround in the kitchen. Its three sturdy pot rests support a range of flat- and round-bottomed pots. The fuel entrance is in front, in an arch across the base (ITDG/GTZ, 1992). It was produced and disseminated under the Women and Energy Project (WEP), started in January 1983 as part of the Special Energy Programme (SEP) of the Ministry of Energy and funded by the German Technical Cooperation Organization (GTZ). After a three-year research period (1983–5), the project completed the design, testing and systematic production of the improved energy-saving Maendeleo woodstove.

Training and dissemination began early in 1986 in five pilot districts, with the aim of duplicating the dissemination strategy in other districts if it proved successful. In 1988 a portable version of the Maendeleo was developed and was well received. In 1991 the project spread its activities to 23 more districts and at present operates on a national level. The stove achieves an average efficiency of about 30 per cent and when in use in the field may give a fuelwood saving of about 50 per cent compared with the three-stone fire. Other benefits include reduced cooking time, minimal attention, reduced smoke and incidence of burns, and cleaner and more hygienic working conditions.

Production is achieved through women's groups and individual potters. The producers are given training in all aspects of the manufacturing technology of the Maendeleo liners, as well as basic training in business management and marketing to promote sustainability. The producers are also provided with basic production equipment such as moulds, kilns and workshops. In total, there are over 40 production centres for ceramic liners, of which more than 33 belong to women's groups. Their total monthly production is about 10,000 but they have the potential to produce over 15,000 fired liners. By the end of 1993, over 180,000 stoves had been disseminated by the Women and Energy Programme (GTZ, 1994). By 1994, the total was estimated to be about 250,000. In an effort to come up with a sustainable dissemination system, the project adopted a semi-commercial approach whereby the commercial production centres produce the liners and then various organizations with extension programmes at grassroots level disseminate them (Muriithi, 1995).

Recently the Maendeleo liner has been introduced to Uganda by CARE-Uganda and the Intermediate Technology Development Group (ITDG-Kenya). An evaluation of CARE-Uganda's Stove and Household Energy Programme (SHEP) indicates that there is a market for liners among urban households in south-western Uganda who use firewood for cooking. In addition, liners can be produced by the existing fired-clay charcoal stove producers with little or no additional training (Turyareeba, 1993a).

An improved stove programme started in Zimbabwe in 1986 after the University of Zimbabwe, through its Development Technology Centre (DTC), came up with an efficient improved woodstove known as the Tsotso stove (Fig 2.20). It is a portable, metal, single-pot, wood-burning

Box 2.5
Explanatory notes for Maendeleo projection graph (Figure 2.19, p. 60)
————————————————————*————————————————————

The business-as-usual scenario illustrates the current state of affairs in the dissemination of Maendeleo woodstoves in Kenya. Four programmes are already in place and their efforts have brought about the current dissemination rate of 16,411 stoves per year.

Kenya has 54 districts (as of January 1996). For each household to have a Maendeleo stove by the year 2020, at least one Maendeleo stove programme is required in each of these districts. Hence if four programmes can disseminate 16,411 stoves per year, then 54 programmes will disseminate.

$$\frac{54 \times 16,411}{4} = 221,548$$

The lower case has been plotted using the business-as-usual growth rate of 16,411 per year while the favourable case has been plotted using the growth rate that would be seen with 54 programmes disseminating Maendeleo stoves, i.e. 221,548 stoves per year.

It is well known that 80 per cent of Kenya's population is found in rural areas. The Maendeleo stove is targeted at rural dwellers as they mainly use wood for cooking. Assuming each household has an average of eight family members, it is possible to find out how many rural families there are in any given year in Kenya.

stove constructed from sheet metal with vermiculite insulation enclosed between inner and outer cylindrical walls. The combustion system is extremely efficient and the stove will effectively burn small pieces of wood and other waste. Before 1986, several organizations had made attempts to introduce improved stoves (based on the Lorena model) in Zimbabwe but soon ran into difficulties. They failed to establish the needs of the target groups first and did not look at stove design scientifically. This disappointed the target group which got stoves that did not suit their needs. Thus by 1988 a half-dozen agencies had managed to disseminate only 4,000 improved stoves, some six years after starting their work and having spent more than US$160,000.

The stoves introduced earlier were based on the famed Lorena high mass stove. A major complaint about this stove was its inability to provide space heating during the winter months, when night temperatures

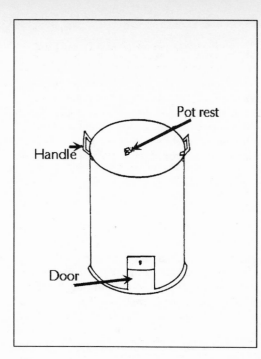

Figure 2.20
The Tsotso stove
Source: Adapted from Walubengo, 1990a.

Table 2.6 Improved stoves disseminated in selected countries

Country	Rural	Urban	Total	Year
Kenya	180,000	600,000	780,000	1993
Tanzania	–	54,000	54,000	1991
Uganda	–	52,000	52,000	1995
Ethiopia	22,000	23,000	45,000	1993
Rwanda[+]	–	30,000	30,000	1991
Sudan	1,380	26,580	27,960	1992
Zimbabwe	10,000	10,880	20,880	1994
Burundi[+]	–	20,500	20,500	1993
Somalia[+]	–	15,400	15,400	1988
Malawi	–	3,700	3,700	1991
Botswana	–	1,500	1,500	1994
Lesotho	800[*]	670	1,470	1993

+ civil strife in these nations has almost certainly reduced the number of stoves in use drastically.

* installed in schools

– Not available

Sources: Katihabwa, 1993; Kammen et al, 1994; Alemayehu, 1993; Getta, 1990; Kammen and Kammen, 1993; GTZ, 1994; Gay et al, 1993; World Bank, 1991; Karekezi, 1988; Ali and Hood, 1992; Kismul et al, 1990; Otiti, 1991; Otiti, 1993.

can fall below zero. The other complaint was that the stove was not capable of holding the large drums used for beer making. These facts could have been assessed easily enough if the stove programmes had first carried out a 'needs assessment' survey. By contrast some 10,000 DTC Tsotso stoves had been disseminated by the end of 1988, two years after introduction, at a cost of US$17,000. The Tsotso stove programme proved more successful because the team went out to the target group and established their needs. Once the stove was designed, it was taken out for field tests and altered to suit the users (Walubengo, 1990a).

Table 2.6 shows the number of improved stoves disseminated in selected countries within the region.

INSTITUTIONAL STOVES

Improved institutional stoves have been disseminated in several countries within Eastern and Southern Africa. In most institutions in Kenya, firewood is used for cooking in inefficient traditional stoves or models which are only marginally better than the three-stone fire. As a consequence, enormous number of trees are being cut down faster than they are being planted to provide wood energy for institutions. In response to this problem, the Bellerive Foundation, an NGO based in Ruiru, Kenya, developed a fuel-efficient institutional stove. Field evaluation and feedback from institutions that have installed this institutional stove to replace traditional systems indicate that when it is properly operated fuel costs for catering can be reduced by 75 per cent or more. Bellerive institutional stoves (Fig 2.21) come in various sizes ranging from 12 to 200 litres. Investment costs range from US$147 to US$1,364 (exchange rate Ksh55 = US$1), including installation costs, supplementary equipment, training for cooks and maintenance contracts. By January 1992, 500 institutions had been fitted with Bellerive institutional stoves (Bellerive Foundation, 1992).

Another institution involved in the production and dissemination of institutional stoves in Kenya is a private company known as Rural Technologies Enterprises (RTE). To meet the cooking needs of different institutions, RTE has developed a wide range of highly efficient stoves which ensure maximum heat retention and economical fuelwood consumption. RTE offers a range of single-pot institutional stoves, with volumes ranging from 25 to 300 litres. The price range of these cooking systems is US$270–910. It also offers multi-pot institutional stoves for hotels, restaurants and home economics laboratories (RTE brochure, undated).

Production and dissemination of institutional stoves in Uganda started in the mid-1980s with two producers who designed the stove models they disseminated, mostly adopted from models produced in different parts of the region, particularly Kenya and Tanzania. Currently, there are many producers, one of which is Joint Energy and Environment

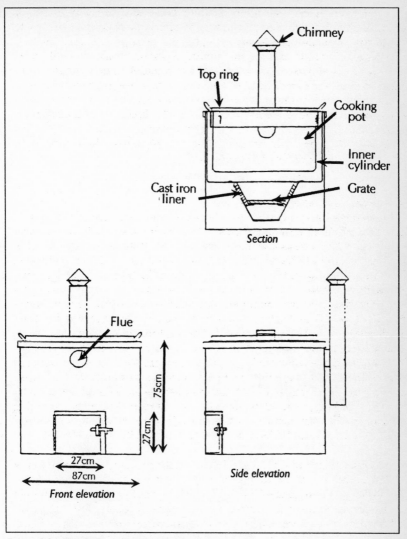

Figure 2.21 The Bellerive institutional stove
Source: Adapted from Bellerive Foundation, 1993.

Projects (JEEP). Usika Crafts Ltd also produces and disseminates an institutional stove with a brick cylindrical structure and a metal chimney, fuelled by firewood or agricultural residues. The stove is built on site and supplied with a suitable pan. Black Power Ltd also produces and disseminates the Black Power institutional stove: a cylindrical, sinking pot

Box 2.6
Economic analysis of viability of institutional stoves

There are approximately 5,000 hospitals, schools, colleges, prisons and dispensaries in Kenya. The larger institutions have to prepare meals for up to 1,100 people per day, while the smaller institutions have to prepare meals for only 30 (Walubengo and Joseph, 1988). Fuelwood and charcoal are the main sources of energy for many of these institutions. In most of these institutions, firewood is used in inefficient traditional stoves or other models which are only marginally better. As a result, operating costs are high and fuel bills are increasing. A suitable response option to the above problem is the introduction of institutional cooking systems such as the Bellerive institutional stove.

Total annual fuelwood consumption in tonnes for institutions providing three meals a day

School population	Open fire (3-stones)		Protected fires		Improved jikos		Bellerive institutional stoves	
	A	B	A	B	A	B	A	B
100	27	35.1	22	28.6	8	10.4	6	7.8
200	54	70.2	44	57.2	16	20.8	12.1	15.6
300	81	105.3	66	85.8	24	31.2	18	23.4
400	100	130	87	113.1	32	41.6	24	31.2
500	134	174.2	109	141.7	40	52	29	37.8

A: Schools that operate on a termly basis
B: Institutions operating throughout the year
Source: Bellerive Bulletin, No. 9, 1994.

Changing a cooking system from an open fire to an institutional stove would yield a school catering for 100 students on an annual basis a huge saving of 21 tonnes in fuel. Using fuelwood costs in 1988 of Ksh120–200 per tonne if bought in bulk, the payback period for the institutional stove is shown in the table below.

	Using fuelwood cost of Ksh120 per tonne	Using fuelwood cost of Ksh200 per tonne
Investment cost per person as Ksh 110	4 years 3 months	2 years 6 months
Investment cost per person as Ksh 150	5 year 10 months	3 years 6 months

Considering the lifespan of an institutional stove, given heavy duty construction, is 10 years, no matter what scale is used, for at least 6–7 years the institution will be reaping a stream of savings from the use of an improved institutional stove.

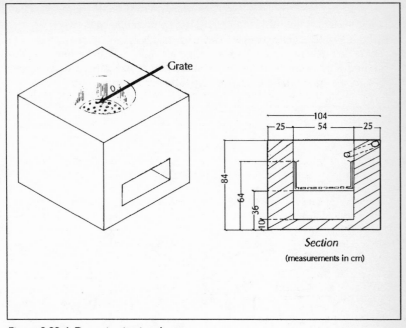

Figure 2.22 A Duma institutional stove
Source: Otiti, 1992.

design with a chimney. The stove is also supplied with a pan and, like the other institutional stoves, uses mainly firewood and agricultural waste. It can also be adapted for charcoal. Rwashana and Associates Co. Ltd is a company which produces the RAC institutional stove. The stove body is made of 22s gauge sheet steel, insulated with a mixture of clay and straw. The stove has a pot seat collar which is made of 3 mm mild steel and a cast-iron fire box. A suitable aluminium pan is sold along with the stove (Turyareeba, 1992).

For Tanzanian public institutions that use wood as fuel, the Centre for Agricultural Mechanization and Rural Technology (CAMARTEC) has developed different sizes of improved woodstoves with chimneys. The main aim of these stoves, designed for use in institutions such as schools and hospitals, is to reduce running expenditure through reduced wood-fuel consumption. Since 1989, woodstoves of 100 and 200 litres have been produced with their locally manufactured stainless steel cooking pots. Known as Duma stoves (Fig 2.22), they are made in Arusha at the CAMARTEC workshop and about 20 to 30 are sold each year: 100 stoves had been sold by 1992 (Otiti, 1991).

Small-scale biogas
Small-scale biogas plants are mostly found on family farms. The plants

have digester sizes of between five and ten cubic metres with a biogas output of two to four cubic metres per day, equivalent to between 40 and 80 MJ per day (Ellegard, 1990).

There are many simple biogas plant designs but only one will be presented here – the floating drum plant which has gained widespread acceptance (Fig 2.23). It consists of the following components:

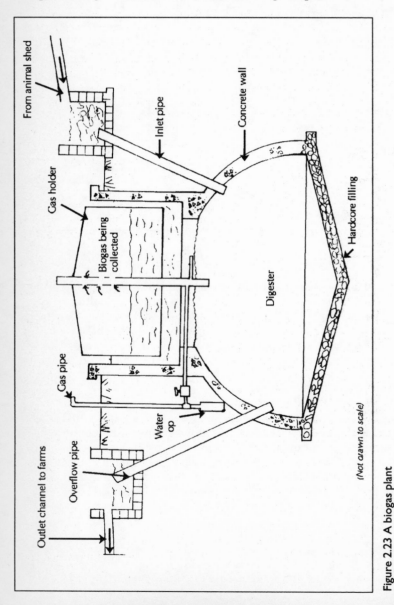

Figure 2.23 A biogas plant
Source: Adapted from GTZ/SEP, 1987.

- Mixing pit;
- Inlet and outlet pipes;
- Digester;
- Gasholder;
- Gas pipes, valves and fittings;
- Slurry store.

In the mixing pit, water and animal dung (most preferred) are mixed to form a homogeneous mixture (substrate). Any fibrous materials are removed from the mixture before the material is allowed to flow into the digester. The feed is led straight into the digester through the inlet and the digested substrate flows out through the outlet pipe. The digester of a biogas plant accommodates the substrate during the digestion process (bacterial activity) and is usually made of bricks and concrete. The substrate is broken down by bacterial activity producing biogas.

The pattern of gas demand, however, does not always coincide with the production. For this reason, the gas produced is collected and stored in a gasholder. Most gasholders in the region are made of 3mm thick steel sheets. Normally, steel is susceptible to intense moisture-induced corrosion. Consequently, the gasholders require proper surface protection coats which should be reapplied annually. A well-kept gasholder can be expected to last for 8–10 years in a dry climate. Polyethylene pipes are used for gas supply over long distances between the plant and the kitchen.

Once the digester is fed with fresh material, an equivalent volume of the old digested material is displaced from the digester, through the outlet pipe, to the slurry store. This material, which is rich in plant nutrients, can then be used as fertilizer. The slurry store container should be made large enough to hold a few days' slurry. This allows the farmer to plan better when and how to apply the fertilizer to the crops.

Selected benefits of biogas plants include the fact that biogas fuel can be used to replace partially or completely conventional fuels such as gasoline and diesel for lighting and cooking; a farm's energy requirement can thus be supplied by the biogas plant. Additional benefits can be derived from the use of the system's waste products or sludge as supplementary feed for hogs, or alternatively as fertilizer and irrigation water for animal forage. Production of biogas can thus serve as a waste treatment device to control pollution. Two major drawbacks must be set against these benefits: a biogas system needs significant attention from the operator and the expense of installation can constitute a very substantial investment for rural farmers.

Two countries that have made significant progress in small-scale biogas are China and India. China had more than 7 million biogas plants by the mid-1970s, while India had installed more than 280,000 biogas plants by 1983. The failure rate of the Chinese biogas plants is as high as 50 per cent, however, while India's is higher than 30 per cent (Ellegard,

1990). One of the few countries where success seems to have been relatively unblemished is Nepal, where a commercial approach to the implementation of the plants was adopted.

REGIONAL STATUS
Biogas is another small-scale biomass energy technology that has attracted considerable attention in the region over the last three decades (Wauthelet *et al.*, 1989; Traore, 1984; Manawanyika, 1992; Peters and Kijek, 1992). As shown in Table 2.7, one of the largest biogas programmes in the region is in Tanzania, where over 1,000 units have been installed (Ministry of Water, Energy and Minerals, 1993).

Table 2.7 Number of biogas digesters in selected countries

Country	Small < 100m³	Large > 100m³	Year
Tanzania	1000*	–	1993
Kenya	500	–	1993
Burundi**	152	63	1989
Zimbabwe	>100	–	1992
Uganda	10	–	1995
Botswana	–	1	1984
Malawi	–	1	1992

* Some of these plants may be large digesters
** Since the outbreak of civil war in the early 1990s, the status of biogas digesters in Burundi has not been known.
– Not known or not available
Source: Rubindamayugi and Kivaisi, 1993; Ministry of Water, Energy and Minerals, 1993.

The history of biogas in Kenya dates as far back as the mid-1950s. But the Ministry of Energy's first official biogas training and plant construction programme was launched in 1983/4 in Meru district, with the assistance of the GTZ/SEP. In the early stage of the programme (until late 1986) all biogas activities were concentrated in Meru. To date, the national figure of biogas plants in Kenya is estimated to be about 500. Initially, the numerous SEP training courses focused on only one biogas plant design, the reason being that at that early stage too many designs would have caused confusion and hampered the dissemination process. The result has been the training of several enterprises in the construction of more than 80 floating drum plants in Meru district in the first phase, and more than 400 plants in other parts of the country between 1982 and 1992. This gives an average annual rate of 50 plants, of which 85–90 per cent are family plants with a capacity of ten cubic metres (SEP, 1993).

In Uganda biogas technology was introduced by the Church of Uganda in the early 1980s when two Indian-type (floating drum) biogas digesters were installed on church property. These digesters acted as good demonstration units, leading to the construction of several more digesters in

Ankole district. Available information indicates that these digesters worked for a number of years, after which they developed problems that were sometimes due to lack of maintenance. A Nepalese digester was also installed at Mbarara, but never functioned. The Church of Uganda initiative was followed by a government pilot project implemented by the former Ministry of Animal Husbandry and Fisheries with technical assistance from the People's Republic of China, in which seven digesters were installed in eastern Uganda. Because adequate technical capacity to monitor and maintain these digesters was not developed, however, all but one malfunctioned after 1987. The remaining digester (in Tororo district) is still operational.

Another programme funded by the World Bank and implemented by the Ministry of Natural Resources established 10 biogas digesters with a total gas capacity of 262 cubic metres. These biogas digesters included three for secondary schools, six for individual farmers, and one portable demonstration unit (two cubic metres). The programme employed an expatriate biogas expert who designed and supervised the construction of digesters. The recipient provides all the necessary materials and pays for all the local labour. The biogas expert was not understudied by a local counterpart in the Ministry. This left the sustainability of the project in doubt. Initiatives by private individuals from local biogas engineers/technicians have been made but with questionable results. Four small demonstration biogas digesters, each with a gas capacity of three cubic metres, were installed at institutions in the remote Karamoja region in 1991/2. While they functioned during the rainy season, they could not get feedstock (cow dung and water) during the dry season as the nomadic people of Karamoja migrate with their herds (Turyahikayo et al., 1995).

In Zimbabwe, a community biogas project for small-scale dairy farmers is currently under way. This project is aimed at demonstrating a wide range of biogas applications in rural areas of Zimbabwe at Rusitu Dairy Scheme in the Eastern Highlands. The project also aims at providing biogas equipment for cooking, lighting and shaft power. The project emphasizes domestic and farming applications on small, zero-grazing dairy farms, where confined cattle produce sufficient dung and other waste for use in biogas generation. Two digesters have been installed, one in Beatrice and another in Rusitu. The Rusitu plant takes advantage of the sloping terrain so that substrate flows into the digester easily. The digested slurry is used as fertilizer in the farmer's gardens. The demonstration biogas digester in Beatrice is for commercial farmers. Funding for the project was provided by the Commonwealth Science Council (CSC) in 1992 (Biomass Users Network, 1995).

Small-scale briquetting
Briquetting of biomass waste has been proposed as one of the ways in which fuel shortages in developing countries might be alleviated. Several wastes are available for this, including groundnut shells, rice hulls, straw

of various cereals, sawdust, papyrus and bagasse. Charcoal fines are also suitable for briquetting. Agricultural residues in their raw form are generally not good quality fuels. They burn too quickly to be used for cooking purposes. They also produce too much smoke and not much heat as a result of which they are fuels of a last resort. Briquetting these residues turns them into good quality fuels (Walubengo, 1988). Briquettes may be fashioned very simply by hand, but their heat value increases if they are pressed using simple devices such as presses made from rope, wood or metal.

Key advantages of briquettes include the fact that they are a good quality fuel that is often cheaper than ordinary charcoal; that they burn longer owing to the high pressure applied during briquetting; and that they encourage the use of agricultural wastes that would otherwise not be used profitably. Indirectly, they minimize waste disposal in rivers, lakes and useful land, prevent environmental pollution and save money which can be used to purchase other items. One major drawback of briquettes is that agricultural waste is used as a feedstock and fertilizer; this could eliminate an important source of nutrients to soils, leading to lower farm yields.

The first operation in producing briquettes is the chopping of the chosen material, for which a machete, broad axe or hand-operated straw chopper may be employed. The next step is to blend it with a suitable binding material – starches from corn, wheat or cassava, glues, fish wastes – which can be done in a cement mixer or a specially made cylinder drum mixer. Next it is necessary to compress the material in some kind of press. Manual briquette presses have been developed by the Bellerive Foundation and Volunteers in Technical Assistance (VITA). They consist of a mould and a piston. The piston can be operated by the hitting power of a hammer or by the pressing power of a lever. One of the main advantages of the hand-operated briquetting press is its relatively low cost (US$360). Disadvantages are its low production rate of about 5 kilograms per hour or 50 kilograms in a 10-hour day, and its high production costs.

REGIONAL STATUS

Briquetting of biomass waste has been practised in Kenya for a long time now. In Nairobi, a paper manufacturer makes briquettes out of sawdust and wood shavings using two types of presses: a Thai screw press and a piston press. The briquettes are then burned in the factory boiler. It is claimed that the company saves Ksh60,000 (1US$ = Ksh54) per month using this briquetted fuel, which is a substitute for oil. The sawdust and wood shavings are obtained from a neighbouring sawmill (Walubengo, 1988). A few individuals have tried to manufacture carbonized briquettes using hand presses. Production rates are so low, however, that it is not worth the effort (Walubengo and Kimani, 1991). According to a survey carried out in Kenya by Walubengo (1989), briquettes are more likely to succeed if introduced as a fuel for industrial or institutional use. There are two main reasons for this. First, briquettes burn better in large furnaces. Second, it may be necessary to introduce a new stove to burn briquettes in households.

In Uganda, attempts at small-scale biomass briquette production have been made. Black Power installed a briquetting plant in 1986 and the system was mainly manual. The raw material base was coffee husks and sawdust. Initially, Black Power was producing 5 tonnes/month of charcoal briquettes. However, machinery started breaking down and production went down drastically. Now, there is almost no production. Black Power sells what little is produced at US$0.15/kilogram, trying to out-compete ordinary charcoal in the market. Simpler technologies are being promoted, mainly by women's groups, and they seem to be doing well so far.

The YWCA has produced a manually operated plant which uses some portable parts. The Association is already replicating the effort in several parts of the country. The Uganda Small-Scale Industries Association (USSIA) is also supporting at least four briquetting groups. The rural women involved use old tins or pots instead of kilns for carbonizing, a process that takes more than 24 hours. The moulding of the briquettes is then done by hand. The more elementary method of briquetting which is popular among rural women is binding waste biomass with banana peels or soil, moulding with hands, and then sun drying. The raw materials are not carbonized (Turyahikayo et al., 1995).

A project to evaluate the technical and material potential of the briquetting technology in Zimbabwe was carried out between 1992 and 1994 at NIJO Farm, owned by the Agricultural Rural Development Authority (ARDA). Its objective was to use crop wastes to produce fuel briquettes that can partly substitute the present consumption of fossil fuels: coal, charcoal and firewood. Crop wastes used during the project were maize stalks and cobs, coffee husks, cotton stalks, soya beans, sunflower stalks, farm grass, pine saw dust, teak sawdust, groundnut shells and leucaena seed pods. Briquettes of good quality were produced and tested during the pilot phase and distributed for use among rural and urban households; they were found to be acceptable. Engineering companies that are in a position to provide back-up services to briquetting technology in Zimbabwe were identified. A small briquette market for household use was also identified. NORAD provided funds for project equipment and consultancy. The Biomass Users Network (BUN) provided funds for project management, manpower, communication, documentation, project vehicle maintenance and infrastructure development (BUN, 1995).

In Sudan, large bagasse blocks are made using brick presses with molasses as a binder. In some areas, charcoal dust is mixed with clay, made into balls and used as a fuel. However, only small quantities of briquettes are produced in this manner (Walubengo, 1990a).

3

Solar Energy Technologies

This chapter focuses on the use of solar energy in the form of sunlight and as a source of ambient energy. Exploitation of energy from the sun dates back to the advent of civilization. Solar energy has long been used for drying animal skins and clothes, preserving meat, drying crops and evaporating sea water to extract salt (EIC, undated). Solar energy continues to play a crucial role in the survival of our planet, especially in the global climate and plant photosynthesis.

The amount of solar energy (insolation) falling on the earth from the sun is estimated to be about 1.73×10^{14} kilowatts which is about 1.5×10^{18} KWh/year – about 10,000 times more than the world's annual energy consumption (Ahmed, 1994). Because this enormous energy resource has not been utilized fully, a lot of attention is being focused on research and development of solar energy technologies. The two oil crises of the early and late 1970s were an important impetus. Another important stimulus was the need to develop independent solar-driven power devices for space telecommunication vehicles. Telecommunication satellites have been powered by photovoltaic panels ever since 1958, when the Vanguard I was launched (EIC, undated).

Today, solar energy is being utilized at various levels (Martinez, 1992). On a small scale, it is used at the household level in goods such as watches, cookers and water heaters, and in solar architecture houses; medium-scale uses include water heating in hotels and irrigation. At the community level, it is used for vaccine refrigeration in health centres, water pumping, purification and rural electrification. On an industrial scale, solar energy is used for power generation, detoxification, municipal water heating, telecommunications and, more recently, transportation (solar cars).

Solar energy technologies are modular and can be tailored to the power needs of individual applications such as electric calculators, small radios, televisions, computers, lights or electric pumps. Solar electric systems can be expanded easily by adding more modules and batteries (Hankins, 1995). The technology is environmentally benign in terms of global warming or destruction of the ozone layer. Solar devices have long lifespans since they have no moveable parts that can wear out. They are economically viable and competitive, largely due to their low life-cycle costs and high reliability. Maintenance is low since no fuel is consumed. Properly installed, solar technologies are safe. The risk of electric shock to users is minimal because of the low system voltages. Other dangers familiar to users of rural appliances, such as explosions in the case of kerosene lamps, are non-existent *(ibid.)*. Solar energy technologies thus significantly enhance the quality of life of the end users.

Some of the key constraints on using solar technologies include the need for sophisticated manufacturing processes, available only in a few developed countries. These processes have negative environmental impacts. A major problem in disseminating solar technology is the high initial capital cost and long payback periods. In the Seychelles, for example, solar water heaters have a payback period of about eight years (Razanjatovo *et al.*, 1994). Special training and infrastructure are needed for the installation and maintenance of these technologies. This is a great hindrance, since the process of developing skilled expertise in the region's energy sector is protracted. This, in turn, has led to a shortage of trained technicians to design and install solar systems (Hankins, 1995). Some of the technologies (for example, PV systems) require back-up systems such as batteries for energy storage (Derrick *et al.*, 1994). These batteries have their own negative environmental impacts, especially during manufacture and disposal. The performance of solar systems is weather-dependent, which can increase unreliability in some cases.

This chapter discusses the principles, fundamentals and operation of solar energy technologies in two broad categories:

- Solar photovoltaic technologies; and
- Solar thermal technologies

Solar photovoltaic technologies

Solar cells (Figure 3.1) are produced from wafers of silicon (a form of pure sand) which is chemically treated and then arranged in parallel or in series in a module/panel (GTZ, 1991). The 'photovoltaic effect' occurs when light falls on an active photovoltaic surface. This energy penetrates the cell near the junction between the p-type and n-type silicon. The semi-conductor dislodges an electron, leaving behind a 'hole'. The electrons generated in this process of electron–hole pair formation tend to migrate to the n region in the front contacts and can flow into an external circuit (Open University, 1994).

The main components of a PV system (Figure 3.2) include a module, a battery, a battery control unit/charge controller, a DC–AC inverter (where necessary) and the load (appliances) (GTZ, 1991). Solar cell modules are devices used to convert sunlight into electricity. Modules should be mounted properly so that they can collect maximum energy. How much

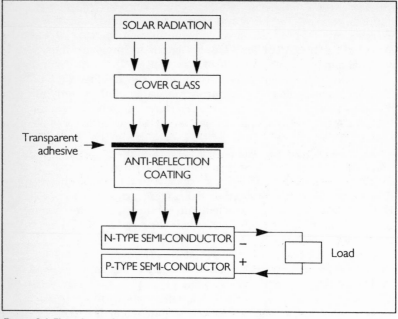

Figure 3.1 Flowchart of a solar cell
Source: Adapted from Ahmed, 1994

a surface should be tilted towards the sun depends on the latitude and at what time of year most solar collection is required. If a surface is tilted at an angle equal to the latitude, it will be perpendicular to the sun's rays at midday. A basic principle that one should remember when choosing a suitable site for the solar panel is that it should be sited as far as possible from shade or shadows as this reduces the panel's overall output. Batteries are used mainly as a back-up system that stores energy collected during sunny days for use at night and during cloudy days. The size of the battery depends on the energy requirements of the system and the budget of the user (Hankins, 1995). The charge controller is used to prevent damage to the battery and other parts of the system due to over-charging and deep discharging. It may also alert the user when the battery or module is not functioning properly.

Important applications of PV systems include (Derrick *et al.*, 1991):

- Rural electrification (lighting and power supply for buildings, power supply to remote locations, portable power for nomadic herdsmen);
- Water pumping and treatment;
- Health care (for storing vaccines and medicines in PV refrigerators);
- Communications (PV-powered remote radio telephones or repeaters);

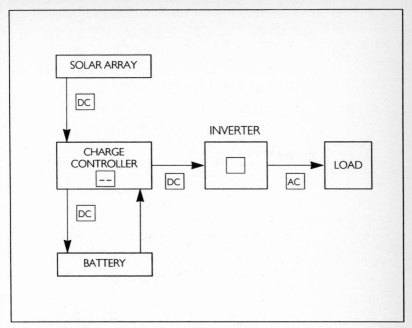

Figure 3.2 Flowchart of main structure of a PV system
Source: Adapted from Derrick et al., 1994

- Agriculture (solar pumps for water pumping);
- Transport and navigation aids (PV-powered navigation and signal lights);
- Security (PV-powered security lights);
- Corrosion protection;
- Household and office appliances (ventilation and air conditioners, calculators, watches, path lights, emergency power and battery rechargers).

The wide-scale use of PV technology has been boosted significantly by a dramatic drop in production costs over the last 20 years (Figure 3.3). The price of PV systems was over US$30 per peak watt (Wp) in 1975, which is expected to fall to US$2 per Wp by the year 2000 (Karekezi, 1994b). This drop in prices can be attributed to improvements in manufacturing technology and mass production of the systems. Yet PV electricity is not yet competitive with bulk grid electricity. Recent estimates indicate the capital costs of PV electricity to be in the region of US$7,000–8,000 per installed KWp, which translates to electricity costs of about US$25 per KWh. By 1992, PV module production was estimated

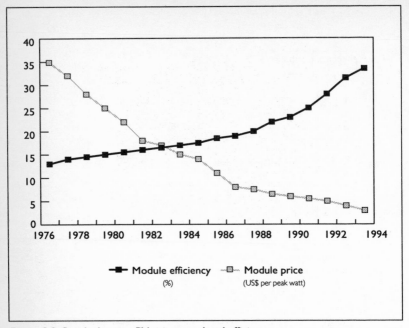

Figure 3.3 Graph showing PV price trend and efficiency
Source: Adapted from Derrick et al., 1993

at 57.9 peak megawatts (MWp) (Ahmed, 1994). Major PV manufacturers (producing over 2 MWp) include: Siemens (USA), Solarex (USA), Sanyo (Japan), Kyocera (Japan), Keneka (Japan), Eurosolaire (Italy), Helios (Italy), Deutsche Aerospace (Germany), Photowatt (France) and BP Solar (UK) (Derrick et al., 1993). Figure 3.4 shows PV module use per region by 1992.

Developing countries offer the most important opportunities for growth of PV sales, although investing in solar PV module manufacture may not be the most appropriate investment alternative since the technology is advancing rapidly. Present manufacturing facilities may be obsolete within a few years time (Singh, 1991). Nevertheless, certain components such as the batteries, cables, regulators and light fittings can be manufactured locally, particularly if suitable manufacturing and assembling facilities already exist.

Regional status
PV refrigerators are being used increasingly in the region for the preservation of medical and veterinary vaccines. They are reliable, with low running costs and long life expectancies (Bokalders, 1989). A typical PV vaccine refrigerator has a low energy requirement of about 2 KWh per day

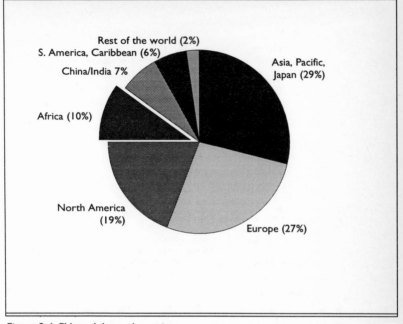

Figure 3.4 PV module use by region
Source: Adapted from Gregory, 1994

which makes it particularly suitable for PV powering. PV vaccine refrigeration has been recognized by the World Health Organization (WHO) and the United Nations Children's Fund (UNICEF) as a suitable technology for preserving vaccines in remote health centres.

The total cost of a PV system suitable for use in a clinic ranges from US$2,700 (refrigeration only) to US$6,060 (refrigeration and lighting), excluding import duties and sales tax (Karekezi, 1992b; Bogach *et al.*, 1992). Although the initial cost of a PV vaccine refrigerator exceeds that of a kerosene refrigerator, sometimes by a factor of two, the running costs of a PV refrigerator are quite low. Field data demonstrate that even on an annualized cost, however, a PV refrigerator is more costly than a kerosene refrigerator (BP Shell, 1991). None the less, on the basis of total cost per effective dose, using a kerosene vaccine refrigerator can be more expensive than using a PV vaccine refrigerator (Derrick *et al.*, 1989). In fact, vaccine losses in a PV refrigerator (about 10 per cent) compare well with losses in a kerosene refrigerator (about 35 per cent) (Derrick, 1993).

PV technology has been acknowledged as a 'power of choice' in the region's telecommunications industry (Annan and Rice, 1991; Durand, 1987). Solar telecommunication systems in use in the region range from small individual radios to large communication systems such as micro-

Table 3.1 Solar photovoltaic systems in selected countries (mainly for lighting applications)

Country	Estimated no. of systems	Estimated installed capacity (KWp)	Year
S.Africa	60,000	2,700	– [a]
Kenya	35–40,000	1,000	1993[b]
Uganda	538	152.5	1993[h]
Zimbabwe	3,000	151	1993[c]
Zambia	2,100	88	1993[d]
Botswana	>2,000	–	1992[e]
Burundi*	1,800	58	1993[f]
Rwanda*	941	29	1991[g]
Djibouti	61	16.2	– [i]

– Not known or not available
* Civil war may have led to destruction of many of these PV systems
Sources: a – Scheffler, undated; b – Acker and Kammen, 1994; c – Hankins, 1993; d – Mbewe, 1994; e – Diphaha and Burton, 1993; f – Katihabwa, 1994; g – Nieuwenhout, 1991; h – Turyahikayo, 1994; i – UNESCO/VITA, undated.

wave repeaters, radio and television repeaters, telephone and fax systems. The underdeveloped transport infrastructure of the region places a high premium on a reliable communications system. Investment in a reliable PV-based communication system can defer costly and difficult-to-maintain investment in conventional road and rail networks in remote areas of the region. Countries in the region utilizing PV power for communications include Kenya, Zambia, Ethiopia, Sudan, Mozambique, Zimbabwe, Botswana, Malawi and Tanzania (BP Solar, 1993), where photovoltaic communications systems have been utilized to improve national networks.

Solar-powered water treatment systems have been used in the region to sterilize water by sand filtration and ultraviolet sterilization. These systems are in most cases combined with solar-powered water pumps. Solar security devices such as alarm systems and electric fences are increasingly common (Durand, 1987). Solar electric fencing has also been designed for herding livestock and for restricting wildlife to the game reserves. In Songa, Kenya, the African Development Foundation (ADF) financed a solar-powered electric perimeter fence to ward off elephants and other wild animals (Katus, 1987).

In technical terms, solar PV lighting has several important advantages that make it competitive with other rural lighting systems such as wood fires, kerosene lamps, pressure lamps and diesel generators. PV systems have begun to demonstrate consistent technical and economic viability. The systems also improve the quality of life of the users dramatically, reduce the use of fossil fuels in decentralized rural lighting applications, create employment and generate income in rural areas (Bachou and Otiti,

Box 3.1. Economic analysis: total cost of rural electrification by use of grid electricity vs solar electricity in a typical Eastern and Southern African country

————————————————— ✳ —————————————————

Grid electricity

Capital cost:-

Grid extension	=$1443.2	
Step down transformer	=	$92.5
Wiring expenses, lighting fixtures, bulbs	=	$325
Total cost	= $1860.7	

Solar electricity

Capital cost:-

100 Ah Battery	=	$101
10 A Charge controller	=	$333
60Wp Panel	=	$550
Wiring expenses, lighting fixtures, bulbs	=	$330
Total cost	= $1314	

Present value of recurrent costs:
Cost for powering a 60W lamp
by grid

4 (lamps) • 60 (Watt) • 5(hours) •365(days)	= 438KWh
(cost of electricity per year)	= US$11.37
4 lamps replacement cost per year	= US$ 2.32
Total recurrent cost	= US$13.69

Present value of recurrent cost for 15 years	= US$152.21

Present value of maintenance costs:

Lamps replacement	$43.87
Battery water replacement	$16.11
Battery replacement	$151.30
Total maintenance costs	$211.28

Lifetime cost
= US $1860.7 + 152.21
= US $2012.91

Lifetime cost
= US $1314 + US$211.28
= US $1525.28

Points to note:
a) Grid extension cost per km = US$8200.
b) Break-even distance = 8.8 km.
c) Step-down transformer serves 50 people (transformer costs US$4625).
d) Estimates are for a 2-bedroomed house with four lamps.
e) Bulb prices are Kshs69 for PV flourescent while the lifetimes are 1 year and 3 years, respectively.
f) Battery for PV system is replaced every 5 years.
g) 1 bottle of battery water worth Kshs100 is used in a year.
h) Exchange rate used is Kshs69 to US$1.
i) Cost per kilowatt : (in Kenya shillings)
            First 50KW = 0.69 cents
            Next 20KW = 1.19 shilling
            Next 20KW = 1.51 shilling
            Extra KW = 2.00 shillings.
j) The tariff in (i) is fixed and does not account for future increments.
k) Present value of recurrent costs is calculated using :
    • 12% interest rate,
    • 8% inflation rate to get the discount factor, after which the present value factor is obtained.
l) Long-run economic benefit of using solar electricity vs grid electricity:
   = US$2012.91 − 1525.28
   = US$487.63

Source: Acker and Kammen,1994. (capital costs only)

1994; Diphaha and Burton, 1993).

Solar PV home lighting systems are becoming popular in the rural areas of the region where, in the foreseeable future, connection to the national electric grid is unlikely to occur because of the difficult terrain that has to be traversed by mains grid distribution networks (Derrick *et al.*, 1989). This is compounded by low population density, characterized by scattered homesteads. Contrary to popular belief, the rural populace in Eastern and Southern Africa do not reside in centralized homesteads but in individual scattered homesteads, which increases the distribution cost of rural grid electrification programmes.

Although reliable, region-wide data on the dissemination of PV technologies have yet to be compiled, available information for selected countries (Table 3.1) indicates growing use. South Africa, Kenya, Zimbabwe, Zambia and Botswana have had encouraging results in terms of the dissemination of PV lighting systems. In Kenya, 35,000–40,000 PV systems have been installed in the rural areas, mainly for lighting (Acker and Kammen, 1994). A third to a half of these systems were sold without charge controllers (Karekezi, 1994b). Solar energy activities are conducted by the private sector, the Ministries of Energy and Health, and NGOs. The private sector undertakes most of the commercialization *(ibid.)*. A number of one-man firms have established shops in rural community centres where installation and after-sales services can be provided (Masakhwe, 1993; Kioko, 1993). There are about 12 suppliers of PV systems and three firms assembling inverters (Hankins, 1992). In the SADC region, there are about 36 distributors and manufacturers of PV systems (Peters and Kijek, 1992), although the Republic of South Africa and Zimbabwe are the only regional manufacturers of PV modules. In terms of manufacturing capacity, South Africa has a total of 2.7 MWp (Scheffler, undated), while Zimbabwe has 151 peak kilowatts (KWp) (Hankins, 1993).

In South Africa about 60,000 PV lighting systems and 1,200 PV water pumping systems have been installed (Scheffler, undated). The South African power utility, ESKOM, has begun installing PV systems in remote rural institutions and households which are uneconomical to connect to the grid (ESKOM, 1992). In conjunction with the Energy for Development Research Centre (EDRC), ESKOM performs tests and evaluation of commercially available photovoltaic modules (Buttle, personal communication, 1995). ESKOM's challenge by the year 2000 is to electrify all rural schools and clinics *(ibid.)*.

Botswana is well endowed with solar energy. It receives about 3,200 hours of sunshine per year (approximately nine hours of sunshine daily). In 1985, solar energy contributed about 16 TJ of the energy consumed, and this contribution is expected to triple by the year 2010 to about 51 TJ, or 0.11 per cent of the total energy demand (Mosimanyane, 1994). PV systems have proved to be economically viable in the country. In contrast to other countries in the region, Botswana has a high number of PV

Box 3.2 PV user's view of the technology
———————————— * ————————————

A survey of Kenyan homes which have installed small PV systems was conducted from July to August 1994. Forty systems ranging from 10 Wp to over 100 Wp clustered in three areas near Nakuru, Meru and Bungoma (in Kenya) were surveyed. The survey addressed different issues like who in Kenya is buying the systems, what the consumers are using the systems for, how well their systems really work, benefits they get from the PV systems and, lastly, the typical problems they face as PV owners.

The survey revealed that most of the Kenyan PV systems are used for lighting. Other uses are for powering radios and televisions. It was discovered that out of the estimated 40,000 PV systems installed in Kenya, 40 per cent of the systems had sufficient problems to impair the system's operation to a significant extent: for example, blackened bulbs, repeated light malfunction and weak batteries – one in four were completely inoperational.

The majority of respondents, even those whose installations had problems, said that they were glad to have bought their systems and that PVs were a good source of power. They felt that PV is the best choice and will become even better if the problems can be ironed out and prices reduced. They also saw that the principal benefit of PVs was that they were the least costly alternative when compared to grid extension or diesel generators.

systems installed in towns. This is mainly a result of government policy, which excludes grid connections to self-help housing projects (Diphaha and Burton, 1993). Another major application has been in reading rooms and halls in nine locations (Mosimanyane, 1994). Every year, the national library service installs lighting systems in 10 primary schools (Diphaha and Burton, 1993). In 1986, about 19 primary schools in Kgatleng district had installed PV systems for lighting. Rural clinics also use PV systems for lighting and refrigeration (Mosimayane, 1994). A total of about 900 homes have installed systems of about 40 watts each. At Manyana village, a pilot project by the Energy Affairs Department has installed 50 PV systems in homes, public buildings and street lighting (ibid). Over 70 PV water pumping systems (about 1 KW) have been installed in the country. Of these, 38 systems were installed by the Department of Water Affairs, 16 by the Department of Wildlife, 12 by other government agencies and the rest by private individuals and companies (Diphaha and Burton, 1993). The national telephone company has a network of 60 PV repeater stations with over 250 PV-powered rural telephone call boxes planned (ibid.). The police also have a communications network with 16 PV-powered repeaters. The Botswana Railways utilizes PV communication systems for remote signalling stations, hot-box detectors and radio communications. Most remote clinics with radio communication systems are powered by PV systems (ibid.).

Solar energy has played a vital role in supplying energy to Lesotho, along with other renewables such as hydro-power, wind and biomass fuels. Solar energy contributed about 1 per cent of the energy demanded in 1990, and is forecast to contribute about twice as much by the year 2010 (Kanetsi and Phuroe, 1994). The government intends to utilize solar energy as a substitute for commercial energy sources and for energy conservation in buildings, commerce and industry. Codes of practice for installation and dissemination of solar PV systems have been prepared *(ibid)*. In the late 1980s, through the Taung/Phamong Project, nine villages were supplied with solar-pumped water *(ibid.)*. The villagers paid for the project through a committee responsible for collection. Meanwhile, Lesotho has been earmarked as SADC's pilot area for a PV electrification project which will carry out a feasibility study in one village to identify the most economical and environmentally favourable means of supplying electricity. If PV happens to be the prime candidate for this project, PV systems will be installed and monitoring of their technical performance as well as evaluation of the viability of a revolving fund will follow. The project will have its results modified (if need be) to serve as a model for other SADC member countries *(ibid)*.

Before descending into the current state of anarchy and civil war, Burundi had registered encouraging results in solar energy development, especially after the 1973 oil crisis. For the first time ever, in the 1977–82 Five Year Plan for Economic and Social Development, the government proposed exploring the supply and use of alternative energy sources (Katihabwa, 1994). The Department of Energy played a significant role in the promotion and implementation of solar energy projects and programmes in the country. The Centre for Alternative Energy (CEBEA) undertook research into ways of exploiting solar energy, while the University Research Centre for Utilization of Alternative Energy (CRUEA) undertook basic and applied research into RETs.

Solar PV technology in the country was mainly used for lighting, telecommunications, refrigeration and water pumping. These systems have accounted for about 57.8 KWp of installed capacity (Katihabwa, 1994). The installation of PV systems was mainly undertaken by the Ministries of Public Health and Rural Development, and by other government and commercial agencies. In 1985, ONATEL, a government parastatal, installed about 41 PV systems (about 6.2 KWp installed capacity) which were used to provide power for telephones in rural communities, institutions and schools. About 6,979 Wp installed capacity was used for lighting and refrigeration in maternity hospitals, schools and missionary houses. The civil war that erupted in 1993–4 led to the destruction of many of these systems and their current status is not known.

Although solar energy sources are hardly used in Uganda, there are at least 538 PV installations in the country which, by 1992, had amounted to a total capacity of about 152.5 KW (Turyahikayo, 1994). The Ministry of Health and various other government corporations have installed PV systems. By 1992, there were 238 PV vaccine refrigerators, amounting to about 60 KW of installed capacity *(ibid)*. These were used in projects which included a health programme financed by the World Bank and the Uganda National Expanded Programme for Immunization, supported by UNICEF.

Solar PV development in the Seychelles has not been significant. In 1987, however, a project undertaken by Developpement des Energies Nouvelles et Renouvelables dans l'Ocean Indien (DENROI) installed a pilot solar refrigeration plant at Pointe Larue. The project was financed by the European Economic Community (EEC) with the Fifth European Development Fund (Razanajatovo *et al.,* 1994). There is also the Alternative Energy Package for Aldabra, a major rehabilitation project established under the Seychelles Island Foundation (SIF). The main objective of the project is to replace the current diesel-fuelled energy facilities with solar PVs and water heaters. The project's estimated capital cost of about US $156,500 would be incurred to meet Aldabra's 1,750 KWh daily energy requirement *(ibid)*.

Recent experiences in the region show that electricity supply can be unreliable, especially in drought periods which adversely affect the generation of hydro-electricity. This provides further justification for the expansion of a decentralized rural electrification strategy with a significant PV component. The cost of a small household PV system would be about US$450–460, excluding sales tax and the import duty still charged in most countries in the region (Karekezi, 1992). Import duties for 45–60 watt PV panels for Botswana is 5 per cent; Malawi 30 per cent; Namibia 20 per cent; Zambia 15 per cent (Peters and Kijek, 1992); and Kenya 31 per cent (in addition to 18 per cent value added tax) (Karekezi, 1994b). Where the duty has been waived, institutional mechanisms to ensure the end-user benefits from the tax rebate are inadequate. In Uganda, for instance, one year after the import duty was waived, there was still no difference in the price of PVs. Suppliers attributed this to a stock build-up before the duty was waived (Bachou and Otiti, 1994). Nevertheless, a study undertaken in Kenya shows that the costs of PV systems can go down if various duties are waived (Karekezi, 1994b). A survey undertaken in the SADC region indicates a large market potential for PV systems ranging from 72 MWp for the business-as-usual scenario to 241 MWp for a scenario in which electrification programmes are pursued aggressively (Bogach *et al.,* 1992). To place the above figures in perspective, the 1992 world-wide annual production of PVs was estimated to be about 57.9 MWp (Ahmed, 1994).

Solar thermal technologies

While heat from the sun (over 300°C) is utilized on a large scale in electricity generation, it can also be used in small- to medium-scale heating, cooking and drying equipment.

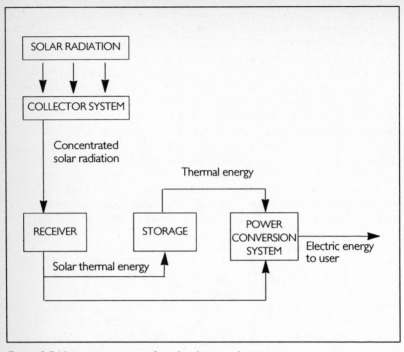

Figure 3.5 Main components of a solar thermo-electric system
Source: Adapted from De Laquil et al., 1993

Solar thermo-electric technologies utilize energy from the sun in the form of heat to generate electricity. The sun's rays heat a fluid from which heat transfer systems may be used to operate an engine (Ahmed, 1994) which drives a power conversion system. In a solar thermo-electric system, sunlight is concentrated with mirrors or lenses to attain a high temperature sufficient for power generation (De Laquil *et al.*, 1993). Parabolic trough systems, central-receiver systems, parabolic dish systems and solar ponds are among those used. As shown in Figure 3.5, the basic components of a solar thermo-electric system are a collector system (which is the panel that collects solar radiation), a receiver system, a transport-storage system (mainly in the form of a fluid that transfers the heat around the system) and lastly a power conversion system (converts energy from one form to another).

Solar water heaters are simple solar thermal applications that transform solar radiation into heat that is used to warm water for bathing, washing, cleaning and cooking (Hankins, 1995). Solar water heaters consist of glass-covered panels with a dark-coloured surface inside. Water (used as the heat transfer fluid) is warmed by the sun and then stored in insulated tanks for later use. There are two main parts of a typical solar water heating system: the flat plate solar collector and the hot water storage tank. Flat plate collectors absorb solar radiation and conduct the heat to cold water that flows through the collector in pipes. Storage tanks are insulated to keep the water hot *(ibid.)*.

Another solar thermal application is the solar drier. There are often two stages in the process: first, solar radiation is captured and used to heat air; then comes the actual drying during which heated air moves through, warms and extracts moisture from the product. Drying takes place in a large box called the drying chamber. Air is either heated in a flat plate collector or directly via a window in the drying chamber *(ibid.)*.

Table 3.2 Various applications of solar thermal systems at various temperature ranges

Temperature range	Applications
Low-grade thermal energy <100°c	Water heating, air heating, drying, refrigeration, space heating, desalination, etc.
Medium-grade thermal energy 100°–300°c	Cooking, steam generation for industrial applications, drying, refrigeration, power generation, water desalination, air heating for industrial applications, pumping, etc.

Source: Dayal, 1989

Active solar thermal technologies include water heaters, cookers, desalinators, dryers, timber kilns, water pumps, solar ponds, refrigerators, air conditioners and greenhouses; solar architecture is an example of a passive solar thermal technology (Dayal, 1989). Annual world-wide sales of solar water heaters are estimated to be about 800,000m^2 (Gregory, 1994). One of the most spectacular developments in solar water heaters is the way in which Scandinavian countries have managed to produce some of the most efficient solar collector systems in the world, although they receive little sunlight: their large solar water heating plants are, in some cases, substitutes for conventional energy sources; in other cases they supplement these.

Solar cookers are increasingly gaining attention all over the world. In the USA, several solar cooking contests and exhibitions have been held over the last few years. On 31 July 1993 the 2nd Annual Solar Cooking Contest was held under the auspices of *Home Power* Magazine (*Home Power* Magazine, 1993). Through India's National Solar Cooker Programme, a part of India's National Programme for the Development

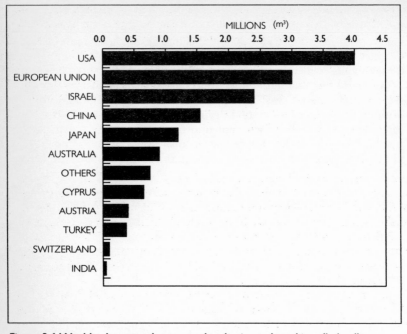

Figure 3.6 World solar water heater market (estimated total installed collector area)
Source: Adapted from Gregory, 1994

and Use of Renewable Energy Sources, about 70,000 cookers were disseminated, selling at a subsidized price of US$30–35 and at US$15 in low-income regions (Kuhnke *et al.,* 1990). To date, about 100,000 solar cookers have been disseminated in the country *(ibid.).* In Pakistan, between June 1985 and June 1987, over 1,780 cookers were sold at a subsidized price of US$18 through the Appropriate Technology Development Organization *(ibid.).* In China, over 100,000 solar cookers, most of them of the reflective type, have been in service *(ibid.).*

On the Asian continent, solar dryers and kilns are in use especially for wood drying. In China, about 16 solar kilns have been installed in various locations in the country (Sattar, 1990). In India, about 22 different types of forced convection solar timber kilns have been developed by the Forest Research Institute (Exell, 1990). In Bangladesh, the Forest Research Institute developed some inexpensive solar timber seasoning kilns which are used by about 15 private and public wood industries *(ibid.).*

Throughout the world, people have used simple materials to construct houses whose interior conditions are able to remain unaffected by the prevailing external conditions. Ancient constructions of such houses have been found in the deserts of the Middle East and North Africa, in English cottages and in North America among the Pueblo Indians *(ibid)*. In spite of its ancient origin, the widespread application of solar architecture has not yet materialized. There has been some attempt to develop the technology, especially in Europe: since 1983, for example, about 50 passive solar homes have been built throughout Germany bearing the famous DOMUS name (Berndt, 1993). In Poland, a 4-storey solar apartment building was designed and constructed in Warsaw to house about 220 inhabitants (Babut, 1990).

Regional status
Solar thermal technologies that have been disseminated in the region include solar water heaters, solar cookers, solar stills and solar driers. With increased efficiency and reduced cost of solar water heaters, small-scale models now have a pay-back period of about 3 to 5 years (Karekezi and Karottki, 1989) as shown in Box 3.3. The diffusion of these systems, however, has in recent years been slower than anticipated. In some countries, liquid petroleum gas (LPG) subsidies make it difficult for solar water heaters to be competitive.

In Africa, as in the case of solar PV systems, limited data on the dissemination of solar thermal systems have been gathered, and the information that is available comes from a few country studies. In Botswana, about 4 per cent of the country's urban population use solar water heaters and about 15,000 solar water heating systems are used by the Botswana Housing Corporation, clinics, mines and the household sector (Mosimanyane, 1994). The government plans to spend about US$1,295,000 on the promotion of solar water heaters and the installation of these systems in government institutional buildings by 1997 *(ibid.)*. It is estimated that between 3,000 and 5,000 units have been installed in Zimbabwe, and about 10,000 units in Kenya (Karekezi, 1994b). In 1993, Uganda's Wilkens Telecommunications Ltd installed a limited number of solar water heaters (16), equivalent to 52.63 square metres of collector area (Turyahikayo, 1994). In Malawi, one company has installed about 950 solar water heaters (RERIC News, 1993b). In South Africa over 136,000 square metres of solar water heating has been installed (Scheffler, undated) and there is a manufacturing history dating back to the 1970s. In 1977, there were about 85 manufacturers, distributors and installation firms for solar water heaters. By 1985, however, only 59 remained (Stassen, 1986). In the Seychelles, the establishment of Enersol, a local manufacturing company, has demonstrated that solar water heaters have great potential for displacing conventional electric and fossil-fuelled water heaters. The solar systems have been installed in hotels and industries (Razanajatovo *et al.*, 1994).

Various types of solar driers have been developed as an alternative to open-air sun drying and other conventional drying methods (Garg, 1990;

Sebbowa, 1987). In Eastern and Southern Africa, extensive research has been carried out to develop reliable solar driers. Some of the countries where research projects into crop drying have been undertaken include Uganda, Zambia, Zimbabwe, Kenya and Mauritius (Brenndorfer *et al.*, 1985). Solar driers of different types and designs suitable for use in the region have been developed. Solar kilns are available for drying agricultural products (such as grain, tea leaves and other crops), fish and timber. In general, research has shown that solar driers perform well and produce better results than the traditional method of drying crops in the open sun. Solar driers can assist in reducing post-harvest losses because dried produce is less susceptible to natural deterioration and insect infestation (Garg, 1990). Existing solar driers are, however, still too expensive for the average small-scale farmer (Sebbowa, 1987). Consequently, only middle- to large-scale farmers can afford them.

Passive solar or thermal-efficient houses in the region have been in existence since the art of constructing houses began in Eastern and Southern Africa. Traditional thatched houses, which are made of mud and wattle, protect their occupants from the heat of the dry season and the cold of the rainy season (Birrer, 1988). In the context of passive solar and thermal efficiency in modern housing and construction, however, there has not been much progress, except at the research level. Experimental passive solar buildings have been designed and built in South Africa, Lesotho and Seychelles (Birrer, 1988; Phuroe and Mathaha, 1995; Razanajatovo *et al.*, 1994).

Solar thermo-electric technologies have not yet been initiated in the region. The only country in the region that may have registered substantive progress in this technology is the Republic of South Africa, but only in terms of research, not application. The research undertaken in South Africa includes examining the potential of solar ponds for electricity generation and storage (Eberhard, 1988).

Box 3.3 Economic analysis of solar energy vs electric geyser energy
Life cycle cost analysis in US$ for a hospital in Lesotho
———— * ————

Project description: A comparison whether Leribe hospital should be fitted with Solarhart 302J solar water heaters (SWH) or a 300-litre electric geyser.

Economic parameters:
1. Years in life cycle = 15
2. Investment rate = 17%
3. General inflation rate = 12%
4. Electricity inflation rate = 14%
5. Discount rate (2–3) = 2%
6. Differential fuel inflation (4–3) = 2%
7. Annual inspection cost = US$278
8. Cost of materials per annum = US$556 (SWH) and US$278 (electric geyser)
9. Present worth factor of 10.38 (for both technologies)

Item	300 litre electric geysers (US$)	Solar water heaters (US$)
Capital equipment and installation:	25,556	86,543
Operation and maintenance:		
Labour		
Year inspection (7 × 9)	2,886	2,886
Material (8 × 9)	2,886	5,771
Energy cost	383,816.7	0
Salvage 20% original price	(485.564)	(1,644.317)
Total life cyle cost	414,659	93,556

NB. Present worth factor is a value applied to a futuristic payment or receipt to find the current value.

Source: Phuroe and Mathaha, 1995.

4

Wind Energy Technologies

Wind is moving air and therefore contains kinetic energy. Wind energy technologies convert this energy into rotating shaft power which can be used for water lifting (windpumps), electricity generation (wind turbines) and machine turning. This chapter discusses two of the most widely used wind energy technologies, windpumps and wind turbines.

The development of wind machines dates back to 2000 BC, when wind energy technologies were used for grinding grain in Persia, the Middle East and Babylon. Ancient ship designs utilized a sail to trap wind energy, thereby moving the ship. On the Isle of Crete, farmers have traditionally used a sail in wind turbines. In the twelfth century, the Dutch developed large horizontal shaft windmills for pumping water, grinding grain, and running saw mills and other machines (Hankins, 1987).

Wind resources

The best places for strong steady winds are the temperate latitudes (between 40° and 50° N and S), and areas which are close to the sea (Figure 4.1, Table 4.1). Wind speeds increase with altitude, making hilltops favourable sites. The fact that winds are intermittent makes some applications such as water pumping more appropriate than others such as direct electricity generation (IIED, 1981). In temperate regions, wind is a good alternative to solar energy, given the lower level of sunshine and comparatively higher wind activity (Kimani and Naumann, 1993).

In the long run, wind generators are cheaper than diesel generators because of lower running costs. This is particularly true in remote rural locations where the logistics involved in the supply of fuel are often insurmountable. On large wind farms, wind turbines have to be separated by distances of five to ten rotor diameters (Johansson *et al.*, 1993). Despite this, wind plants use only a small portion of the land they occupy, typically less than 15 per cent, and the rest can be used for grazing or farming (Gipe, 1993). The wind industry also has a good safety record, with no reported major incident from wind installations (Johansson *et al*, 1993). As regards security, diesel fuel engines are often stolen, while stealing a windpump or wind turbine is much more difficult (Plas, 1993).

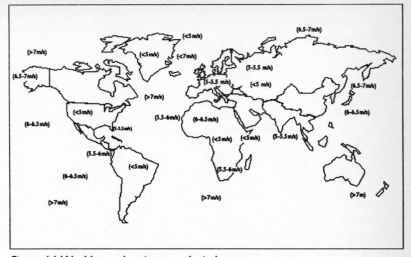

Figure 4.1 World map showing annual wind energy resources
Source: Adapted from *Renewable Energy Technologies and their Applications in the Developing World,* 1986

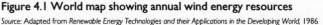

Electricity from wind turbines is thought to be unreliable due to the unpredictability of the wind. Since wind energy converters work only during windy periods, they lie idle during less windy months. Inoperative windpumps and wind turbines discourage wider dissemination. Furthermore, once a windpump is standing still, it needs a rather high windspeed to get it going again. This is referred to as hysteresis (Smulders, 1992). Another disadvantage is that boreholes in the region, for example in Botswana, are sometimes too deep for windpumps to perform adequately.

Excessive variation in wind regimes can affect the cost effectiveness of wind energy adversely. For example, uncertainties in wind availability force Denmark, at times, to sell power at a low price to Norway or purchase it at a high price from Germany. The price of having to buy or sell power at the 'wrong' time must be added to the basic cost of windpower generation, which can make windpower more expensive (Nuclear Forum, 1992). In addition, wind generators have higher initial costs than the competing diesel generators.

The successful exploitation of wind energy is highly site-specific and largely depends on the wind resources of the area being exploited (Christensen *et al.*, undated). The economic viability of wind energy converters depends on the wind conditions that prevail at a particular site. Electricity generation from wind energy requires a wind speed greater than 5 metres per second (m/s) (Mwangi, 1993). For windpumps, lower wind speeds can be sufficient. However, most windpumps will not start below a wind speed of 3 m/s and will furl at about 12 to 15 m/s (Fraenkel *et al.*, 1993).

Table 4.1 Estimate of wind power potential, (average possible production in GW)

World	6050
Africa	1200
Australia	330
North America	1600
Latin America	610
Western Europe	550
Eastern Europe & Former SU	1200
Rest of Asia	560

Source: Sorensen, 1995

Windpumps

A windpump consists of a rotor (made up of blades) connected to transmission and safety systems (Figure 4.2). The rotor is the essential part that converts the power of wind (kinetic energy) into useful shaft power. The rotor is fixed to a steel shaft by means of one or two hub plates. The shaft is supported by steel sleeve or roller bearings or by hardwood sleeve bearings. Rotors for water pumping range from 1.5 to 8 metres in diameter.

The transmission of a windpump conveys the mechanical energy delivered by the rotor to the pump rod. There is a gear box with the main function of reducing the speed in rotations per minute (rpm) of the pump, normally by a factor of about 3. The pump rod then transmits the power to the pump. The safety system is combined with the orientation system. At low wind speeds the rotor is oriented into the wind; with increasing wind speeds the rotor is gradually turned out of the wind so as to limit the speed of the pump and the forces acting on the structure. The functioning of this safety system is based on the equilibrium of aerodynamic forces (acting on one or two vanes and the rotor) and some other force (usually a spring or weight) that serves to counteract the aerodynamic forces. The safety system's main purpose is to protect the wind pump during heavy gusts and storms (Meel and Smulders, 1989).

The tower is what supports the head assembly and raises it over any obstructions into the path of the wind. It also serves as a rig during installation of the pipes of deep well pumps. Tower heights range from six metres for small windmills to 18 metres for larger ones. The most common height is around ten metres.

There are several types of windpumps, classified mainly according to the transmission between the rotor and pumping device. These include piston, rotary and hydraulic pumps. Most common windpumps drive a

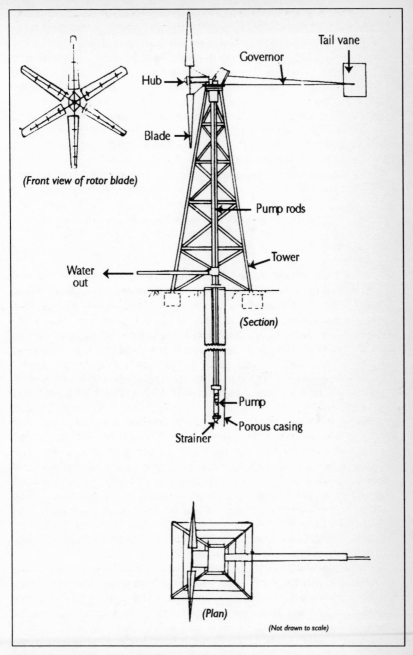

Figure 4.2 Diagram of a windpump
Source: Adapted from Hankins, 1987.

piston pump through mechanical transmission (Meel and Smulders, 1989). Typical applications of windpumps include small-scale irrigation, cattle watering, supplying drinking water and drainage (Box, 1990).

Wind energy activities in developing countries have followed two main paths: the direct use of wind energy for shaft power and electricity generation (Karekezi, 1988b). Wind power for water pumping has gained acceptability because the technology required is simpler and thus more accessible than that for electricity generation (Kimani and Naumann, 1993). The vast majority of windpumps in use in the world today (around 500,000–750,000) are for livestock, village water supply and, to a limited extent, irrigation (Fraenkel et al., 1993).

Argentina leads in windpump manufacture, with an annual production of approximately 2,000 units or 20 per cent of world production (Karekezi and Karottki, 1989). India had 1,962 windpumps in operation in 1988 (Bhatia, 1988), while Mauritania currently has 2,000. Morocco produces 100–200 and Tunisia 50 units per annum (Fraenkel et al, 1993).

Regional status
In Eastern and Southern Africa, South Africa has the largest number of installations, with about 280,000 windpumps (Stassen, 1986). Competition from PV pumps has slowed the installation of new units. The current market is now 800 units per year (Fraenkel et al., 1993). There has been little detailed monitoring of wind data in potentially favourable sites in South Africa, however, and consequently the viability of wind farms, feeding into national or local grids, is still unclear (Eberhard, 1988). Namibia has the second largest number of installations in the region with approximately 30,000 units (Linden, 1993). Kenya is next with 360 units (Table 4.2).

Even in countries with low wind speeds, wind energy can be exploited in specific niches. A typical example is Botswana, which is located between two stable, competing high pressure cells over the Atlantic and the Indian Ocean and therefore has a wind energy potential characterized by relatively low speeds and a high percentage of 'calms'. Average annual wind speeds, an important indicator of the wind energy potential, are in the range of 3 m/s or less (Fig 4.3). While the wind regime in Botswana is thus unfavourable for the economic exploitation of wind power for electricity generation, in some areas windpumps may be viable options for domestic water supply and livestock watering (Mosimanyane, 1994).

In Botswana, water supply is a major constraint on development. There are 15,000 boreholes of which most are deep, with water rest levels often as low as 60–100m. These require high wind speeds for effective windpump operation. Windpumps are competitive with diesel pumps for small- and medium-scale water supply applications, if the wind speed in the least windy month is above 3.5 m/s (Table 4.3). In remote areas where diesel fuel transport costs are high, windpumps can be economical at even lower wind speeds, so long as the water level is high. Windpumps

Table 4.2 Wind energy potentials and number of windpumps in selected countries

Refs	Country	Potential (m/s)	Number of wind pumps
1, 2	South Africa	7.2–9.7[a]	280,000
3	Namibia	–	30,000
4, 5	Kenya	3	360
6a, 6b	Botswana	3	200–250
7	Zambia	2.5	100
8, 9	Tanzania	–	58
10	Uganda	4	13[b]
11	Sudan	3	12
12	Burundi	2.5	1[c]
13	Cape Verde	9–10	–
14	Lesotho	5[d]	–
15	Mozambique	0.7–2.6	–
16	Seychelles	3.62–6.34[e]	–

(a) Highest wind speed recorded
(b) Six of them are not operational
(c) Before the civil war
(d) Highest wind speed recorded at one site
(e) Average wind speeds for two seasons

Sources: (1) Diab, 1988; (2) Stassen, 1986; (3) Linden, 1993; (4) Fraenkel et al, 1993; (5) *Kenya Engineer*, 1994; (6a) IT Power, 1988; (6b) Mosimanyane et al, 1995; (7) Sampa, 1994; (8) Sawe, 1990; (9) Mwandosya and Luhanga,1983; (10) Turyahikayo, 1994; (11) Hassan,1992; (12) Katihabwa, 1994; (13) INforSE, 1994; (14) Kanetsi and Phuroe, 1994; (15) Gielink and Dutkiewicz, 1992; (16) Razanajatovo et al., 1994.

Table 4.3 Cost comparison between a windpump and a diesel pump (US$)

	Diesel pump	Wind pump
Capital cost	6000	10000
Annual operating and maintenance cost	250	100
Fuel cost	292	0
Discount rate	10%	10%
Unit cost (US$/cubic metre)	0.18	0.19

Assumptions:
Lowest monthly average wind speed is 3.5 m/s. Windpump output 20 cubic metres per day at 60 metres head. Diesel pump efficiency 25%. Fuel cost US$0.60 per litre.

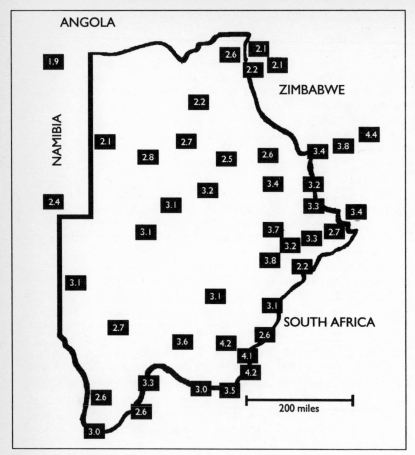

Figure 4.3 Wind map of Botswana (average wind speeds in m/s)
Source: Mosimanyane, 1994; Larson, 1987; IT Power, 1987.

are also economical in many remote cattle posts where small dispersed water supplies are needed for livestock (Box 4.1). Botswana has a large demand for livestock water which can be met by windpumps. There is stiff competition, however, from diesel-powered water pumps imported from South Africa (with no import duty), and also from solar pumps.

In Botswana, there is little information on windpumps except that provided by the Rural Industries Innovation Centre (RIIC) and the Botswana Technology Centre (IT Power, 1988). The majority of windpumps in the country are Climax and Stewart & Lloyds models imported from South Africa. The RIIC is the principal organization in wind energy technology development in Botswana. It began operating a pilot project in 1987 and provides technical support, although the manufacturing and

Box 4.1
User's perspective – windpumps in Botswana

—————————— * ——————————

A survey was conducted in Botswana on owners/users of windpumps. The aim was to determine the ownership, procurement and installation, use, environmental impacts and promotion of windpumps. The survey revealed that 54 per cent of the windpumps were owned by households and 23 per cent by farmers' groups or syndicates. The rest (23 per cent) were owned by the community. The majority of the windpumps (85 per cent) were purchased and the rest were donated. Fifty-six per cent of the respondents purchased windpumps or raised money from the banks to purchase them, whereas 18 per cent utilized group contributions. Most of the respondents purchased the windpumps from the RIIC, the main local supplier. The installation of the windpumps was done by the RIIC in 69 per cent of the cases and by owners and foreign dealers in 23 per cent and 8 per cent of the cases, respectively. Ninety-two per cent of the respondents were of the opinion that the installation was done satisfactorily. The operators had been trained by the supplier in 39 per cent of the cases and, in the remaining cases, had either taught themselves (31 per cent) or been taught by the local technicians (8 per cent).

All the respondents revealed that windpumps were used for pumping water for livestock as well as for irrigation and domestic purposes. Ninety-two per cent of the respondents were of the opinion that the windpump had significantly improved their water supply. Eighty-five per cent thought that windpumps satisfied the water needs of the community. Thirty-one per cent depended on windpumps entirely for their water pumping, while 69 per cent had other systems. The respondents perceived windpumps as a good technology mainly because they were cheaper to use. One of the problems associated with the use of windpumps was the high frequency of breakdowns. Forty-six per cent indicated that they broke down once a year, 31 per cent twice a year and 23 per cent more than three times a year. Major repairs were done by the RIIC (54 per cent), local technicians (8 per cent) or a combination of the two (8 per cent).

The study also investigated the perceptions of respondents of the environmental impact of the use of windpumps. The majority (85 per cent) thought the windpumps improve the scenery, whereas 15 per cent said they do not make a difference. No negative impacts were reported. It was also the view of 92 per cent of the respondents that noise from the windpumps is not a nuisance. The respondents thought that the adoption of the windpump technology was constrained by factors such as the lack of appropriate policies, lack of awareness of the technology, high costs of maintenance and inadequate wind regimes.

Source: Mosimanyane et al., 1995.

installation of windmills is now limited by low demand. The organization has developed a rotary windpump but only 25 of these pumps have been bought and installed.

To date, about 200–250 wind machines have been installed in Botswana, mainly in the agricultural sector for pumping water from boreholes, thus reducing dependence on the use of diesel-powered pumps. Only about two windmills per year are installed, although many more opportunities exist (over 600 boreholes per year). Institutional support in the water pumping field is improving. The Department of Meteorological Services has mounted a major effort to install an array of anemometers in the country to assess further the potential of using wind energy to pump water, and a wind map of the country has been developed (Figure 4.3) (Mosimanyane, 1994). The government is placing some orders for locally produced wind machines, but a bigger market for windpumps exists in the private sector.

Good potential for windpumps exists in Kenya because it has high wind speeds and adequate ground water resources as well as good quality machines manufactured locally, with spare parts and maintenance services available. By 1993 there were 12,000 registered boreholes and the rate of boring was approximately 1,000 holes a year (Borg and Oden, 1995). Over 50 per cent of Kenya has an annual average wind speed of above 3 m/s (Figure 4.4). Many of the windiest areas in Kenya are sparsely populated. This affects the ability to attract investments negatively. The coastal plain, lake basin and highland areas (which are densely populated), on the other hand, have moderate wind speeds.

There are two local manufacturers of windpumps in Kenya, Bob Harries Engineering Ltd and Pwani Fabricators, who manufacture the Kijito and Pwani windpumps respectively. Over 200 of the windpumps installed in Kenya are of the Kijito type. The existing market for windpumps is approximately 30 units/year (Fraenkel et al., 1993). The Kijito is a modification of the Intermediate Technology (IT) windpump. Most installed windpumps are either in donor-funded water supply projects or on large privately owned farms where the main application is domestic water supply.

With the exception of the GTZ-funded Special Energy Programme, there is a lack of general expertise in most aspects of windpumps in the relevant ministries and NGOs. In addition, groups or individuals considering the installation of windpumps for commercial purposes (cattle watering, industrial water supply) lack appropriate financing mechanisms. The Kenya Industrial Estates initiative, whose objective is to encourage small- and medium-scale manufacturers, could be an important source of credit. Increased support from the Kenyan government, and especially from the Ministry of Water Development, is needed for the widespread dissemination of windpumps. Thorough training of district water engineers in all aspects of wind pumping technology is necessary. The Ministry of Agriculture and Livestock Development needs to be

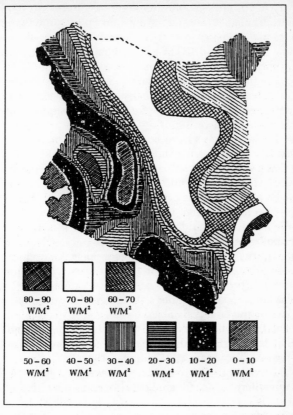

Figure 4.4 Map showing estimated wind power available throughout Kenya
(watts/square metre)
Source: Hankins, 1987

encouraged to promote the use of windpumps for animal watering (IT
Power, 1987).

In Zimbabwe, there are two local manufacturers of windpumps,
namely Stewart & Lloyds and Sheet Metal Krafts. Sales of windpumps are
around 30 units per annum (Fraenkel *et al.*, 1993). In Zambia, the Department of Energy is currently implementing a wind energy project and has
financed a local manufacturer. A windpump has been installed at a test
site near Lusaka (Sampa, 1994).

By 1983, there were an estimated 30 windpumps in mainland Tanzania
(Mwandosya and Luhanga, 1983). Less than a third of these were
operational. There is a Southern Cross Windmills Project in Singida
region where about 10 villages get a regular supply of water pumped by
large multi-blade fan windmills funded by the Australian and Tanzanian

governments. The Ministry of Water and Energy runs several windmill programmes. Ubungo Workshop were building a prototype windmill (Mwandosya and Luhanga, 1983) and Arusha Appropriate Technology Project (now part of CAMARTEC) have completed work on two prototypes being manufactured by a village cooperative society. The Faculty of Engineering of the University of Dar es Salaam is working on several windmill designs, two of which were installed and tested. However, high initial cost made them unaffordable for rural water supply, despite satisfactory performance (Sawe, 1990).

In Uganda, windpumps have been installed by the Roman Catholic Mission, the Church of Uganda and the Karamoja Development Authority (Turyahikayo, 1994). In Djibouti a long-term VITA project has been promoting wind, solar power and energy conservation technologies. The project has been building the capabilities of ISERST, the country's only scientific research institution. ISERST has now collected and organized basic energy information and directed the testing of various alternative energy technologies (UNESCO/VITA, undated).

In Malawi, the Department of Meteorological Services failed to convince the government to provide funds to purchase equipment to collect wind data on a sustainable basis all year round. The Department thus collects data on wind regimes only in a few locations. Consequently, a consolidated wind energy database for the country is lacking. It is clear from the available wind maps that owing to Malawi's highly diverse topographic characteristics, there are major variations in wind patterns between regions and seasons (Kafumba, 1994a). The levels of wind velocity and frequency are considered inadequate for electric power generation, but may suffice for shallow water pumping *(ibid.)*.

Wind turbines

Wind turbines/generators are used to generate electricity (Table 4.4). The components of wind turbines for electricity generation include a two- or three-blade aerofoil rotor to capture the wind (Figure 4.5). The rotor blades are slender with cross sections similar to those of aeroplane wings. The rotational speed of a blade tip is of the order of 150 to 300 km/hr while in operation, depending on the machine size. Other components are: the gearbox, which transfers the aerodynamic torque from the rotor to the electric generator (AC or DC) and the tower (Frandsen, 1991). Wind turbines vary in size. The most common specifications quoted by manufacturers are the diameter and the rated power.

There are two types of wind turbines, horizontal axis wind turbines (HAWTs) and vertical axis wind turbines (VAWTs). HAWTs generally have two or three blades. Their axis of rotation is horizontal. They are employed mainly to generate electricity. VAWTs have an axis of rotation that is vertical and therefore can harness winds from any direction with-

Table 4.4 Typical applications of wind generators

Rotor diameter (m)	Typical rated power in 12 m/s wind	Typical use
1	50 W	Battery charging for lighting and communications in remote locations
2	1 KW	Multi-battery charging and communications
6	10 KW	Heating and multi-electrical uses, probably with some battery storage
14	50 KW	Stand-alone electricity generation for communities (small villages)
20	100 KW	Grid connection, export and sale of output to grid company

Source: ITDG, 1994

out the need to reposition the rotor when the wind direction changes. There are three types of VAWTs; the Darrius VAWT, H-VAWT and V-VAWT. The blades of the Darrius VAWT are curved like a spinning skipping rope. The H-VAWT has two horizontal cross arms that support, at their ends, upright aerofoil blades in the 'H' shape. The V-VAWT consists of straight aerofoil blades attached at one end and inclined in the form of a 'V' (Open University, 1994).

Small-scale wind generators were used and tested in the Antarctic as early as the first post-war expeditions of the 1950s. High failure rates (due to both low temperatures and powerful gusty winds), energy storage problems and the continuing need for complete back-up systems led to their withdrawal, except for a few small field installations for charging batteries for scientific and communications equipment. Recently, tests on larger types of commercial wind generators have been carried out by the French at New Amsterdam Island (1986–8), by the Germans at George Von Neumayer Station (since 1991) and by the Australians in the sub-Antarctic at Heard Island in 1992 and 1993 (Guichard, 1994).

The world's estimated installed wind electricity capacity is about 2,100 MW, equivalent to an investment of US$2–3 billion. By the end of 1990, more than 20,000 wind turbines were operating as grid-connected machines throughout the world. Over 75 per cent of these are found in California, USA and Denmark (Frandsen, 1991). Denmark is the world's leading manufacturer of wind turbines, having manufactured 12,500 turbines of which 9,000 were exported and 3,500 installed in the country (Thomsen, 1994). Wind turbines in Denmark represent roughly 340 MW of the grid's output of 8000 MW (Frandsen, 1991) with unit sizes ranging from 55 KW to 450 KW. High population density, which implies many restrictions on land use, has stimulated interest in off-shore wind turbines.

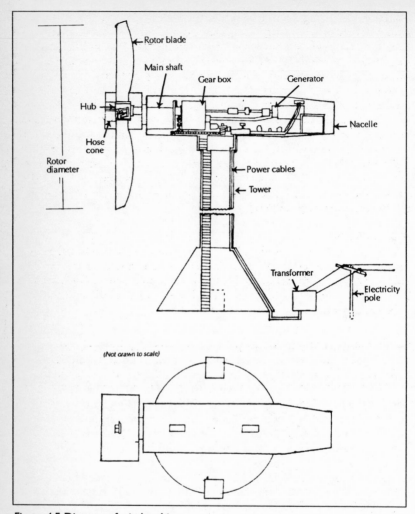

Figure 4.5 Diagram of wind turbines
Source: Adapted from ITDG, 1994

In general terms, wind conditions at sea are believed to be better (Thomsen, 1994).

Over half of the wind turbines in the USA were imported from Denmark, though there are also many local manufacturers (Thomsen, 1994). These gained a lot of government support through legislation and the policies of utilities (Gipe, 1993). In California, more than 15,000 wind turbines have been integrated into existing utility grids and are operated in conjunction with conventional hydro-electric, fossil-fuel and nuclear generating stations. Importantly, the cost of wind-generated electricity has decreased substantially during the last several years, to the point where it is now an attractive contender among new generating options. Installed capital costs have also dropped sharply, and wind turbine use has improved considerably, indicating that manufacturing techniques and wind farm operating methods are maturing rapidly (Johansson et al., 1993).

It is estimated that approximately 20 per cent of the land area in the former Soviet Union experiences an annual average wind speed of 6 m/s or more. Fifteen organizations are involved in the development and manufacture of wind power engineering equipment in the former Soviet territories. These organizations manufacture wind turbines rated between 1 KW and 1000 KW (Knyazeva, 1990). India has wind electric generators with a total installed capacity of 120 MW (Sorensen, 1995). Grid-connected wind turbines are also found in Hawaii, Germany, Spain and the Netherlands (Gipe, 1993).

Regional status
The dissemination of wind turbines in the sub-Saharan African region has been very limited (Table 4.5). This is in part attributable to low wind speeds. Other factors include poor maintenance and inadequate operation of wind generators due to the low level of technical skills and maintenance know-how in the region (Karekezi, 1988b).

Table 4.5 Number of wind generators disseminated in selected countries

Refs	Country	Number of wind generators
1, 2	Kenya	3
3	Cape Verde	2
4	Seychelles	2[a]
5	Lesotho	1[b]
6	Rwanda	1[c]
7, 8	Tanzania	1

(a) One broke down.
(b) Was abandoned in favour of solar.
(c) Before the civil war.

Sources: (1) Fraenkel et al., 1993; (2) *Kenya Engineer,* 1994; (3) INforSE, 1994; (4) Razanajatovo et al., 1994; (5) Kanetsi and Phuroe, 1994; (6) UNDP/World Bank, 1982; (7) Sawe, 1990; (8) Mwandosya and Luhanga, 1983.

Nevertheless, electricity generation from wind turbines has been field tested in some countries in the region. In Namibia, a pilot project on wind is being set up by the Ministry of Mines and Energy to prove the viability of wind on a large scale. If this project proves successful, this source of energy may be used more extensively (Linden, 1993). External donors have assisted by financing a programme in which two wind generators were installed in the Seychelles (Razanajatovo et al., 1994). An automatic weather station was also installed for wind measurement. Only one wind generator is operational, however, and this was installed as part of a project financed by the European Economic Community *(ibid.)*. A few individuals and some mission stations in Tanzania use windmills to generate electricity to meet their lighting needs. One such unit in operation is a LUBING wind power generator installed at the Chunya Catholic Mission. The generator produces 400 W at wind speeds in excess of 10 m/s (Mwandosya and Luhanga, 1983). Three wind turbines have been installed in Kenya. The first is a hybrid diesel/wind turbine installed in Marsabit, with a power output of 200 KW. The other two (150 and 200 KW) are installed on the Ngong Hills. All the installations were financed by a Belgian government grant. The two turbines on the Ngong Hills are grid-connected and are run by the Kenya Power and Lighting Company. The project in Ngong is being run on an experimental basis to prove the viability of a wind farm in the area (*Kenya Engineer*, 1994).

5

Small Hydro Technologies

This chapter discusses the fundamentals of small hydro-power (SHP) technology before assessing its potential and use world-wide and in Eastern and Southern Africa. Human kind has used the energy of falling water for many centuries, at first in mechanical form and by further conversion to electrical energy since the late nineteenth century (WEC, 1992). Water power or hydro-power are terms given to power extracted from energy in fast-flowing streams or rivers (Power Guide, 1994).

Hydro-electric technology is well-established and has been producing power at competitive prices for about a century. It is the principal source of power in some 30 countries, and provides about a fifth of the world's annual electrical output. Hydro-power stations include some of the largest artificial structures in the world. Present day hydro-electric plants are the end product of 2,000 years of technological advance, from the creaking wooden water wheel, converting a tiny percentage of the available power into useful mechanical output, to the modern turbo-generator spinning at 1,500 rpm and producing electric power at efficiencies which can reach 90 per cent (Open University, 1994).

Historically, hydro-power was developed on a small scale to serve localities in the vicinity of the power plants. With the expansion and increasing load transfer capability of transmission networks, power generation tended to be concentrated in increasingly larger units and to benefit from economies of scale. Rising conventional energy prices and concern for the environment have revitalized interest in small hydro. Technological developments have also accompanied the revival of this power source (Power Guide, 1994).

Gravity gives water above sea level potential energy. Consequently, fast-moving water has kinetic energy which can be harnessed to do useful

---

Box 5.1 Small hydro: a note on terminology

———————————— * ————————————

Small hydro is often categorized into mini and micro hydro. No consensus has been reached on the definition of mini and micro hydros (Johansson et al., 1993). In this chapter, consequently, the term small hydro power (SHP) covers both mini and micro hydro of under 10 MW. The term hydro, when used alone, should be understood as inclusive of both large and small hydro.

Box 5.2 Essential characteristics of a hydro volumetric site

✳

The essential characteristics of a hydro volumetric site are the effective head (the height H through which the water falls) and the flow rate (the number of cubic metres of water per second, Q). The power, in kilowatts, carried by the water is roughly 10 times the product of these two quantities:

As each cubic meter of water has a mass of 1000 kg, the power is given by

$$p = (1000Q) \times 10H$$

More conveniently, p can be expressed in kilowatts, in which case:

$$p(KW) = 10QH$$

where Q is the number of cubic meters per second, p is power in kilowatts, and H is the head in meters (Open University, 1994).

The conversion of energy carried by the water into electrical energy is done by a turbo-generator: a rotating turbine driven by water and connected by a common shaft to the rotor of a generator. The head and the required power are critical in determining the most suitable type of turbine for a site (Open University, 1994).

The electric power output will be less than the input: resource estimates, therefore, must take into account energy losses. In any real system, the water will lose some energy as a result of frictional drag and turbulence as it flows in channels and through pipes, and thus the effective head will be less than the actual head. These flow losses vary greatly from system to system: in some cases, the effective head is no more than 75 per cent of the actual height difference, in others as much as 95 per cent. Then there are energy losses in the plant itself. Under optimum conditions, a hydro-electric turbo-generator is one of the most efficient machines, converting all but a small percentage of the input power into electrical output. Since the efficiency is always less than a 100 per cent, the output power becomes:

$$p(KW) = 10nQH$$ where n is the efficiency expressed as a fraction and H is now the effective head.

---

work (Hankins, 1987). Hydro-electric power is derived from harnessing the power released when water passes through a vertical distance usually referred to as the 'head' (Jackson, 1993).

There are many uses of water power which do not involve the generation of electricity. The kinetic energy of moving water can be used directly and indeed this was the sole mode of use until the mid-19th century. The most common uses of small hydro power were irrigation and water supply. Water wheels (Fig 5.1) and the vertical axis Norse wheel or the *ghatta* were the most common. These were made from wood with a few wearing parts made from metal or stone. Later, water wheels drove air bellows used to power machines during the industrial revolution. These machines were gradually developed to fairly high efficiencies (Power Guide, 1994). Now, however, such direct uses account for only a very small fraction of the total.

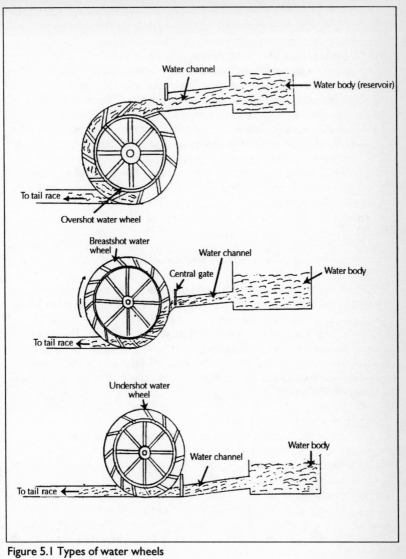

Figure 5.1 Types of water wheels
Source: Power Guide, 1994.

Water wheels are among the oldest hydro-power devices and consist of large slow-spinning wheels with attached paddles or buckets which are turned by the force of moving water. Traditionally, they operated grind-stones, threshers, blowers, waterpumps, lathes, saw blades and, with gearing, began to generate electricity (Hankins, 1987). By the end of the eighteenth century, three main types of water wheels were in use: the undershot, overshot and breastshot water wheels (Figure 5.1). Two of these had remained virtually unchanged for well over 1,000 years.

The undershot wheel was driven by the pressure of water against its lower blades which dipped into the flowing stream. The overshot wheel was driven by water falling on the blades from above. The blades have closed sides, making them effectively buckets. The breastshot wheel, a later development than the other two, is a compromise between them. The water is channelled between parallel breast walls and strikes the paddles at about the level of the wheel axle.

Key components of a modern small hydro scheme

The key physical parameters for an SHP scheme are the head, the civil works and the electro-mechanical equipment (Figure 5.2). Civil works are carried out before installing the turbine, generators and transmission equipment (Gullberg, 1994). The main physical works are the dam, the spillway or diversion weir, and the water passages to the powerhouse. The dam directs the water into the powerhouse through water passages. The powerhouse contains the turbine with the mechanical and electrical equipment (WEC, 1992).

Turbines
Hydro turbines convert the energy in falling water into rotating mechan-ical energy. The energy in the rotating shaft may be used directly to operate a mill and grinding equipment or hooked to a generator to produce electricity (Alward *et al.*, 1979).

A turbine consists of a set of curved blades designed to deflect the water in such a way that it gives up as much as possible of its energy. The blades and their support structure make up the turbine runner, and the water is directed into the blades by channels and guide vanes or through a jet, depending on the type of turbine. The speed of the runner blades relative to the velocity of the moving water is a critical determinant in the efficiency and suitability of the turbine. The main relevant features are:

- The water speed is limited by the available head;
- The blade speed depends on the rate of rotation of the turbine runner, and is thus related to the desired rate of rotation of the generator – usually between about 200 and 1500 rpm;
- The speed of the blade tip also depends on the diameter of the

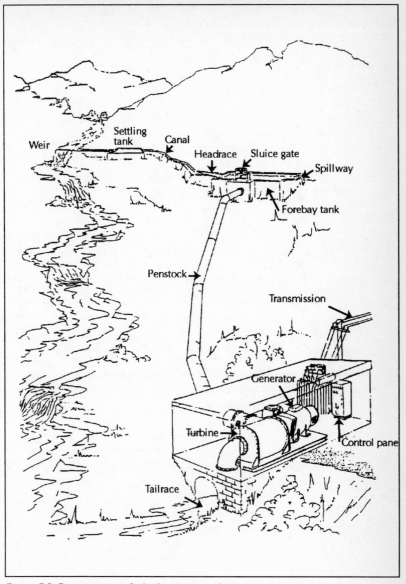

Figure 5.2 Components of a hydro-power scheme
Source: Drawing by the authors..

runner, which in turn depends on the power required (Open University, 1994).

As shown in Appendix 2, turbines are broadly divided into three groups – high, medium and low head – and into two categories, impulse and reaction turbines (Figure 5.3) (Holland, 1983). The impulse turbines convert pressurized water into a high speed jet through a nozzle while a reaction turbine runs completely filled with water. The flow of water creates pressure differences across the blade, thus causing rotation. Present-day turbines come in a variety of shapes. They also vary considerably in size, with runner diameters ranging from as little as a third of a metre to six metres and more *(ibid.)*.

Modern turbines operating under optimum conditions are extremely efficient machines. Efficiencies of 95 per cent can be achieved – but only by maintaining exactly the right speed and direction of the incoming water relative to the blades. This may lead to another problem. If demand falls, the output can be reduced by reducing the water flow. To maintain a constant supply frequency, however, the rate of rotation of the generator needs to remain the same at any power level. An unchanged runner speed with a lower water speed means that the angle at which the water hits the moving blades is altered, so the efficiency falls.

IMPULSE TURBINES

Impulse turbines are generally more suitable for small hydro installations than reaction turbines because they have the following advantages:

- Greater tolerance of sand and other particles in the water;
- Better access to working parts;
- Easier to fabricate and maintain;
- Better part flow efficiency.

The major disadvantage of impulse turbines is that they are generally unsuitable for low-head sites *(ibid)*.

The Pelton wheel is an example of an impulse turbine. Essentially a wheel with a set of double spoons or cups mounted around the rim, it is driven by a jet of high speed water hitting each cup in turn. Because the energy is delivered in a series of short impulses, it is called an impulse turbine. Other examples of impulse turbines are the Cross-flow turbine and the Turgo wheel (a variant of the Pelton wheel, the difference being that the double cups are replaced by single cups) (Open University, 1994).

REACTION TURBINES

The most common reaction turbines are the Francis and Propeller turbines. In both types the specific speed is high: reaction turbines rotate faster than impulse turbines given the same head and flow conditions. The important consequence is that a reaction turbine can often be coupled

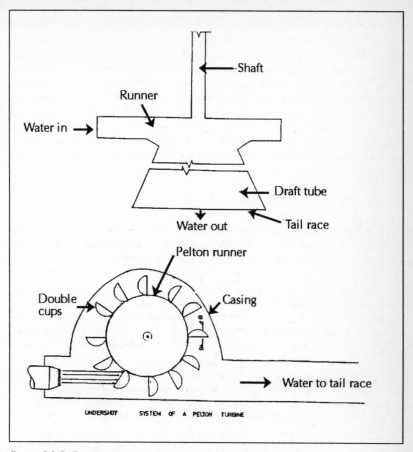

Figure 5.3 Differences between impulse and reaction turbines
Source: AEDDC, 1995.

directly to an alternator without requiring a speed-increasing drive system. On the whole, reaction turbines require more sophisticated fabrication than impulse turbines because they involve the use of larger and more intricately profiled blades, together with carefully profiled casings (Open University, 1994).

Hydraulic ram pumps
Hydraulic ram pumps, or 'hydrams', pump water from a stream or river up to a place where it is needed and combine the functions of a turbine and a water pump in one simple unit (Figure 5.4) (Hankins, 1987). Water is led down the pipes as in the case of most turbines, but the resulting flow is periodically stopped by means of the impulse valve. This rapid

valve closure causes a pressure surge, known as water hammer. Another valve called the delivery valve opens near the peak of this pressure surge and allows a small portion of the water through to the high pressure side of the device. From here the water is led by the delivery pipe to the higher point where the water is required. The pressure surge limits the size of the hydrams to a few hundred watts per unit, but units can be operated in parallel for larger outputs. At powers of under 500 W, hydrams are generally cheaper than the equivalent pump-turbine set, and will operate at similar or better efficiencies. The overall efficiency of most commercially available hydrams is at least 50 per cent (Power Guide, 1994).

These systems have broadly the same civil works components as small hydro schemes. Hydram penstocks, however, are generally termed 'drive pipes' and are designed on different criteria. They need to be sufficiently rigid and strong to transmit water hammer pressure surges. The hydram unit is fitted to the end of the drive pipe. From here most of the water will be exhausted into a tailrace, but a portion will be diverted into the high pressure side of the pump, and from there to the delivery pipe (the pipe connecting the hydram to the point of use of the pumped water). Normally there will be a storage tank at this point.

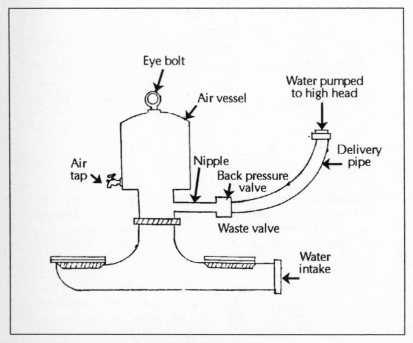

Figure 5.4 Components of a hydraulic ram pump scheme

Source: Adapted from Jandu Plumbers Ltd.,1996.

Pumped storage systems

Pumped storage systems (Figure 5.5) are being developed increasingly in a number of countries. In the case of SHP systems, however, this is still at the pilot stage. The development of these systems is due to the need for back-up power in times of variation in output. At present, one of the most widely used means of storing electrical energy in very large quantities is to use it to pump water up a mountain. The principle used is that electrical energy is converted into gravitational potential energy when the water is pumped from a lower reservoir to an upper one, and the process is reversed when it runs back down, driving a turbo-generator on the way. The economics of the technology depends on the fact that a suitably designed generator can run 'backwards' as an electric motor; the machine which converts mechanical energy into electrical energy can equally well carry out the reverse process, and a suitably designed turbine can also be run in both directions. Thus the turbine extracts energy from water as a turbine and delivers energy to the water as a pump. The complete reversal thus converts a turbo-generator process to an electric pump process. The cost saving of these dual machines is significant (Open University, 1994). Although as always there will be losses in

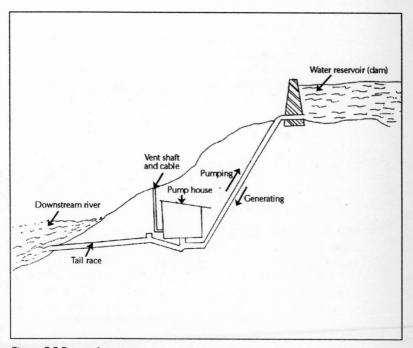

Figure 5.5 Pumped storage
Source: Adapted from Open University, 1994.

Box 5.3 Economic analysis for small-scale hydro-power

——————————— * ———————————

This analysis is based on a case study of *Small Hydro and Grid Extension for Rural Electrification: Alternatives and Complementarities* conducted in the town of Jinka, Ethiopia.

Alternative sources of energy:

1. *Small hydro plants:* Preliminary studies identified a site that would enable the inexpensive harnessing of hydro energy. Groundwork design of the relevant structures suggested that a small hydro plant with installed capacity of 600 KW would cost US$1.45 million.

2. *Grid extension:* The nearest town with grid electricity supply is 225 km distant. Applying unit costs of high voltage transmission lines under construction in Ethiopia in 1988, total investment required for the extension was estimated to be US$17.1 million.

3. *Diesel:* It would require two generating sets of 300 KW each, including generation and distribution panels, transformers, etc. A fuel storage tank, minimum building requirements and site works were also included in the estimated cost of US$0.8 million. The operating sets need to be replaced after the fifteenth year of service.

Investments and energy costs:

Maintenance costs for the small hydro and grid extension are taken to be 1.5 and 1 per cent of the annualized costs respectively. The annualized maintenance cost for the diesel plant is estimated at 15 per cent of the investment. Fuel costs are computed additionally.

Main findings:

The case study demonstrates (Figures 5.6 and 5.7) that supplying electricity to Jinka and the rural communities in its environs from the small hydro site 25 km away would be the least-cost option in annualized foreign exchange costs at any time in the project cycle, in comparison with the diesel plant and grid extension.

Source: Haile and Hailu, 1990.

---

energy, efficiencies of up to 80 per cent can be achieved. To make full use of the pumping facility, a low-level reservoir of at least the capacity of the upper one must be available – or must be constructed *(ibid.)*.

Small hydro, unlike some sources of energy, has the great advantage of multiple use: energy generation, irrigation and water supply. In addition, SHP is a very reliable technology that has a solid track record. The high capital investment is amortized by long service life and low maintenance requirements (*SHP News,* No.2, 1994). Small hydro development mainly targets the rural areas where grid connections do not reach, thus promoting rural industrial growth and improvement in the general welfare of the people (Ranganathan, 1992). It is worth noting that the decentralized nature of hydro sources suits the dispersed nature of rural populations (Inversin, 1986). It has been demonstrated in many countries that small hydro can make important contributions towards rural development (Holland, 1983). If implemented correctly, small hydro can offer opportunities for employment creation. Construction is straightforward and involves simple processes which offer opportunities for a large degree of local participation, in terms of both labour and materials (see Table 5.1, Fig 5.8 and Fig 5.9) (WEC, 1992).

In comparison with conventional sources of energy, small-scale hydro development is considered more favourable environmentally. With small hydro, there is no air pollution, no waste disposal and no fuel costs (Inversin, 1986). Usually small hydro does not involve the construction of significant storage; in general, it avoids the significant environmental impacts associated with large-scale hydro, including loss of habitat, change in water quality and siltation *(ibid.)*.

Among the advantages that hydro technologies have are the limited maintenance required and the continuous availability of power (Fraenkel *et al.*, 1991). This is important in the light of the fact that small hydro

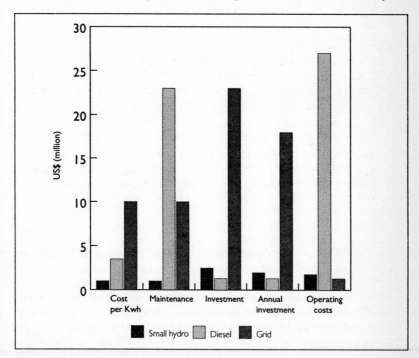

Figure 5.6 Cumulative annualized foreign exchange costs of alternative electricity supply for Jinka area

Source: Haile and Hailu, 1990.

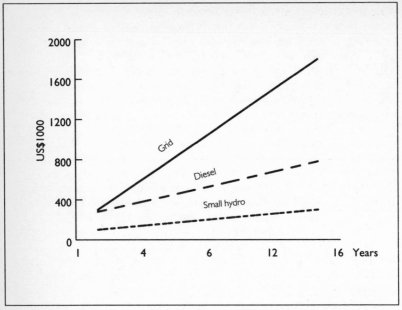

Figure 5.7 Comparative costs of alternative electricity supply sources for Jinka town

Source: Haile and Hailu, 1990.

utilization tends to be decentralized. Thus, with little maintenance required, a great cost reduction can be achieved (Box 5.3, Fig 5.6 and Fig 5.7). This also helps reduce the importation of necessary technical know-how to service these systems.

Environmental concerns are driving changes in the design, construction and operation of SHP technology (Johansson *et al.*, 1993). For instance, the diversion of water from natural channels and its passage through a turbine is inevitable and may create negative impacts due to fish mortality or impediments to the movement of migratory fish species (WEC, 1992). In developed countries where environmental aesthetics are taken into account, most penstocks are buried to reduce visual impact (*Hydronet* 2, 1994). Surface-mounted penstocks may interfere with the paths and tracks used by local people, or with farmers' fields (Gullberg, 1994). The river banks or any canal diggings for the small hydro project may be vulnerable to erosion *(ibid.)*. This may lead to sedimentation of the river and could interfere with the turbines. Two small hydro plants experienced sedimentation problems in Lesotho (Phuroe and Mathaha, 1995). Small hydro plants are also susceptible to damage by floods and silt (Turyahikayo *et al.*, 1995).

Small hydro-power is almost always obtained from river-driven plants

Table 5.1 Capital cost example for a 40 KW small hydro plant

Activity	US $	%	L	I
Pre-feasibility study	500			
Feasibility study, funding applications	1,000			
Design study (detailed surveys, production of tender documents, specifications, legal aspects, planning permission)	2,000			
Sub-total	3,500	4.0	✔	
Site preparation (Access tracks, clearing, temporary accommodation, etc.)	2,000			
Civil works (installed costs)				
Intake weir	4,000			
Headrace canal	1,000			
Setting tank	1,500			
Canal	3,000			
Forebay tank	2,000			
Penstock + supports	20,000			
Powerhouse, tailrace	2,000			
Sub-total	35,500	40.3	✔	
Electro-mechanical works (delivered to site)				
Turbine-alternator set	20,000			
Load control + ballast tank	5,000			
Power house, switchgear, protection	2,000			
Overhead line to demand point	4,000			
Installation costs	6,000			
Sub-total	37,000	42.1		✔
Other costs				
Insurance, water abstraction licence	1,000			
Supervision of contractors	3,000			
Contingency (10%)	8,000			
Sub-Total	12,000	13.6	✔	
TOTAL	88,000	100.0		

L – Local content
I – Import content
Source: Gullberg, 1994.
Note: The above table is purely an example. In practice the above figures may vary widely, depending on local circumstances (Fraenkel et al., 1991). It should also be noted that the total costs are more than indicated above. This is because one has to take into account the fact that, in typical circumstances, the total costs cannot be fully raised by the end users; most likely it will be met by a loan from a bank, thus incurring interest payments.

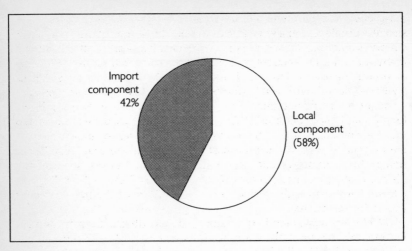

Figure 5.8 Comparative expenditure using local and imported small hydro materials

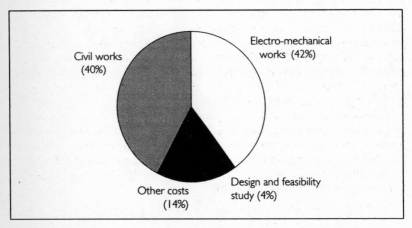

Figure 5.9 Capital costs of a small hydro plant

that lack the reservoir capacity to store water. Consequently, severe seasonal variations in power output may occur (Johansson *et al.*, 1993). It is also a site-specific technology and sites that are well suited to the harnessing of water power and close to a location where power can be exploited economically are not always available (Fraenkel *et al.*, 1991). Some small hydro technologies have been developed to counter the above drawbacks. The Rainbow micro hydro, developed in Australia, is consistently efficient over a wide range of sites. This is important when water supply is marginal since it has the ability to suit any site with a head of 5 metres or more. The technology has a turbine that can be adjusted to keep on producing useful amounts of power even when flow rates are as low as 0.2 litres/second) with heads greater than 40 metres (*Hydronet* 2, 1994).

Small hydro development is often associated with high initial cost (Sampa and Sichone, 1995). The economics of hydro depend on the location and condition of the use to which the power is put. Major costs are associated with the capital cost of equipment (Intermediate Technology Brief, undated) and especially the importation of some of the electro-mechanical components such as turbines. Table 5.1 and Figures 5.8 and 5.9 illustrate the typical cost of a 40 KW small hydro scheme for generating electricity.

The lowest-cost small hydro systems are usually built locally and are used mainly for mechanical applications such as milling. They can cost as little as US$200/KW. The most expensive are usually 'turn-key' electrical systems in remote areas which use high-quality imported Western equipment and contractors. These may reach as high as US$ 10,000/KW (Fraenkel *et al.*, 1991). A more detailed study (Table 5.1) shows, however, that most of the initial costs can be reduced by the involvement of the local end users. In the table, the letter 'L' represents activities which can be undertaken locally (57.9 per cent of the costs) while those represented by the letter 'I' (42.1 per cent of the costs) would have to be imported. In contrast to large-scale conventional energy systems, SHP can provide significant local added value, with over half of the construction expenditures made locally. Consequently, SHP potential for generating local jobs is much higher.

A large number of small hydro plants have been installed world-wide, often providing the only source of power in remote regions (Inversin, 1986). In 1986 hydro-electricity (including large-scale hydro-power) contributed 14.5 per cent of the world's total generated electricity (Johansson *et al.*, 1993). Recent international surveys on hydro-power facilities (capacities below 10 MW) reveal that:

1 Small hydro plants are currently under construction or are being planned in 100 countries;
2 Total installed capacity of small hydro facilities in 1989 was 23.5 GW, 38 per cent of which was generated in China;
3 Small hydro potential (up to 2 MW) is in the order of 570 TWh/year, or 3.8 per cent of the world's total technical power potential (Johansson *et al.*, 1993).

In many instances, small hydro is considered to be one of the cheapest renewable energy options. For instance, in Germany 1 KWh of hydro-power costs DM0.14 compared with DM0.35–0.90/KWh for wind energy, DM1.75 for solar thermal, and DM0.30 for PV systems (US$1= DM1.53).

Europe's exploitable small hydro potential (including Eastern and Central Europe) is estimated to be some 400 TWh/year, of which about 150 TWh/year is considered economically feasible. In 1991, small hydro accounted for slightly more than 1 per cent of the European Union's electricity generation, with about 12,000 developed sites in Western Europe translating to an installed capacity of approximately 6,300 MW. This may be compared with the EU's exploitable small hydro potential, which reaches 21 per cent of the total existing (both large- and small-scale) hydro potential (*Hydronet* 2, 1994).

A programme in Switzerland plans to attain a 5 per cent participation for small hydro in the country's total energy production by the year 2000 *(ibid)*. In the UK, 15 proposed small hydro schemes with a total capacity of 14.5 MW will be offered 15-year contracts to supply power (*Hydronet* 3, 1994). It was also proposed that five small hydro plants be built in Wales, with a total capacity of 4.6 MW (*SHP News* 2, 1994). Another 600 KW plant has been installed in Devon, UK (*Hydronet* 2, 1994). Since 1990, the Romanian Electric Authority (RENEL), has conducted rehabili-

Table 5.2 Developed small hydro sites in Western Europe

Existing plants in the EU countries

Country	No. of plants	Capacity (MW)
Germany	ca. 4600	1380.00
France	ca. 1400	ca. 1000.00
Spain	853	876.00
Italy	369	285.50
England	70	20.00
Denmark	60	10.50
Portugal	50	150.00
Ireland	28	5.00
Belgium	20	20.80
Greece	10	41.00
Luxembourg	7	0.65
Netherlands	7	36.00

Existing plants in the European Free Trade Association countries

Country	No. of plants	Capacity (MW)
Austria	ca.1400	ca. 430.00
Sweden	ca. 1200	ca. 320.00
Switzerland	980	680.00
Finland	235	ca.300.00
Norway	228	806.00
Iceland	19	43.00

Source: Hydronet 2, 1994.

tation studies of its small hydro stations and is also planning some structural changes (*SHP News* 2, 1994). Approximately 30 per cent of hydro-power potential in Slovenia has been exploited and there are about 290 privately instituted SHP schemes. Moreover, construction of new small hydro schemes (up to 40) is to be encouraged in the future, with the number of installations expected to double (*Hydronet* 3, 1994).

In South America, many small hydro installations are found in southern Chile. In Argentina, two small hydro plants (15 KW and 30 KW) have been built *(ibid.)*. Peru has a widely scattered population, many of whom have access to small hydro sites, and more manufacturers are now involved in hydro-power generation (Power Guide, 1994).

Pacific Hydro of Australia owns 50 per cent of Northern Mini Hydro Corporation (NMH), which operates three stations generating 11.6 MW in the Philippines. Pacific Hydro plans to expand into Malaysia. The Philippines seeks to refurbish the installation of 90 small hydro electric generators with a total capacity of 40 MW (*SHP News* 2, 1994). Recently, GTZ helped the country implement a 720 KW plant. GTZ has another programme in Indonesia to implement new small hydro schemes (*Hydronet* 3, 1994). Also in Indonesia, a 2.4 MW plant begun in in late 1994 was to be completed by 1995 (*SHP News* 3, 1994). In Western Samoa, a 4 MW project is to be completed through funding from the Asian Development Bank (*SHP News* 2, 1994). The government of India plans to develop 19 small hydro plants. Five will be built by the government and 14 will be offered to the private sector (*SHP News* 3, 1994). Work on two other plants, a new 1 MW small hydro and a 3.75 MW plant, was scheduled to be completed in the latter part of 1995 and 1996 respectively *(ibid.)*. The prospect of generating power and profit through SHP has attracted interest from the private sector in Sri Lanka. A plant is being upgraded to provide 100 KW of power and work was in progress on an 800 KW grid-connected scheme; another 60 KW grid-connected scheme was to be commissioned soon (*Hydronet* 2, 1994). By 1986, 40 plants ranging from 5 KW to 15 KW had been installed in remote rural villages in Pakistan. More were under construction (Inversin, 1986).

China covers a vast territory with over 5,000 rivers and a catchment area of 100 square kilometres. It is therefore not surprising that it was one of the earliest countries to harness water resources for energy production (*SHP News* 3, 1994). The technical potential for small hydro is approximately 220 TWh/year and the country had installed 37 per cent of this by 1989 (Johansson *et al.*, 1993). Small hydro development in China has been phenomenal. In 1949, the country had only 50 hydro-electric power stations producing 56 MW (Hankins, 1987). In 1950, China embarked on a small hydro power programme (Johansson *et al.*, 1993) and by 1960 there were 45,000 units producing 200 MW *(ibid.)*. By the end of 1993, the number of small hydro stations totalled 45,645 with a total installed capacity of 6,003 MW *(SHP News* 3, 1994). China has long been the world leader in terms of the number of modern small hydro systems installed

(Power Guide, 1994). These usually operate in isolation or connected to local grids. In the countryside, the combination of small hydro systems with reservoirs is stressed and optimized systems are being widely adopted. Since the technology of small hydro has come to maturity, it occupies an important position in rural China (*SHP News* 3, 1994).

The harnessing of water power in Nepal is not a new phenomenon: traditional water wheels for agro-processing have been in use for centuries in the rural areas, with the first modern hydro power installed in 1911 (*SHP News,* 3, 1994). Hydraulic ram pumps have been manufactured since the early 1980s (Power Guide, 1994) and have been used mainly for water supply. Small hydro turbine and electrification schemes have been found to be viable options for meeting the energy needs of the rural population in remote areas of Nepal (*SHP News* 3, 1994). To date, the country has about 25,000 operational small hydro units. Several institutions have been involved in small hydro development. For instance, a private non-profit agency, United Mission to Nepal (UMN), has worked in this field since 1963. The agency formed the Butwal Technical Institute (BTI) in 1963 to train young people to work in hydro-power and to promote development and dissemination of small hydro technologies.

The Nepalese government has also undertaken small hydro power programmes (Inversin, 1986) and has assisted UMN's electrification efforts. In 1984 it sanctioned privately instituted small hydro projects under 100 KW, eliminated licensing requirements and granted approval for charging unrestricted tariffs. Deregulation of small hydro projects has stimulated private involvement. The government also planned to install 80 small hydro turbines within the 1994 financial year (*SHP News* 3, 1994). Another institution involved in similar activities is the Centre for Rural Technology (CRT). It has assisted a private developer, for example, to generate 1.5 KW of electricity from an improved *ghatta* (traditional water mill). Out of an estimated 25,000 traditional *ghattas* still in existence in Nepal, only about 250 have been improved so far. An electricity company also plans to develop small hydro-power for sale to the national grid (*Hydronet* 2, 1994).

It is well known that much of the unexploited potential for small hydro is in remote areas of Africa (*Hydronet* 3, 1994). Most attempts at promoting hydro-power technologies, however, have focused on large-scale applications for generating electricity. Identified technologies were perceived in the light of large-scale power generation. Consequently, attractive opportunities for small hydro systems were not exploited fully (Karekezi and Turyareeba, 1995).

The Eastern and Southern African region is endowed with a large number of permanent streams and rivers feeding the major rivers: the Blue and White Nile, the Zambezi, the Orange and the Limpopo (Figure 5.10). The region also contains much of the watershed of the Congo. Most of the rivers and tributaries provide excellent hydro-power development potential (Karekezi and Turyareeba, 1995) for all the countries in the

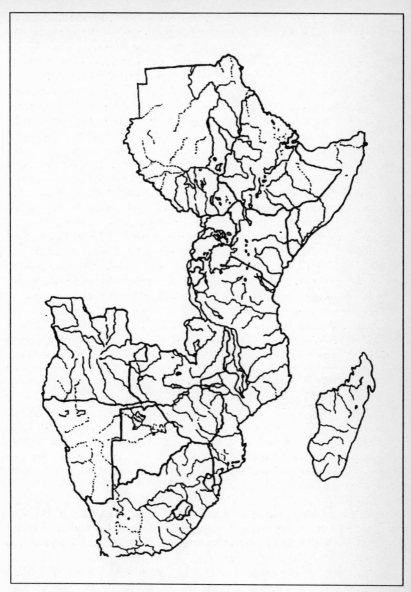

Figure 5.10 Map of drainage, Eastern and Southern Africa

Table 5.3 Small hydro-power sites identified in selected countries

Country	Number of sites
1. Madagascar	Over 100[1]
2. Burundi	Over 100[1]
3. Kenya	Over 100[2]
4. Uganda	22[1]
5. Lesotho	22[3]
6. Zambia	20[4]
7. Rwanda	8[1]

Sources: 1. Karekezi and Turyareeba, 1995; 2. Hankins, 1987; 3. Phuroe and Mathaha, 1995; 4. Sampa and Sichone, 1995.

Table 5.4 Small hydro-power utilization in selected countries

Country	Harnessed (Small) (MW)
Mauritius	6.70
Kenya	6.28
Burundi**	5.17
Somalia	4.80
Zambia	4.50
Tanzania	4.00
Lesotho	3.54
Malawi	1.52
Botswana	1.00
Rwanda**	1.00
Uganda*	0.50
South Africa	0.40
Swaziland	0.30
Mozambique	0.10

*Other stations of total capacity 6.81 MW are not operational.
**Outbreak of civil war may have affected the performance of existing small hydro installations
Source: Karekezi and Turyareeba, 1995.

region except Djibouti. Attempts have been made to harness both large and small hydro potential, although in the Seychelles and Botswana potential is restricted to small hydro schemes (Karekezi and Turyareeba, 1995).

There is limited information on small hydro sites in the region. While experience to date has raised awareness of technical options for disseminating small hydro in Africa, the results of many of the initiatives have been disappointing, largely because of the unexpected complexity of developing, selecting and implementing these options. One constraint has been limited access to information on small hydro, particularly in terms of resource assessment (Karekezi and Turyareeba, 1995). Table 5.3 shows the number of sites identified in selected countries.

Lesotho has substantial hydro-power resources with four small hydro plants (Phuroe and Mathaha, 1995). Before the initiation of the giant Lesotho Highland Water Project, the Lesotho Electricity Company (LEC), a government parastatal, was responsible for the supply of all electric power through the national grid and from the small hydro generation plants, some of which are not connected to the grid (Bhagavan and Karekezi, 1992). A number of studies have been undertaken to estimate the potential for small-scale hydro-power and 22 sites have been identified as shown in Table 5.5 (Phuroe and Mathaha, 1995).

Four of the above sites have been developed with a total installed capacity of 3.4 MW. It should be noted that two of the above (Mantsonyane and Semonkong) have experienced problems due to drought while the other two (Tlokoeng and Qacha's Nek) have experienced problems of sedimentation. A notable example is a 15 KW plant which used to be run by expatriate workers which fell into disuse after they left. This is probably because the expatriates left no one with the skills and interest to keep it going (Phuroe and Mathaha, 1995).

Uganda, despite limited experience with small-scale hydro-power development, has demonstrated the viability of the technology in commercial activities such as mining and also in social services. Most of the potential for small hydro lies at the extreme ends of the power grid in the western and eastern parts of the country where 22 sites for development have been identified. These sites are concentrated in the mountainous areas. The government is in the process of implementing three of these sites, with an estimated total capacity of 13 MW. By 1970, the country had five small-scale hydro-power installations. The fifth one stopped operating in the same year. This installation was damaged by floods and silt interfered with the turbines. It was closed down when the town it operated in was connected to the grid and is now earmarked for rehabilitation. A few other small hydro plants existed before 1970: these were mainly systems designed to provide mechanical power for running grain mills. They belonged to white and Asian entrepreneurs but fell into disuse after they left (Turyahikayo et al., 1995). No doubt the running of these systems would have been taken up by the local authorities if better organizational skills had existed in the country.

The Church of Uganda diocese plans to install a 120 KW plant which will replace a diesel generator at Kuluva hospital, a few kilometers from Arua town, and will also be used for grain milling. In March 1994 the European Development Fund (EDF) sponsored a survey of small hydro sites with potential for development which focused on the West Nile region. The survey identified 76 sites with potential ranging from 2 KW to 566 KW. As a follow-up, the programme plans to ensure that most of the mechanical equipment will be fabricated in Uganda, with most of the construction work undertaken by local personnel under the supervision of expatriate staff. World Harvest Mission is sponsoring a feasibility study for small hydro-power from the Nyabuka river in the foothills of the

Table 5.5 Existing studies and projects on small-scale hydro-power in Lesotho

Project	Capacity (KW)
Likhebaneng	4500
Mosetleto	2500
Mantsonyane	2000
Lethena	2000
Mokhotlong B	1500
Mokhotlong I A	800
Mokhotlong	795
Mokhotlong I B	700
Tlokoeng	670
Motete	524
Qacha's Nek	400
Semongkong	340
Mokhotlong N	242
Mokhotlong S	205
St. Teresa	200
Sehlabathebe	150
Semokong I	120
Lesobeng	110
Sehlabathebe	100
Pitseng	70
Sehonghong	70
Ha Ntsi	30
TOTAL	18026

Source: Phuroe and Mathaha, 1995.

Table 5.6 Small hydro stations in Uganda, 1970

Name	District	Installed capacity (MW)	Remarks
Mobuku	Kasese	5.4	Operating
Kikagati	Mbarara	1.23	Closed in 1970
Maziba	Kabale	0.50	Being uprated to 1MW
Kagando	Kasese	0.06	Needs rehabilitation
Kisizi	Rukungiri	0.01	Uprated to 0.06 MW in 1984

Source: Turyahikayo et al., 1995.

Rwenzori mountains, aiming to involve the local community and political leaders (Turyahikayo et al., 1995).

Zambia has several sites for small hydro development. The estimated potential is 45 MW, found mainly in the northern and north-western parts of the country. The exploited potential of small hydros is slightly more than 10 per cent of the total. A pre-feasibility study conducted in 1982 identified five sites for small hydro; they could not be developed, however, in the prevailing economic conditions. Another study in 1986 concluded that small hydro-power sites near districts connected to the grid were not economically viable at that time and could not be developed. The study recommended the development of two other sites, one with a total capacity of 3–5 MW. Another study, conducted in 1992, concluded that there were 10–20 sites for small hydro in three districts, although many of these were not favoured by the hydrological conditions. The Zambia Electricity Supply Corporation (ZESCO) is scouting for funds to finance an updated study and re-evaluation of these potential sites. Only two schemes are connected to the main grid; a 5 MW and a 1 MW plant. Hydraulic rams were also recommended to supply water and for small-scale irrigation (Sampa and Sichone, 1995).

Small hydro systems have been in use in Kenya since 1925 (Karekezi, Majoro and Ewagata, 1994): introduced by the European settlers, they fell into disuse after independence because of the shortage of qualified personnel to repair them and the government's concentration on grid electricity programmes. Investments in hydro-power development have concentrated on schemes for large dams with little investment in small ones. Many utilities prefer large centralized investments which are considered easier to manage (Karekezi and Turyareeba, 1995). Some plants, however, are still operating in parts of the country which have high rainfall. A study estimated that there are more than 100 sites which are 25 km or more from the grid and economically feasible. There are many more potential sites for plants which would produce less than 10 KW. A visit by AFREPREN to the Brooke Bond Tea factory in Kericho, Kenya, revealed that the company has initiated several SHP schemes, as early as the 1920s and as recently as 1995, ranging between 400 KW and 800 KW in capacity. The Tenwek Hospital in the same region developed a donor-funded SHP plant with a capacity of 400 KW, commissioned in 1990. Water wheels are also still in use in a number of sites. Many Kenyans are

Table 5.7 Existing sites and committed small hydro plants in Kenya, 1987

River	Capacity (mw)	No. of units	Year installed
Tana	8.0	2	1954
Maragua	7.4	4	1952
Maragua	6.4	3	1933
Kuja	2.2	2	1958
Thika	2.0	2	1925
Tana	1.5	3	1955
Sosiani	0.4	2	1952
Maragua	0.4	1	1933

Source: Hankins, 1987.

solving their water problems with small-scale hydro-power and it is estimated that there are over 2,000 hydraulic rams pumping water around the country, and at least three companies making high-quality hydrams (Hankins, 1987).

Adding a major electrification component to small hydro schemes designed for direct shaft (mechanical) power is often not cost-effective, as demonstrated by Madagascar's Ampefy project (Box 5.4). Experience in a number of developing countries, notably Nepal, shows that the most successful small hydro schemes are primarily designed for direct shaft power with electrification remaining a secondary and less important objective (Karekezi, 1989).

There are some isolated small hydro schemes connected to the main power grid in Ethiopia. In 1992 the country had the capability to design and construct small hydro plants with a generating capacity of up to 5 MW. Most of the hardware and electro-mechanical equipment could be manufactured locally. The bulk of rural electrification in Ethiopia over the coming 20 years will be carried out through linkage to the main grid or through the development of isolated small hydro units matched to local requirements (Ranganathan, 1992).

There are six privately owned small hydro stations in Malawi (mainly on tea estates). Before the civil war in Rwanda, small hydro provided 2 per cent of the total generation capacity (1983) (Karekezi and Turyareeba, 1995). There is only one known small hydro in Somalia, a 4.8 MW small hydro commissioned in 1983 (Ahmed, 1988). It is not known whether the station is still operational. In Tanzania, a 40 KW small hydro station was built in a church in 1988 and is still functioning well (SEI, 1994). In Zimbabwe, a power corporation has started construction of a 700 KW hydro plant for electrification of a canning factory; the plant will be connected to an existing line (*Hydronet* 3, 1994).

**Box 5.4
The Ampefy project**

———————————————— * ————————————————

A seminar conducted in Madagascar led to the evaluation of the energy needs of the country. This also provided an opportunity to assess the institutional capacity of the local energy agencies. The seminar recommended that efforts to develop low-cost renewable energy resources for the rural areas should be intensified. A subproject was designed to address one of the most important objectives of the Energy Initiatives for Africa (EAI) project which was to develop alternative, low cost and indigenous power resources for agro-processing in African countries. The above concerns led to the initiation of the Hydropower for Agroprocessing subproject in Ampefy, Madagascar. The project developed a pilot agroprocessing installation that would provide rice milling facilities using hydropower. The selection of hydropower was based on the great potential that exists throughout Madagascar with its abundant water resources and ideal topographic characteristics. The central and most important activity of the subproject was the design, manufacture and installation of a 64KW small hydropower station for agroprocessing and electricity generation. By the end of 1987, the hydropower station (64KW) had been constructed and commissioned. This was followed by the construction of a 15KW small hydropower at another town in the country. The design of the turbine and other associated equipment was effected by a university student.

(Karekezi, 1989a).

Part 3

Factors Influencing the
Dissemination of Renewable Energy Technologies
and Strategies for Future Development

6

Institutional Development

One of the key factors influencing the implementation and promotion of renewable energy technology programmes in the region is the existing institutional infrastructure. Although not accorded as much attention as other factors such as finance, a conducive institutional framework has often been shown to be a prerequisite for successful technology dissemination. Institutions should provide the enabling environment required to ensure that regulations are adhered to.

The important institutional actors in the renewable energy sector are government and the commercial agencies. Key agencies in government include Ministries of Energy and their respective departments, including research institutes. Government agencies are particularly important in the regulation and licensing of key institutions operating in the energy sector. Support from government is crucial where the technology being promoted is not commercially viable in the short term and there is uncertainty about its future prospects (Kjellström, 1994).

Table 6.1 and 6.2 shows the importance of interventions in competitive technologies. Despite the two countries having almost the same potential, positive institutional and policy interventions in Cyprus have realized a much higher solar water heaters (SWH) installed capacity than Malta's.

Table 6.1 Solar water heaters (SWHs) in Malta and Cyprus: the impact of policy

	Malta	Cyprus
Population	400,000	700,000
Latitude	35°50°N	34°34°N
Annual kWh/m^2	1986	1910
Electricity cost (ECU/kWh)	0.062	0.076
Cost of 2m^2 SWH (ECU)	800	700
Total installed cap (m^2)	> 1,000	626,000
Annual sales (m^2)	200	30,000
Market growth (annual)	0	3–5%
Major interventions	None	Indirect • Testing facility • Advisory services • Hotel loans

Source: Gregory, 1994

The commercial agencies, largely guided by the profit-making incentive, include financial institutions and the producers and distributors of various systems (Kjellström, 1994). Apart from government and commercial agencies, other important actors include non-governmental organizations (NGOs) (often facilitators in RET dissemination), consultancy firms and consumers.

Government structure and policy

Experience in the region shows that the introduction and success of any RET is, to a large extent, dependent on the existing government policy. Government policies are an important factor in terms of their ability to create an enabling environment for RET dissemination and mobilizing resources, as well as encouraging private sector investment (Sampa and Sichone, 1995). Government agencies have played an important role in providing public education on RETs through seminars, publications and posters. In certain cases, however, they have been impediments to the dissemination of RETs in the region: government restrictions on the activities of energy-related NGOs and bilateral agencies are common, for example.

Most of the early institutional initiatives in the region were driven by the oil crises of the early 1970s and late 1970s. In response to the crises, governments established either an autonomous Ministry of Energy or a department dedicated to the promotion of sound energy policies, including the development of RETs. For example, Zambia responded by outlining policy proposals in its Third National Development Plan (1979–83) to develop alternative forms of energy as partial substitutes for conventional energy resources. The plan singled out the research and development programmes of various RETs. The government established the National Energy Council (NEC) and the Department of Energy (DOE) in 1980 and 1983 respectively, after recognizing the need for institutions charged with the responsibility of implementing such programmes (Sampa and Sichone, 1995).

Unfortunately, once the energy crisis subsided, government support for energy development and RET activities diminished significantly. Now most of the remaining support is at the rhetorical level. Consequently, in many countries of the region, official support on energy issues is being wound down. Diminishing policy support for energy issues is demonstrated by the limited budgetary allocation to Ministries of Energy or, in certain cases, the downgrading of these ministries into minor departments in larger ministries responsible for mineral resources and the environment as well as energy. In addition, many countries do not have an independent Ministry of Energy. Consequently, energy programmes are handled by low-level departments. Even where a Ministry of Energy exists, its role is often confined to minor energy activities with limited influence on energy policy, investment and financial issues, which are perceived as the preserve of either the Ministry of Commerce, the Ministry of Finance or the national utilities. In Uganda in 1983 energy affairs were under the Ministry of Power, Posts and Telecommunications, re-named the Ministry of Energy in 1986 to indicate that energy issues had attained a higher profile. In 1991, however, the Ministry of Energy was reduced to a department of a larger Ministry of Water, Energy, Minerals and Environment Protection, renamed the Ministry of Natural Resources in 1993, thus removing the word 'energy' from the Ministry's title altogether.

There are a few exceptions. In Kenya prior to 1979, for example, energy sector issues related to policy and management were scattered over several ministries. The Ministry of Power and Communications handled electricity, the Ministry of Finance handled petroleum pricing and the Ministry of Environment and Natural Resources tackled woodfuel development and management (Nyoike and Okech, 1993). The Ministry of Energy in Kenya was established at the end of 1979, after the Kenyan government realized that the sector presented a growing challenge to the country's socio-economic development. Budgetary allocations to the Ministry of Energy, however, have continued to be inadequate. In many countries in the region, government activities in the energy sector continue to be widely dispersed; as a result, there is a vacuum of authority in decision making on RETs. According to Turyahikayo et al. (1995), the energy sector in Uganda is poorly managed, coordinated and planned, a situation aggravated by slow bureaucratic practices in most government departments.

Most governments in the region do not have a clear-cut policy on the development and promotion of RETs, which continue to be undertaken within an energy planning and policy vacuum. As a result, RET development follows an *ad hoc* path, with little recourse to national energy plans which are rarely available or else out of date and inadequate (Karekezi, 1988b). A survey carried out in Botswana revealed that about 57 per cent of the respondents had no knowledge of government policies designed to promote the use of RETs, including wind pumps (Mosimanyane *et al.*, 1995). In Malawi the policy vacuum has meant that the majority of RET dissemination efforts have not only been *ad hoc,* but have operated largely as informal sector activities outside the framework of government machinery, thus failing to mobilize the fiscal support of the central government and its major donors (Kafumba, 1994a). A study on wind energy undertaken in Kenya reported that Dutch aid officials would have been interested in financing wind projects if there was an official wind energy policy strongly supported by the government (IT Power, 1987) .

Most of the countries in the region place more emphasis on the petroleum and power sectors, which supply a small portion of total energy consumption, than on renewables (particularly biomass) which supply the needs of a larger portion of the population. Biomass energy consumption is often not covered in official national statistics. In Kenya,

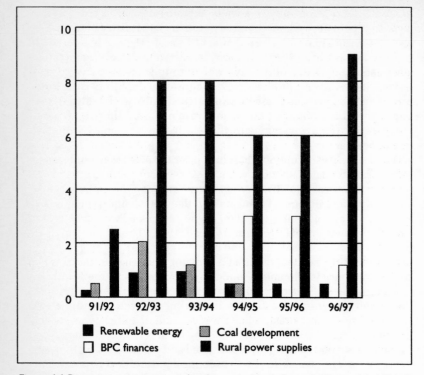

Figure 6.1 Botswana energy sector development expenditure (million pula), 1991–7
Source: Ministry of Finance and Development Planning (MFDP).
BPC = Botswana Power Cooperation

wind energy does not feature in the National Energy Programme. Botswana is one of the few countries with an official budgetary allocation to renewables but, as shown in Figure 6.1, the allocation to RETs is significantly lower than those made to power (Botswana Power Cooperation) and conventional rural energy programmes.

More proactive government support for RETs can yield encouraging results, as demonstrated by the Brazil ethanol programme. The success of the programme was, to a large extent, attributable to strong government support through incentives both to the sugar cane growers and to the ethanol plants. The Brazilian government also established a price policy to ensure remuneration of the ethanol producers and guaranteed that it would purchase all the ethanol produced within an established physical limit (Hall *et al.*, 1993). In contrast, policies pertaining to ethanol production, distribution and sale in Kenya have not been established. The pricing of gasohol is a highly bureaucratic process, worked out by at least two ministries (Ministry of Energy and Ministry of Finance) in addition to the entire Cabinet, the oil companies and the Kenya Pipeline Company.

In 1991, the price of power alcohol was Ksh7.60 per litre, while the ethanol plant required a minimum of Ksh11.60 per litre to turn a profit (*Standard,* 1991).

In some countries, however, RETs are beginning to attract significant government support. The government of Zambia is planning to incorporate the use of renewable sources of energy in government-funded projects. It also plans to sensitize government ministries and departments to the potential of PV systems (Sampa and Sichone, 1995). The government of Botswana in its National Development Plan VII (1991–7) has demonstrated support for the development and promotion of RETs by setting aside a total of US$1.3 million for renewable energy programmes (Mosimanyane *et al.*, 1995), although this is far below the amount allocated to conventional energy sources.

Parastatals and utilities

The existing institutional framework in the region is largely characterized by the monopolistic or oligopolistic practices of parastatal electricity utilities and multinational oil companies respectively. Oil and power sector companies usually have a *de facto* or *de jure* monopoly on production and distribution of energy, making it difficult for RETs to penetrate the market.

The major obstacles to the wider deployment of large-scale biomass energy power generation in the region are institutional. Questions regarding the legality of the generation, distribution and sale of power by institutions other than the national utility hamper wider dissemination of this important technology. Even when the national or local utility agrees to purchase power generated by independent producers such as sugar companies, price setting becomes the sticking point. Many national utilities have no institutional interest in fostering competing sources of electricity.

In some countries the Electricity Act prohibits independent power producers and distributors from selling power directly to consumers. They can only generate it for internal consumption, since all power generated for commercial purposes has to be sold to the national utility, which often quotes a prohibitively low price. This predicament is well illustrated in the case of Kenya where the national utility (KPLC) has refused consistently to pay more than its own saved operating costs for electricity deliveries from sugar mills (Nyoike and Okech, 1992). In Mauritius, the equipment installed in the sugar factories is sufficient to double the current level of electricity generated, but the low prices provided by the national utility to independent power producers removes the commercial incentive (Baguant, 1990).

In the case of small hydro development, large utility monopoly makes it difficult for the private sector to invest in hydro generation. It is believed that the continuous supply of power to the grid by the Mobukusi small hydro station in Uganda is prohibited by the near-monopoly held by the Uganda Electricity Board (UEB) (Turyahikayo *et al.*, 1995). The existing Electricity Act (Chapter 135, 1964 edition) gives UEB a near-monopoly of power generation, transmission and distribution in the country. UEB reserves the right to grant or refuse to grant a licence to any other party for the generation of power, be it for own use or sale to other parties *(ibid.)*.

The Corporate Act that established the Electricity Supply Commission (ESCOM) in Malawi gives it near-monopoly powers in electricity generation and complete monopoly status in electricity transmission and distribution. All private producers have to obtain generation licences from ESCOM, whose decision is subject to ministerial approval. In the case of transmission and distribution, private generators are barred from selling their power to other users and can only sell to ESCOM for eventual distribution (Kafumba, 1994a). In Zambia, the previous government policy was to concentrate on power generation, transmission and distribution in one giant national power utility for supposedly 'strategic' reasons. Consequently, the Zambia Electricity Supply Corporation (ZESCO) has dominated the industry (Sampa and Sichone, 1995) and independent renewable energy power producers have failed to emerge.

The region's governments need to limit the monopoly powers enjoyed by the utilities in order to create an environment conducive to independent power generation from bagasse, wind or small hydro. A few countries have begun to enact more liberal laws: in Tanzania, the Ministry of Energy has agreed to allow the GEF-financed plant to sell the electricity generated from a planned urban waste biogas plant to TANESCO at the market price. The Ministry has also indicated that the plant can negotiate special arrangements with companies located near the facility to directly supply them with electricity (GEF, 1993). Similar reforms of the legislation and regulatory framework governing the power sector in Uganda are being contemplated (Turyahikayo *et al.*, 1995). In contrast to the power sector, where the monopoly is centred on state corporations, the petroleum sector is dominated by private enterprise oligopolies which are subsidiaries of multinational companies closely linked to their parent international companies. They are able to collude with these parent companies outside the region in the aggressive pursuit of their interests. The multinational companies constitute an important obstacle to the successful use of ethanol in the transport sector. In Malawi, the multinational oil companies are unwilling to increase the ratio of ethanol in gasohol, thus denying the ethanol company a chance to attain full capacity utilization and expand its operations. In Kenya, after the introduction of power alcohol into the market by the Agro-Chemical and Food Corporation (ACFC), implementation of the gasohol take-up programme was slow and eventually ground to a halt owing to the reluctance of oil companies to blend the product with gasoline and pay a remunerative price for gasohol as recommended by the government (Awori, 1995). ACFC is currently forced to rely on the ethanol export market to survive after attempts to produce power alcohol for local use failed.

Only proactive and overt policy support from governments can change the status quo. In Zimbabwe, the National Oil Company purchases power alcohol from the producers and ensures that the power alcohol is used. Since ethanol has proved environmentally benign, governments could promote ethanol use by restricting the amount of lead fumes from car emissions through a policy that accounts for environmental damage in the prices of fuel.

Research institutions

The region's RET research and development programmes are hampered by numerous constraints. Some of the problems identified include deficiencies in manpower, clear objectives, direction, analytical skills, adequate facilities and incentives for researchers (Othieno, 1993; Turya-hikayo, 1994). Most of the RET research institutions are faced with severe financial constraints. Funding scientific research is not a priority of most of the governments in the region, which typically spend less than 1 per cent of their GDP on research and development. In addition, the large corporations involved in energy-related activities which could provide important support do not conduct or contract out research work on RETs (Othieno, 1993). The NGOs which are known to be actively involved in RET promotion in the region are involved in extension work and rarely undertake research activities.

For example, the limited budget allocated to the African Regional Centre for Solar Energy (ARCSE) in Burundi by the member countries is insufficient to provide even basic requirements for research and development in RETs. The centre is now inoperative. The Appropriate Technology Centre (ATC) at Kenyatta University was not able to mobilize a level of funding that would allow it to provide testing and research facilities on a continuous basis – despite being the centre for most of the cookstove testing and research in Kenya (Karekezi and Masakhwe, 1991).

It is not surprising, therefore, that most of the research activities in this field are externally funded (Othieno, 1993). The Kenya Renewable Energy Development Project (KREDP), which led to the development of the famous Kenya Ceramic Jiko (KCJ), was a four-year bilateral project between the US government and Kenya which consisted of a US$4.8 million grant from the US plus US$1.7 million provided by the government of Kenya in the form of staff time contributions (Karekezi and Masakhwe, 1991). The Botswana Renewable Energy Technology Project (BRET) was jointly funded by USAID and the Ministry of Mineral Resources and Water Affairs (Mosimanyane et al., 1995). The Swedish International Development Authority (SIDA) also funded a large-scale investigation of wind energy potential throughout Botswana.

The dearth of research activities means that few of the region's countries have an energy data bank in place. Base-line information on resources such as small hydro, solar and wind energy is poor and unreliable. The data available on wind in Mozambique (measured two metres from the ground) was collected for agricultural purposes (Lopes and Macamo, 1994). The same situation exists in Tanzania where the meteorological data used in calculating wind power potential suffers from three main limitations (Mwandosya and Luhanga, 1983):

- Wind velocities were obtained at two metres;
- Obstructions were found close to wind speed measuring equipment; and
- Most of the data was collected using unreliable methods.

The region also lacks a comprehensive inventory of activities in the renewable energy sector and this has led to difficulties in formulating appropriate policies and plans. In Botswana, the figures released on solar systems installed are broad estimates because no records on imports from South Africa are kept (Diphaha and Burton, 1993).

In Botswana the potential for renewable energy sources is not quantified, while in Mozambique the main barrier to wind energy technology dissemination is lack of appropriate wind data. There are very few research institutions that focus on ethanol and bagasse power generation, although sugar cane industries are found in virtually all countries of the region.

There are some exceptions: for example, the Ethanol Company Limited (ETHCO) of Malawi has financed efforts to search for alternative ethanol feed material using woody biomass thinnings from Viphya Pulp/Paper Plantation (Kafumba, 1994a). In Kenya, the Meteorological Department and the Special Energy Programme are making an effort to increase the reliability of wind data suitable for wind policy formulation (IT Power, 1987). Between 1985 and 1987, the Department of Meteorological Services in Botswana, in collaboration with Botswana Technology Centre, Rural Industries Innovation Centre and the Department of Water Affairs, installed an array of anemometers throughout the country at a height of 10 metres. This provided baseline data on wind speeds and assessed the potential for using wind energy to pump water in the country (Mosimanyane et al., 1995). The data collected also enabled analysts to select geographical areas that have potential for wind pumping systems and to advise on the appropriate size of such units (ibid.). In the same vein, the basic data on solar radiation being compiled in Botswana by the Department of Physics at the University of Botswana will be of value in solar systems design and sizing (Diphaha and Burton, 1993).

Unreliable estimates are sometimes used to establish resource availability. For instance, the number of animals a country possesses is often used to determine biogas potential. This is misleading because the statistics account for diverse types of livestock management systems without taking into consideration the extent to which non-zero grazing systems (which are unsuitable for biogas production) are practised in the region.

The region's poor baseline information on RETs is exacerbated by inadequate RET documentation and library services. Information on past experiences that would help to avoid duplication and the recurrence of past errors has been dumped instead of being transferred to libraries. In spite of almost two decades of accumulated commercial experience, lack of accurate information inhibits the market penetration of renewable energy applications. Karekezi and Masakhwe (1991) cite the example of how it became difficult to obtain documentation and information on USAID's ten-year effort to introduce RETs in sub-Saharan Africa because key documents were dumped after the cessation of the programme. More extensive publication of books, journals and newsletters on RETs is needed urgently. The existing documentation units that cover RETs should instal computerized documentation systems such as CDS-ISIS for easy access to and retrieval of vital information.

Private sector

The term 'private sector' refers to a wide range of commercial firms ranging from a one-man backstreet informal sector operation to large subsidiaries of multinational corporations. Although private sector concerns are largely driven by the need to make profit, their dynamism and willingness to take risks has been instrumental in the dissemination of RETs. Local small- to medium-scale RET companies are usually more innovative than RET subsidiaries of large multinational – usually oil – companies (Masakhwe, 1993). Small companies are also more labour-intensive and make greater use of local resources. Labour intensity enhances their contribution to the development of the national economy while greater recourse to local human and material resources enhances sustainability (Karekezi and Masakhwe, 1991).

The private sector, therefore, is important in promoting the wide-scale use of RETs and ensuring long-term sustainability. The benefits of private-sector participation at the early stages of a project include faster commercialization of new RETs, reduced public sector funding, increased competition and possibly more cost-effective prices for the new RETs. This was clearly demonstrated by the case of the KCJ (discussed in Part 2) and PV systems in Kenya (Karekezi, Ewagata et al., 1995). The rapid growth of the solar industry in Kenya is largely attributable to the role played by the private sector (Walubengo and Kimani, 1993).

Under normal circumstances, the private sector creates an environment of competition that lowers commodity prices but can lead to quality problems if not properly monitored. The PV industry in Kenya provides compelling evidence of this fact. Many poor-quality PV systems (incorrectly sized, coupled to the wrong type of battery, fitted with inadequate controls) were sold to many users at very low prices. While this generated short-term sales income for the firms that scrambled to meet this increased demand, the long-term impact of poor field performance on the PV industry has been negative. Customer confidence was seriously eroded, which may undermine the industry's long-term future. This is also one of the main setbacks in the Seychelles solar industry, where there are no regulations restricting the import of electrical appliances with inappropriate ratings and low efficiencies (Razanajatovo *et al.*, 1994). While the role played by the private sector is crucial, additional support is required in quality control and standardization.

Non-governmental organizations

Indigenous non-governmental organizations (NGOs, sometimes referred to as voluntary agencies) have been instrumental in reaching grassroots communities in RET dissemination programmes because of their flexibility and innovativeness (Sampa and Sichone, 1995). NGOs tend to prefer small-scale and simple but innovative technical solutions to local energy problems. They have been instrumental in training and in providing public education on RETs through workshops, training courses, newsletters, books, posters and calendars. In general, however, NGOs have limited their attention to small-scale RETs, mainly in the biomass sector (improved stoves, household biogas plants and small-scale improved charcoal production). Due to limitations in expertise and financial resources, very few NGOs have worked on modern large-scale RETs such as PVs for power production, wind farms and co-generation.

In certain cases, NGOs have begun to compete with private sector RET companies. This has hampered the effective dissemination of RETs. One case is in Kenya where Bellerive Foundation, an NGO charged with the responsibility of disseminating institutional stoves, undertakes stove production and marketing. Since the organization received grants from donor agencies, Bellerive stoves were sold at subsidized prices. Prices were no longer determined by market forces and this gradually drove out private manufacturers. This is in complete contrast to the successful KCJ project in the country, where NGOs largely stayed out of the commercial production and marketing process.

In a study of key factors for the successful dissemination of RETs, Karekezi and Masakhwe (1991) compared the KCJ and PV systems in Kenya. The KCJ programme relied on the substantial involvement of indigenous NGOs while the PV sector had virtually no input from this source. While the absence of NGOs appears not to have prevented commercialization of PVs in Kenya, the dissemination process would have benefited from an institutional framework for raising user awareness and lobbying for increased policy support. In particular, obtaining information on PVs is difficult since it remains with individual firms who are unwilling to share it *(ibid.)*.

In the dissemination of stoves in Kenya, NGOs were an important channel for information and the provision of free technical support. This kind of support structure was missing in the PV dissemination and has resulted in a very limited retention of institutional memory. As a result, agencies starting to work in this field are not able to tap the valuable experience of previous efforts. The development of local NGOs is thus an important element in RET dissemination in the region and should be an important component of any effort to promote their wide-scale use.

A 1982 report by the World Bank recommended that the Ministry of Energy in Kenya consider extending the role of the numerous NGOs working on energy-related activities. These range from information dissemination to agro-forestry and the introduction of more efficient fuelwood and charcoal stoves. The Ministry could then act as a clearing house for information and advice about NGO activities (Nyoike and Okech, 1993).

Coordination

Another major institutional bottleneck in the promotion of RETs in the region is the poor coordination between the various agencies involved in RETs. This is the cause of overlapping responsibility, duplication and redundancy in both research and policy formulation, hindering the implementation of innovative renewable energy initiatives and programmes (Karekezi and Masakhwe, 1991).

Lack of coordination in NGO activities in Kenya led to the failure of numerous windpump projects. Each attempt to design windpumps started from scratch, ignoring all previous work (IT Power, 1987). A study undertaken in Kenya on the Kijito windpump recommended that Bob Harries Engineering Limited (the manufacturer) cooperate with other pump suppliers, drilling companies, convenient distributors or hardware shops to reinforce its marketing and distribution network. Cooperation would have resulted in more cost-effective expansion of the market size and lowered the cost of maintenance back-up provision (Borg and Oden, 1995).

Disparities in research can be attributed, in part, to insufficient collaboration between the diverse disciplines involved. Most of the research on RETs in the region is spearheaded by natural scientists with little understanding of the social issues affecting the targeted consumer. This is exemplified in the case of solar water heaters where there has been inadequate consultation between engineers, economists and architects, and the technology has been developed without taking into account the type of user, the acceptable cost of the system, the size of the system that would suit the user's needs and related installation problems (Bassey,

1992). Solar cookers developed without thermal storage facilities only function during sunny weather and mainly at midday – in sharp contrast to the traditional cooking habits of the region, where people cook mainly in the evenings. This demonstrates why users' needs should be addressed and their participation ensured at all stages of project development.

It is evident that those projects in the region that were able to forge a stronger collaborative link between key agencies and actors in both the formal and informal sector registered a more encouraging level of success (Karekezi, 1988b). Greater coordination should also be promoted within government. For a national windpump programme to be successful in Kenya, closer coordination between the Ministry of Energy, Ministry of Water Development, and the Ministry of Agriculture is essential. Ideally, windpump policies should be consistent across all the ministries concerned and require a high level of inter-ministerial cooperation (IT Power, 1987). In Madagascar, an inter-ministerial *ad hoc* commission was established for effective policy coordination of small hydro development in the country.

Poor coordination among institutions involved in the biogas project in Lesotho was the main reason why only 20 per cent of the digesters were functioning after ten years. The Department of Energy responded by establishing a committee with the primary objective of coordinating renewable energy activities in the country. The committee's membership included government departments, parastatals and private agencies, but its work was marred by poor attendance at meetings and gradually it ceased to operate. Only those institutions (DOE and ATS) which had policies and a budget on RETs continued to participate (Kanetsi and Phuroe, 1994).

Forums such as seminars and exhibitions where key RET actors meet and exchange ideas should be encouraged, and closer links between engineers/natural scientists and social scientists involved in RETs should be forged: this is why the African Energy Policy Research Network (AFREPREN) stresses a balanced representation of natural and social scientists in its research programmes. Support for information networks can also alleviate the problem of duplication. Collaboration in the flow of information can be achieved through links between new and existing networks and institutions such as AFREPREN, the Commonwealth Science Council, the Global Windpump Evaluation Programme (UNDP/World Bank/Netherlands Government), and the Gasifier Monitoring Programme (UNDP/World Bank) (Karekezi, 1992a; Bassey, 1992).

Box 6.1
AFREPREN

---------------------------- * ----------------------------

AFREPREN – The African Energy Policy Research Network – brings together over 90 African energy researchers and policy makers from 16 countries in Africa who share an interest in energy research and the attendant policy-making process. The key objective of the network is 'to strengthen local research capacity and to harness it in the service of energy policy making and planning'. Its formation was motivated by the realization that there was a gap between energy research and the formulation and implementation of energy policies in Africa, and especially sub-Saharan Africa.

Initially there was an imbalance between the number of policy makers and the number of researchers in the composition of the members of AFREPREN. Today, the balance is almost at par: about half the network's members are policy makers and the rest are researchers, including both natural scientists and social scientists. The engineers and natural scientists make up about 60 per cent of the AFREPREN researchers, while the rest are from social and economic disciplines. Recruiting more members from social research backgrounds is a priority.

This approach ensures that the policy maker, who is the primary target of all the findings of the AFREPREN research programme, is involved in all aspects of the network. It also has a positive influence on goals such as capacity building and relevance.

Source: Christensen and McCall, 1994.

Table 6.2 Institutional incentives for RET dissemination and promotion in the region (see ranking procedure in Appendix 5)

Country	Rank	Institutional incentives
Botswana	110	• Government undertaking research and projects that mainly deal with renewables • Renewables in the National Development Plan VII (1991–7)
Zimbabwe	110	• It is mandatory for all the gasoline used in the country to be blended with ethanol • Establishment of codes of practice and conduct for PV manufacturers to install and provide guarantees
Kenya	108	• Creation of a gasohol zone where no pure gasoline was to be sold, thus facilitating market for gasohol • Policy on SHP development was under discussion in 1983 • National masterplan covering all activities in hydro-power • Improved stove research and development through funding by USAID under the Ministry of Energy • Installation of a hybrid wind system by the Ministry of Energy and KPLC in collaboration with the Belgian Development Cooperation
Tanzania	108	• Study by TANESCO on SHP plants • The government established CAMARTEC to implement a large-scale national biogas project • The Ministry of Energy allowed TAKAGAS biogas plant to sell electricity to the grid through TANESCO at market prices • The use and development of biogas technology has been emphasized in the country's energy policy • Research, development and field testing of a number of solar devices
Uganda	107	• UEB is involved in development of SHP schemes of 500 KW capacity and above • Liberation of the power sub-sector will pave way for private SHP development for sale of power to the grid • Government has implemented two donor-supported biogas projects • The Department of NRSE is encouraging local artisans to make burners fitted with biogas units. The Department plans to buy all the burners that are produced • The Department of Environment Protection is involved in the dissemination of improved stoves for rural households
South Africa	106	• Opened a US-sponsored factory in Johannesburg to begin producing PV panels to electrify 10,000 rural towns, schools, clinics, etc. per year under a restructuring programme • ESKOM has a PV rural electrification programme

Table 6.2 cont.

Country	Rank	Institutional incentives
Lesotho	106	• A 1981 study by a French company that identified 9 sites for SHP development • Appropriate Technology Section established in 1978 • Government's Village Water Supply (VWS) has installed about 43 water-pumping windmills
Malawi	106	• Construction of a biogas digester in 1994 by ETHCO capable of producing 60 cubic metres of gas per day • An ethanol:gasoline blend of 15:85 in 1983 • Biogas demonstration units are being established by the Ministry of Women, Children's Affairs and Community Services in training institutions
Zambia	106	• Standards and codes of practice for SHP systems • Feasibility study by the German government on hydro sites • The Department of Energy through the Improved Charcoal Stove Project has been disseminating improved cookstoves
Madagascar	104	• Provision of hydrological data by the national meteorology agency and the electric utility for the evaluation of SHP potential • National energy policy recognizes SHP as an option for power generation
Mauritius	103	• The St Antoine sugar factory (plus other sugar factories) was allowed to sell excess electricity to the grid by the Central Electricity Board
Seychelles	102	• The Ministry of Community Development has incorporated solar water heaters in their housing schemes
Ethiopia	102	• Collection of relevant radiation data to enable planning of solar energy development
Sudan	102	• USAID study on the SHP potential • Sudanese Islamic Bank has expressed interest in future participation in new briquette production plants • In March 1988, the Rahad Corporation in collaboration with Tenant Union decided to establish a company to develop cotton stalk carbonization and briquetting into a commercial enterprise
Somalia*	102	• Faculty of Engineering was planning to undertake theoretical and experimental studies in solar energy
Burundi	102	• Resource assessment studies by UNDP and GTZ for SHP development

*Civil war likely to have halted most of the iniatives listed in the table

7

Financing and Economic Issues

This chapter examines the financial factors affecting RET dissemination in the Eastern and Southern African region and how such factors have hindered or facilitated their dissemination. The chapter begins by examining the rationale for investing in RETs, assessing their economic viability and technical feasibility. It goes on to discuss methods of lowering costs such as local production, government subsidy policies and appropriate financing mechanisms.

Financing and economic issues play a major role in the formulation of RET policies. Earlier studies have established that the main obstacle to implementing renewable energy projects is often not the technical feasibility of these projects but the absence of low-cost, long-term financing (News At Seven, 1994). This problem is complicated by competition for limited funds by the diverse projects and becomes critical if the country is operating under unfavourable macro-economic conditions. Governments and private enterprises must therefore seek creative ways of financing RET projects.

All the agencies involved in the RET field require funds before embarking on their programmes. The manufacturer and the supplier require capital to invest, while the consumer will need the income to purchase. They all have to weigh the opportunity cost before undertaking the venture selected. This includes assessing the risk factor, amortization period, lifetime and internal rate of financing. The challenge, therefore, is to develop a financing model in which these technologies can be made affordable to the consumers at a price that ensures that the industry remains sustainable. Even poor people can often afford purchases, if these are financed in a way that will allow them to make repayments without compromising their standard of living (Gregory, 1994).

PV power can be more cost-effective than grid extension (Table 7.1) in meeting the energy needs of rural villages with about 100 to 200 dwellings (each requiring between 0.5 and 2.0 KWh/day) that are between 8 and 35 kilometres away from the nearest available utility point (US Department of Energy, 1987). Depending on the cost of diesel fuel and the intensity of local insolation, PV systems can be more cost-effective than diesel generators for rural loads requiring up to 3 to 8 KWh of daily power on an annual basis *(ibid.)*. Experiences outside the region, in Sri Lanka for example, show that people are willing to pay in excess of their current energy expenditures for kerosene and batteries because they value the quality of light, the cleanliness of the systems and the ability to power small electronic devices such as televisions and radios (Schaeffer, 1993).

A life-cycle cost comparison between kerosene and photovoltaics for lighting reveals that PV systems are less costly by about 29 per cent (Derrick, 1993). A study in Kenya comparing PV and diesel generators revealed that at equal import duty and VAT rates, PV appears to be more expensive for locations close to the grid. But for locations far from the grid, the cost per KWh for PV systems is lower (Karekezi, 1994b). For oil-importing countries, the operating cost of a diesel or gasoline system (generator) is tied to international oil prices and the prevailing tax regime. Its long term recurring cost is therefore less predictable than that of a PV system (Wade, undated).

PV vaccine refrigeration also competes well with kerosene vaccine refrigeration in terms of cost per effective dose (Derrick, 1993). In the context of vaccine losses, a PV vaccine refrigerator is more reliable

---

Box 7.1 Comparative economic viability: PV portable lanterns versus kerosene wick and pressure lamps

———————————— * ————————————

A survey carried out in the SADC region sought to compare PV technologies to conventional technologies on the basis of their annual cost over a 20-year period. The annual economic costs of a kerosene wick lantern, a kerosene pressure lamp and two types of PV lanterns were calculated. It was found that the annual economic cost of using a kerosene wick lantern at base fuel cost for an average of 4.5 hours per day was approximately US$14–18, while a typical annual economic cost for using a pressure lantern would range from US$39 to US$52, depending on the cost of kerosene. The annual economic cost of operating a self-contained PV lantern, where the array is an integral part of the lantern itself, would be an estimated US$40, while that of a portable plug-in PV lantern would be considerably lower, at US$25.

From these findings, it appears that the PV lanterns are close to being cost-competitive when compared with the kerosene wick lantern and the pressure lamp. A comparison of the photometric characteristics of the light produced by kerosene lamps and PV lanterns showed, moreover, that a PV-powered fluorescent lamp produces a better quality of light than a pressurized kerosene lamp.

NB: The economic costs excluded all import duties, surcharges and sales taxes. All costs are given in constant 1991 US$ and the discount rate used in this analysis was 12 per cent.

Source: Bogach et al, 1992, p. 21

Table 7.1 Comparison of grid, generator and PV for rural electrification in Kenya

System	Nominal life (years)	Approximate installation costs (Ksh)	Typical system running costs (Ksh/yr)
Grid connection	N/A	30,000–120,000+	2,500–3,000*
500 W diesel generator	5	45,000–55,000	4,000**
50 Wp PV system	15–20	65,000–90,000	2,800***

* 720 KWh per year at KPLC charges
** Minimum fuel and operating costs
*** Battery replacement once every 3 years
Source: Hankins and Bess, 1993

because there are fewer vaccine losses (10 per cent) compared with a kerosene refrigerator (35 per cent). This means that more people can be vaccinated in a health centre that uses a PV vaccine refrigerator. PV installations of about 3,000 Wp for vaccine refrigeration purposes are considered to be economically viable, especially where fuel availability is a serious problem (*ibid.*).

In a village with 1000–2000 inhabitants and water usage of 20–40 litres per person, PV power can be more cost-effective than either hand pumps or diesel generators (US Department of Energy, 1987). A study undertaken in Khartoum, Sudan shows that the annual operating and management cost for a diesel pump (US$250) is twice as much as that of a windpump (US$100).

The Leribe Hospital in Lesotho, fitted with a Solarhart 302J solar water heater, made an annual saving of US$383,816.7 on the energy costs of an electric geyser (Phuroe and Mathaha, 1995). Solar water heaters installed in a hotel in Seychelles to supplement electricity for water heating made electricity savings of 3.72 units per bedroom, equivalent to a pay-back period of about 10.3 months on the capital outlay (Razanajatovo *et al.*, 1994).

An economic analysis based on a case study of small hydro and grid extension for rural electrification in Jinka town (Box 5.3, Fig 5.6 and Fig 5.7), Ethiopia indicated that in remote areas small hydro would be the least-cost option in annualized foreign exchange costs, as compared with diesel plants and grid extension (a diesel plant's operating costs must be met mainly in foreign exchange for fuel, lubricants and spare parts).

Savings made on fuel, for example, may be used for further investment in the technology. The Kenya Power and Lighting Company (KPLC) has an operating cost of Ksh7.5 per KWh, excluding fuel, transport and fixed costs, in running a wind generator – thus making a saving of Ksh4 million (US$60,000) on diesel fuel per year. This represents a pay-back period of 6 years, after which further investments can be made (Kruger Consult, 1993).

It is more economical to generate electricity from large scale biomass RETs, such as bagasse, than from petroleum-based fossil fuels. Owing to the monopolistic nature of utilities in Africa, however, bagasse-based co-generation has not expanded as rapidly as was expected.

The pre-feasibility study undertaken prior to the launch of the GEF Pilot Project in Tanzania, indicated that the price of petrol is US$0.55; thus, if the GEF project could produce biogas equivalent to 30,000 litres of petrol a day, then the country could save US$16,500 per day that it would have spent on petrol. Calculations indicated that these savings could be realized during the third year after establishment because of lower operating costs (GEF, 1993).

Improved stoves are designed to reduce heat losses and to increase combustion and heat transfer efficiency. According to Wickramagamage (1992) to cook the same type of food a traditional institutional stove consumes 528 kg of firewood as compared with only 92 kg for the improved institutional stove. One of the stoves developed by CAMARTEC in Tanzania has a fuel-saving range of 70–85 per cent. The Duma stove, also from Tanzania, has a fuel saving of 40 per cent compared with traditional metal stoves, a lifespan of between six and nine years and a pay-back period of about one and a half years (Karekezi, Ewagata *et al.*, 1995).

In Kenya, average daily charcoal consumption with an improved stove fell to 0.39 kg per person per day from 0.67 kg per person per day for a traditional stove. This adds up to a total yearly savings of 613 kg per family, with a value of about Ksh1,170 (US$64.7). Savings of the order of US$15 to US$84 are substantial for families in countries like Kenya where the average annual GNP per capita is only $370 per year.

The above examples clearly indicate that RETS are cost-competitive in a growing number of applications. The question, then, is why they have not been developed fully and disseminated. Some of the financial and economic impediments to RET dissemination are discussed below.

Pricing issues

Pricing policies in many Eastern and Southern African countries continue to be a major barrier to RET development and dissemination. Distorted taxes and fees have affected fuel choices, technology choices and total energy demand. Pricing distortion has led to high initial costs and a small market for RETs, as is shown below. Policy options such as tax rebates and local manufacture and/or assembly incentives are proposed.

The initial cost of most RETs is very high, as shown in a survey carried out in ten Southern African countries which estimated the price of a 25

Table 7.2 Costs of 18–53 Wp solar lighting systems in Kenya

Item	Cash price US$	HP price US$	HP deposit US$	Monthly payment	Months of payment
18W Panel	446	595	118	32	15
33W Panel	491	655	132	35	15
40W Panel	537	716	146	38	15
53W Panel	652	871	174	47	15
Charge controller	216	286	58	15	15
Cut out	216	288	58	15	15

HP – hire purchase
Source: Karekezi, 1994b.

cubic metre biogas unit to be about US$1,500 for a Chinese-type fixed-concrete dome unit and US$2,400 for an Indian-type floating-steel dome (Peters and Kijek, 1992).

Table 7.2 gives the cost of various solar models in Kenya. These costs are relatively high as compared with *per capita* incomes in the region. The result is that in Kenya in the 1980s and early 1990s, PV users were generally in the middle-income group with an annual income of about US$3,000 and above (Karekezi, Ewagata *et. al.*, 1995): RETs thus had a low market base. More recent figures indicate that PV technology is now within reach of lower-income groups (Figure 7.1). The average cost of a 200-litre solar hot water system in Botswana is equivalent to a teacher's salary over six months, although salaries in Botswana are some of the highest in the region (Diphaha and Burton, 1993). Typical 1991 prices of 200-litre copper collector SWHs and plastic collector SWHs in Southern Africa were estimated to be US$ 450 and US$ 790 respectively (Peters and Kijek, 1992).

The survey of Southern African countries also established that the annualized cost of a low-head PV pumping system (7.5 cubic metres per day) is about US$492, while the total cost of a clinic PV system is about US$5,525 including import duties and sales tax (Bogach, *et al*, 1992). The total cost for the construction of a solar bio-climatic house in the Seychelles was US$34,000 (Razanajatovo *et al.*, 1994), whereas the income budget in Seychelles is estimated to be about US$600–800 per month and rarely above US$1,600 per month (*ibid.*).

Prices of windpumps in several sub-Saharan African countries have been estimated to range from US$2,500–5,000, limiting wind pumping to large- and medium-scale farmers and rural institutions (Bogach *et al.*, 1992). A study of windpumps in Botswana shows that only a few people can afford the required capital and that over 57 per cent of windpumps were acquired through grants and donations (Mosimanyane *et al.*, 1995). The Kijito windpump, manufactured in Kenya, costs between US$3,000 and US$12,000, depending on rotor size, pump size, depth and distance of the site from the factory (Borg and Oden, 1995).

The total cost of an improved stove in Uganda used to be in the range US$6–US$9, about three times the price of a traditional stove (Turya-reeba, 1993a). This relatively high price is the key barrier to the wide-scale dissemination of the improved stove. High inflation rates in the country affected the purchasing power of the population, who found investing in RETs prohibitive (*ibid.*).

The above RET price examples demonstrate that RETs are not affordable to many low-income consumers (Kanetsi and Phuroe, 1994; Sampa, 1994; Katihabwa, 1994), especially to small-scale landholders unaccustomed to making decisions based on life-cycle costs (Cabraal *et al.*, 1981). Low *per capita* incomes, lack of available long-term capital in some countries and high capital costs combine to restrict the ability of the consumer to pay for a RET system (*ibid.*). The effect of high prices on the adoption of RETs by the target group is directly related to the priorities of target groups and the interests of different stake holders. Energy savings, environmental issues and reducing convertible currency expenditure are not necessarily major concerns of low-income households whose priorities primarily relate to day-to-day survival. One major reason for high RET prices is the taxes imposed on them by governments. Cumulative duty (import duties plus various surcharges on components) on RETs in Malawi is estimated to be

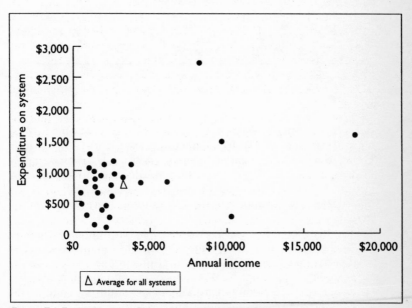

Figure 7.1 Expenditure on PV systems versus annual income, Kenya
Source: Adapted From Acker and Kammen, 1994

Table 7.3 Duties and taxes for PV equipment, Kenya (1993)

Item	Heading/code	Description	Import duty %	VAT %
Batteries*	8507.20.00	Other lead acid	37	18
	8507.30.00	Ni-Cad	37	18
	8507.40.00	Nickel-iron	37	18
Lighting equipment	8513.10.90	Other lamps	37	18
	8539.31.00	Fluorescent lamps	37	18
Controllers	8536.90.00	Electric apparatus for protecting elec. circuits	31	18
PV panels	8541.40.90	PV cells and light-emitting diodes	31	18
	8541.10.00	Diodes, transistors	31	18
Pumps	8413.70.00	Other pumps	12	5
Fridges	8418.22.10	Unassembled, elec.	31	18
	8418.10.10	Unassembled, combined, elec.	31	18
	8418.21.20	Assembled elec.	50	18
DC generating sets	8502.30.30	Assembled solar DC	12**	5
	8502.30.20	Unassembled	12**	5
	8502.30.90	Assembled	12**	5

* Only locally made batteries accrue 18% VAT
** Derived from 1992 figures
Source: Karekezi, 1994b

as high as 75 per cent (Karekezi, 1994b). In Zambia, a solar home lighting system with a value of US$934 attracted sales tax and import duty amounting to about 70 per cent of the price, while a solar water pumping system with a value of US$12,391 attracted sales tax and import duty amounting to about 56 per cent (Sampa and Sichone, 1995). Table 7.3 indicates duties and taxes imposed on PV equipment and DC generating sets in Kenya.

High priority should be given to reducing these heavy import and sales taxes throughout the region. In September 1994, the government of Zambia provided fiscal incentives to purchasers of photo-sensitive devices by issuing Statutory Instrument No.114, which announced the removal of duty and sales tax on PV equipment. The impact of this measure on the penetration of RETs is being monitored, however, with a view to determining the market response (*ibid.*). It is believed that one of the reasons why a number of agricultural facilities and church missions have

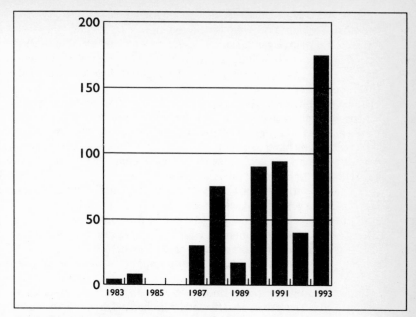

Figure 7.2 PV applications in Uganda (1983–93), annual installations
Source: Adapted from Turyahikayo (1994)

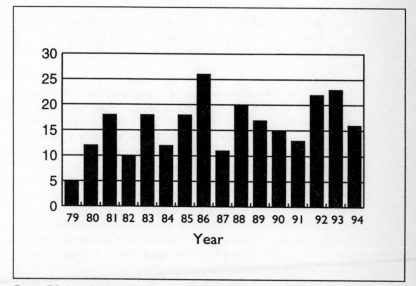

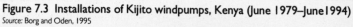

Figure 7.3 Installations of Kijito windpumps, Kenya (June 1979–June1994)
Source: Borg and Oden, 1995

solar systems in Zambia is because donor agencies, church organizations and agro-business ventures were exempted from paying sales tax and import duties (*ibid.*). In Uganda, taxes on solar gadgets (58 per cent for PV) were removed in 1992/3 but reintroduced in the 1993/4 budget (Turyahikayo *et al.*, 1995). Figure 7.2 shows that there was an increase of over 300 per cent in PV installations in 1993.

It is incorrect, however, to believe that tax exemption on RET equipment on its own can lower prices. Dealers are sometimes reluctant to lower prices, so as to reap higher profits. Other factors such as institutional mechanisms have to be strengthened. An increase in the number of dealers in the market may be needed to create competition and force prices down.

In 1986, the government of Kenya exempted potential purchasers of windpumps from a 17 per cent sales tax, in addition to an earlier removal of import duty on steel. This cut the cost of manufacture of windpumps and helped create an environment in which locally manufactured windpumps could compete with imported ones (IT Power, 1987). Figure 7.3 shows that the highest sales of Kijito windpumps were recorded in this year.

Landlocked countries have limited access to port facilities and consequently end-user prices are affected by higher freight and insurance costs (IT Power, 1992). One option for landlocked countries is to embark on local manufacture. This can reduce some of the overhead costs such as transport. Past local manufacture initiatives in the region have recorded encouraging results. These include the manufacture of cookstoves, windpumps and solar water heaters. Even local assembly can make a major difference. In the Seychelles the local company, Enersol 92, imports the main components of SWHs and assembles them locally. Since the company's inception, the price has actually declined by about 30 per cent (Razanajatovo *et al.*, 1994).

In other cases, local assembly of RETs may not have real cost advantages. There is still the need to import most of the materials required for the manufacture of these technologies. Depending on configuration, 70 per cent of the cost of a PV module is the cost of PV cells which are not produced in the region (Peters and Kijek, 1992). Assembling parts of PV modules using imported wafers, therefore, relieves only a small portion of the foreign exchange burden (Cowan, 1992).

The limited market for RETs in the region is also responsible for the high initial cost of most of the systems. Sub-Saharan Africa accounts for less than 10 per cent of the market for wind and PV pumps. Sena Kangoeli Solar Systems, one of the pioneer companies distributing and installing solar energy systems in Lesotho, ceased its services in 1989 after five years of operation because it had been importing solar products at high prices and there were not enough customers (Phuroe and Mathaha, 1995). Small markets have ensured that the production of some RETs remains low. Although photovoltaic array costs have continued to decline, they

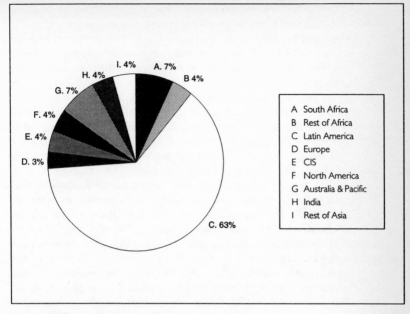

Figure 7.4 Potential world market for windpumps
Source: Adapted from Fraenkel et al., 1993

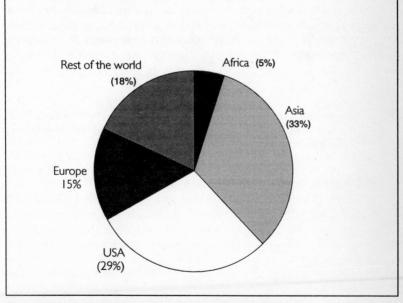

Figure 7.5 World market for PV pumps for remote applications
Source: Adapted from Barlow et al., 1993

have not fallen as far as was envisaged, partly because the expected volume of production has not been reached. In contrast, the drop in the price of the KCJ can be attributed to increased production. The initial cost of the KCJ was high but competition soon lowered the price from a peak of US$15 to a current average price of US$3 per stove (Karekezi, 1994a). This shows that increased production of RETs by a wide range of manufacturers can create competition and lead to major reductions in costs and prices.

If subsidies on conventional fuels were removed and consumers were asked to bear the full cost of generation, distribution and consumption, many RETs would become cost-competitive. In most of the region's countries, social and environmental costs are not taken into account in determining the actual price of conventional fuels. The pricing structure of conventional energy systems needs to be reviewed to ensure that energy prices reflect long-run marginal costs and, wherever possible, incorporate the environmental costs associated with conventional systems. This will ensure a level playing field. In Uganda, high taxes on petroleum products immediately made PV systems more competitive (Turyahikayo et al., 1995).

Inconsistent government decision-making distorts consistency and stability in policy, important ingredients in the RET promotion process. This has led to hesitation about new investment based on renewable energy sources and reduced interest in funding research and development (Kjellström, 1994). Furthermore, some of the region's countries are faced with constant currency fluctuations and forex shortages, coupled with rigid and opaque import regulations (Razanajatovo et al., 1994; Hankins, 1993; Peters and Kijek, 1992). Kozloff sums up the impact of macro-economic structural adjustments on energy prices in developing countries (Kozloff, undated).

> To date the primary manner in which international development organizations have influenced energy price signals is through structural adjustment mandates, whose goal may include controlling inflation or making energy prices more cost based. In any case, structural adjustment plans have been developed with little attention on how they might affect energy supply technologies.

On the other hand, liberalization of the economy also makes foreign exchange more available of by eliminating bureaucratic processes and delays. Some economic changes taking place in the region's countries are thus encouraging the dissemination of RETs.

Government investment policies and subsidies

Priority is not given to RETs during government budgetary allocations in most cases (Mosimanyane, 1994; Turyahikayo, 1994). In Tanzania, the budget of the entire Renewable Energy Division in the Ministry of Energy and Water Resources is less than that allocated to a single departmental section; the Bamboo Water Section (Katyega, personal communication, 1994). In Botswana, out of US$22.02 million allocated for energy sector development expenditure in 1991–7, renewable energy received only US$ 1.3 million (or about 6 per cent) (Mosimanyane, 1994). This is, however, beginning to change in some countries: for example, in 1993 a programme was launched by the Department of Energy in Zambia with an initial budget allocation of US$128,000 to install photovoltaic technologies for water pumping, lighting and medical refrigeration (Sampa and Sichone, 1995).

In most Eastern and Southern African countries, budget allocations to renewable energy development are negligible, if they are made at all. In Botswana and Zambia, governments have a commitment to RET development that other countries should emulate. In a study conducted in Botswana, 85 per cent of respondents believed that providing incentives and government assistance in the form of credit facilities would increase uptake of windpumps (Mosimanyane *et al.*, 1995). Subsidies, however, have the attendant problem of not creating a sustainable programme.

In comparative terms, the power sector enjoys lavish levels of investment and high subsidies but serves only a small portion of the population. In contrast to PVs, grid electricity is subsidized in many countries (Karekezi, 1994b). Unlike RET investments, which bear the full brunt of import duties and sales tax, electricity generation equipment for conventional systems is often imported duty free, especially if it is procured in the context of a grant, bilateral loan, multilateral grant or loan agreement programme.

Governments have invested heavily in the petroleum sector, ensuring that it has an extensive infrastructure. In most countries in the region, petroleum fuels such as kerosene and diesel are subsidized, making RETs less competitive against conventional fuel technologies (Cabraal *et al.*, 1981). This gives diesel generators an unfair advantage over RETs (such as PVs) in rural electrification applications, especially since diesel generators also attract lower import duties than PVs. In Kenya, for example, diesel generators have a cumulative tax of only 17 per cent while PV panels face a punitive 49 per cent (Karekezi, 1994b).

Financing mechanisms

Organizations which finance renewable energy technologies range from conventional financial institutions such as commercial banks to government-sponsored bodies. The region lacks suitable financing mechanisms such as loans, hire purchase, delayed payments and subsidies through which the low-income groups can afford to procure RETs (Kanetsi and Phuroe, 1994; Sampa, 1994; Turyahikayo, 1994; Katihabwa,

Table 7.4 Financial institutions: capacity for RET funding

Country Source	Malawi Smallholder Agricultural Credit Admin. (Minis. of Agri.)	Malawi Indefund Ltd	Malawi National Rural C. Programme (Small Enterp. Dev. Organ.)	Mozambique Development Bank	Namibia Landbank of Namibia (Ministry of Agriculture)	Namibia Comm. Bank of Nam. Rural Credit Programme	Swaziland Swazi Developt & Savings Bank
Financial institute's experience with PV tech.	None	Some	None	None	None	None	None
Home mortgage interest rate	None	None	None	6–10%	14–18%	19.5–20%	17–20%
Home improt loan rate	None	None	None			19.5–20%	
Collateral				None	Machinery	Home/bond	Land title, livestock, hard assets
Institutional /comm. loan interest rates	12.20%	16.5–18.5%	16% rural 18% urban	20–35%	18%	20%	5%
Collateral	Equipment, livestock	Machinery, land	Equipment, personal effects				
Further PV info. required by financial institution	General information	Technical specs, life cycle comparison, possibly pilot projects	Cost of panels, appliances, installation, maintenance, general effectiveness	Technical, finan. & economic viability	Technical information, performance	Cost savings info, social benefits	Reliability, life cycle, salvage value

Source: Kafumba, 1994

1994). According to Gregory (1994), the main barrier is not the availability of capital *per se* but limited access to credit facilities, since even in poor areas the population often has savings (though usually deposited in informal credit institutions). As argued earlier, even poor people can often afford purchases if these are financed in a way which allows them to make payments without compromising their standards of living (Gregory, 1994). In the rural areas, the financing mechanism must cater for unexpected adversities such as drought, very low producer prices for cash crops, and civil conflict (*ibid*.).

Some private enterprises finance RETs by allowing payments to be made in instalments. This has been common among PV agencies in Kenya (Kimani, 1993) and in Lesotho. In Kenya, one solar agent was installing PV systems after a down-payment of 40 per cent, the remaining 60 per cent to be paid in instalments: this facility has been withdrawn, however, because of defaulting. Proper follow-up procedures for credit or delayed payments can help to overcome this problem. Regulations for loans have the traditional collateral requirements (Gregory, 1994), prohibitive for many potential consumers. Some of the conditions set by local funding agencies in selected Southern African countries are shown in Table 7.4.

A study undertaken for AFREPREN on Uganda's experience in mobilizing financial resources to promote RETs established how the unfavourable requirements of banking institutions affected dissemination. The study noted that banking institutions laid down strict conditions for RET investors and this deterred potential users. Conditions required by banks included a feasibility study conducted at the applicant's expense, land titles as collateral and high interest rates. In addition, the banks required portfolios of project sponsors and managers, data on past and current operations, approximate value of existing investment, a valuation report, balance sheets, audited accounts, income tax clearance certificates, raw materials procurement plans, and the marketing strategy for the finished product (Turyareeba, 1993b).

Furnishing this information is a herculean task for small-scale entrepreneurs who do not keep such detailed records. Moreover, using land titles as security presented difficulties because people often did not have land titles – and, if they did, the land was not owned by a single individual or company but by a family. In addition, the interest rates charged by the Ugandan banks were extremely high. In cases where a sound feasibility study was conducted, there was no guarantee that a loan would be secured. Consequently, there were few applicants for these loans, even though they were available.

In order to increase access to loans, banks should find alternatives to the collateral requirements. But since the bank policy may not change in the near future, one possibility is to encourage potential consumers to form self-help groups or cooperatives so that they can acquire loans through cooperative banks, most of which do not have stringent collateral requirements. As shown in the case of solar technologies in many developing countries and the dissemination of micro-hydro technology in Nepal, the involvement of local credit agencies is crucial in ensuring continuity when external support ceases. More importantly, the borrower gains access to the immense local know-how and expertise that is found in most local credit institutions. Many have a nationwide network in place and would eliminate, therefore, the need to incur the high costs associated with the establishment of a national outreach programme.

Through their fiscal policies, governments should encourage financial institutions to provide loans to small-scale projects (Table 7.5). In an attempt to promote the wider application of RETs, the government of Zambia intends to introduce additional fiscal incentives such as offering guarantees to banks willing to lend to income-generating activities based on RETs. This will be done by establishing a RET 'Guarantee Account'. A potential donor has already been identified. The banks that are willing to lend to RET projects will be identified, their loan conditions ascertained and agreements drawn up for their participation in the scheme (Sampa and Sichone, 1995).

Funding for the Solar Rural Electrification Programme in Zambia will come from the Rural Electrification Fund (REF), established by the government in early 1994. The money in this fund is raised through a 15 per cent sales tax on electricity earmarked for the Rural Electrification Fund (*ibid.*). In Ghana, a levy on petroleum products is used to develop RETs. Financing through revolving funds can be important: the government of Zimbabwe, in collaboration with GEF and UNDP, hopes in this way to disseminate about 9,000 PV lighting systems in the period 1993–7 (Mandishona, 1994). Plans are under way to implement such a fund in Lesotho. A US-funded project, Renewable Energy for African Development (REFAD) and the Kingdom of Lesotho, through its Department of Energy, will establish a revolving fund. A number of financial and development institutions with experience in this kind of undertaking have been approached and are prepared to administer it once the funds have been released (Kanetsi and Phuroe, 1994).

Experience with other sectors which have benefited from such schemes alerts one to the danger that dedicated funds can be hijacked by beneficiaries other than the intended ones. For example, a renewable energy fund can be diverted to petroleum distribution network development. Another danger is the absence of sufficiently developed institutional machinery for carrying out recovery of the loan. Leasing of RETs such as PV systems spreads the costs over a period of years. Leasing programmes can be operated by local distributors who rent out the systems to farmers in the area to pump water for irrigation; when the season is over, they use the same systems for battery charging (Cabraal *et al.,* 1981). Electricity utilities can develop programmes similar to the non-grid Remote Area Power Supplies (RAPS) established by ESKOM (the South African power utility), whereby smaller PV systems (less than 150 W) are subject to repayment of the initial costs, plus interest, over a period of 5 years, after which the system is possessed by the customer (Cowan, 1992).

International and regional development banks and aid organizations remain important sources of loans and grants for renewable energy programmes. Bilateral assistance institutions provide grants, mainly on condition that the equipment and other requisite materials be purchased in their country of origin. Other government-sponsored philanthropic institutions may provide grants with various levels of restriction (Shepperd and Richards, 1993). NGOs, which in the main are humanitarian aid organizations, have not been suitable creditors as they are accustomed to managing donations and not credit. Examples of RET projects funded by multilateral organizations in the region include the GEF large-scale biogas plant in Tanzania; the EEC/UNDTCP (United Nations Department of Technical Cooperation for Development) bio-climatic house project and solar kilns projects in the Seychelles; the World Bank improved stoves project in Burundi; the FAO/UNESCO biogas and solar projects in Lesotho; and the GTZ and European Development Fund small hydro projects in Uganda.

RET projects can be financed through a 'two pot' financing system whereby, out of one pot, multilateral organizations provide funds for the capital portion, while funds to meet the operating costs come from the local fund, which is the second pot. If the funds to cover operating costs are not diverted to other uses, this can provide sustainable funds and investment (Little, 1987).

Under the Global Environment Facility financial assistance programme of catering for incremental cost, the climate-friendly RETs have the advantage of being an important option for mitigating the emission of greenhouse gases and therefore qualifying for GEF funding.

One of the methods currently being used to finance utilities in developing countries is the BOOT (Build, Own, Operate, Transfer) system (Brew-Hammond, 1994). Under the BOOT arrangement, the power plant will typically be operated by a foreign firm for a period of about 10 years. After the ten-year period, the plant is handed over to the host country. This strategy provides a mechanism for minimizing the risk exposure for private foreign investors and thereby attracting them to energy projects in developing countries that would otherwise have some difficulty in obtaining financing (*ibid.*). This is an ideal method of financing many small hydro and large-scale biomass projects. Studies undertaken in Zambia have revealed a number of sites to be technically and economically viable and these could be financed by BOOT schemes. Most of the major cities are already faced with waste disposal problems and large-scale biogas projects funded under BOOT schemes could be an important response option.

It is worth noting that the applicability of the financing mechanisms discussed above differs from region to region and none can be prescribed as absolute for all environments. Those countries that wish to increase their market for renewable energy systems must assess carefully what financing and support mechanism will best suit their national, regional, social, cultural and economic conditions (Gregory, 1994). That is why the traditional money lenders and credit systems in Africa – *susus* in Ghana, *fingongs* in Northern Tanzania, *equbs* in Eritrea and *tontines* in Senegal and Rwanda – should not be disregarded. These organizations are all traditional, informal savings organizations which can include both rotating and accumulated savings and credit. They not only fit into the social and cultural norms in which they operate, but are also adaptable to low-income local conditions because of their very low overheads (Gregory, 1994).

Local production issues

Despite local production being a potentially attractive option for lowering the cost of RETs, its viability in the region has not been demonstrated. Below, we assess past performance and outline strategies to mobilize this important economic and technical option.

The region does not have adequate industrial capacity to manufacture the more sophisticated RETs and therefore can only import them from developed countries, often at prohibitive cost (Thomsen, 1994). Large-scale production and manufacture of RETs is capital-intensive. For example, the total cost of a 40 KW small hydro plant is estimated to be about US$90,000 (Gullberg, 1994). The total cost of the Chakata Falls small hydro project in Zambia, based on 1986 prices, was US$ 4.25 million for an initial development of 700 KW, including an 11 KV line to one of the towns (Sampa and Sichone, 1995). The large-scale biogas plant in Tanzania, whose predicted life cycle is 25 years, will cost a total of US$ 4 million for the plant and US$1.5 million for the training and capacity-building elements (GEF, 1993). The financial costs of installing gasification units in the Indian Ocean islands of the Seychelles was estimated to be in the US$2,000–2,800/KW range compared with conventional power stations with costs in the range US$1,000–1,500/KW (Razanajatovo *et al.*, 1994). The Zimbabwean ethanol plant, which is believed to have the lowest capital/litre cost in the world, required US$6.4 million (1980 prices). The start-up capital for the manufacture of Kijito windpumps in Kenya by Bob Harries Engineering Limited was almost Ksh2 million (US$34,483) (Borg and Oden, 1995). We can deduce from these figures that under the current unfavourable macro-economic conditions existing in the region, investment costs are prohibitive. Regional planners, investors and policy makers need to develop innovative modalities for attracting capital or minimizing the total cost per unit produced.

Lending agencies and especially banks give low priority to renewable energy options. RETs are considered a new option at its embryonic stage of development. Some of the more complex RETs are considered immature and unproven in commercial terms. A good example is large-scale biogas technology. This is no more complex than the existing operational commercial establishments in Denmark but, according to a GEF analyst, it is clear that multinational, regional and national banks are unlikely to give loans to such an enterprise until its feasibility is fully demonstrated in Africa (GEF, 1993).

Large lending institutions are always reluctant to fund small-scale non-conventional energy projects and prefer investing in large-scale power projects using well-known, familiar technologies, such as hydro-electric dams or thermal generators. Some of the reasons given for such a bias include (Shepperd and Richards, 1993) the following;

- These institutions are known to be oblivious to and sceptical of new technologies that are seldom included in standard country develop-ment plans;
- Renewable energy technologies require regulatory and institutional infrastructure that seldom exists in developing countries;
- Small projects are more difficult to administer than fewer, large centralized projects, even though they are often more attractive technically.

One way to overcome the above constraint is for governments to expand the financing of research and development and demonstration projects aimed at educating the public about renewable energies. The Tanzanian large-scale biogas project is a good example of such efforts. It seeks to demonstrate, within the African context, the technical, economic, environmental and energy-producing benefits of using organic waste to produce gas. Its success is expected to remove the financial barriers facing other developing nations that might wish independently to replicate such a project (GEF, 1995).

RETs that are still in the pilot phase usually record much higher costs per unit of capacity. These pilot projects are small in size and, as a result, incur higher transaction costs such as those of planning and developing project proposals, assembling finance packages and soliciting supply contracts with the utility (Kozloff and Shobowale, 1994). Small projects implemented by utilities do not enjoy economies of scale, since the design approach and standards used are mostly based on those for large projects, thus increasing the overheads (Foley, 1993).

In an attempt to institutionalize small-scale energy funding, the World Bank's Energy Management Assistance Programme established its pro-gramme on Financing Renewable Energy for Small-Scale Energy Users (FINESSE) to 'provide workable approaches to financing infrastructural problems that hinder the spread of renewable energy technologies' (Shepperd and Richards, 1993). This involves the bundling of discrete renewable energy projects into large programmes that can be financed by major bilateral and multilateral financing agencies.

Much of the equipment needed for many renewable energy tech-nologies can be fabricated in developing countries (World Bank, 1985). Renewable energy plants should be designed to make maximum use of the locally available resources and equipment in the construction phase, as was the case in the Zimbabwean ethanol project: the Kenyan plant

Table 7.5 Financial incentives for RET dissemination and promotion in the region (see ranking procedure in Appendix 5)

Country	Rank	Financing
Botswana	109	45% duty on PV equipment removed by government in June 1986. VAT and duty exemption on all PVs imported by donors. US$1.3 million set aside for renewables in the National Development Plan VII. Grant schemes for the purchase of windpumps. 71.5% of windpumps acquired through these.
Kenya	108	Donor and technical assistance for the Maendeleo stove project by GTZ. The KREDP was supported by a US$4.8 million grant plus US$1.7 million provided by the government. Removal of 45% duty on PV equipment by the government in 1986. Exemption of VAT and duty on all PVs imported by donors. 17% sales tax exemption for Kijito windpump fabricators for all windpumps sold to projects and NGOs.
Zimbabwe	107	GEF is funding a solar electric systems project with the aim of installing 9,000 units in rural households. Government grants, donor funds under bilateral/multilateral agreement for NRSE. Soft loans for end users who are envisaged under the GEF and local financial institutions. PV and biogas technologies are subsidized by government plan to reduce/remove taxes, duties and levies on other NRSE components, especially imported ones. R & D section under the Department of Energy budget is allocated funds for NRSE promotion.
Uganda	107	Donor funded scheme, e.g. by the World Harvest Mission. Government policy on tax exemption on imported RET components, devices and systems. A loan of UK£59,000 in aid of biogas pilot project was provided by China under an agreement for economic and technical cooperation. The World Bank provided a loan of US$1.03 million for a Department of NRSE project. Government increased taxes on petroleum imports to discourage their wasteful use. This has led to their substitution by other sources of energy, e.g. biomass as a source of heat energy in industries.

Table 7.5 contd

Country	Rank	Financing
Burundi*	107	US$1.9 million investment for SHP development by the Department of Water and Rural Electrification. US$40,000 is yearly allocated to NRSE R&D by government. Funds are also provided by EEC. Biogas digesters are built at government expense and the cost is recovered from the beneficiary (with subsidies) in instalments. Funds are provided by by GTZ. A government- and GEF/UNDP-funded project on production and commercialization of mechanical windpumps scheduled for February 1996.
Lesotho	106	Funding of two SHP plants by the Norwegian government. Annual total budget of the Division of Renewable Energy is US$51,000. SADC to establish a revolving fund for PV rural electrification project. Government provided a US$407,000 investment for a SHP project.
Zambia	106	Government intends to offer additional fiscal incentives such as guarantees to banks willing to lend to NRSE projects. The Department of Energy had an initial budget allocation of US$128,000 to install photovoltaics. In 1984 government provided fiscal incentives such as offering guarantees to banks willing to lend to NRSE projects. The Department of Energy had an initial budget allocation of K40 million to install photovoltaics. In 1984 government provided fiscal incentive on photosensitive devices by issuing Statutory Instrument No. 114 that led to removal of duty and sales tax on such systems.
Tanzania	104	Government financial support for development of biogas production. Government partly funded and supported gasification projects to help sawmills meet high investment costs. Government hoping for funding from the UN's Technical Cooperation Development Unit for methane gas project.
Mauritius	101	The Mauritius Research Council provided financial assistance for co-generation.
South Africa	101	The Foundation on Research Development provided financial aid for research into energy from landfill gas and sewerage.
Seychelles	102	Exemption of tax on imported solar water heaters.

*The ongoing civil war is likely to have negatively affeted the initiatives outlined in this table.

could have minimized its initial costs if it had replicated the Zimbabwean strategy. The estimated total investment cost of Kenya's ethanol plant is US$15 million (Karekezi, 1994d), compared with the Zimbabwean plant's US$6 million. The use of local labour, expertise and technology helps reduce the high overheads created by foreign consultants and contractors (Inversin, 1986). Of the US$90,000 required to build a typical 40 KW small hydro plant, about 59 per cent can be spent on local materials and services.

Another way of resolving the funding issue is to integrate RET programmes into the local and national development agenda rather than implementing them in isolation. RET projects should no longer be viewed as social and welfare matters but as catalysts for development. They can be related to other socio-economic contexts such as health, agriculture, water development, gender and environmental conservation. In that way they are likely to receive more donor and government attention. Improved stoves received attention because it was believed that they could reduce deforestation and indoor air pollution, create employment and empower women (Karekezi, 1994d).

According to Sampa and Sichone (1995), one strategy for small hydro that should be considered in Zambia is the articulation of the development and use of water resources for power production, irrigation and potable or industrial water supply on existing or potential sites. This will have the effect of reducing the project cost by allocating costs amongst the various competing users. In Uganda, small hydro projects supporting income-generating activities such as mining have been successful (Turyahikayo *et al.,* 1995). In line with the government of Lesotho's objective of creating employment, the SADC's PV power generation scheme and the Renewable Energy For African Development (REFAD) project have placed emphasis on supplying power to income-generating activities rather than lighting homes (Kanetsi and Phuroe, 1994).

Even well-established renewable energy manufacturing concerns face severe financial problems. Despite being in the market for 10 years, Bob Harries Engineering Limited, manufacturer of Kijito pumps in Kenya, can show no cumulative profit. It owes creditors an estimated Ksh15 million (Borg and Oden, 1995). A possible solution to this problem would be diversification into products to be sold alongside RETs. This serves to overcome the risks involved in establishing a dedicated RET business enterprise. A good example is Kenya's Botto Solar Company, where the owner produces other items such as cooking pots; this offers operational capital when RETs have low sales.

According to Kozloff and Shobowale (1994), producers face a difficult predicament: 'Producers are reluctant to invest the capital needed to reduce costs when demand is low and uncertain, but demand stays low because at current costs the technology is not competitive in large markets.' In such cases, temporary subsidies and grants may be justified to assist potential manufacturers to overcome the initial start-up hurdles and to protect them from the excessive risk associated with start-ups.

Though local production of renewables remains a potential financial solution for developing countries, the above barriers have to be overcome. This underscores the need for a scheme of support for investors through grants, tax credits and other government incentives (Thomsen, 1994).

8

Organization, Management
and Maintenance

Organization, management and maintenance play an important role in the development of renewable energy in sub-Saharan Africa. The impetus behind this is the growing disenchantment over the recurrent need to rehabilitate renewable energy installations (Bhagavan and Karekezi, 1992). While knowledge of technical options for disseminating RETs in Africa has increased significantly with experience, the results of many of the initiatives have been below expectations, largely because developing, selecting and implementing the appropriate technical option have turned out to be unexpectedly complex tasks (Karekezi, 1994).

Poor performance is not just the outcome of external factors such as lack of spares or financial resources but can be traced to institutional and human resource constraints affecting renewable energy organizations. These constraints affect both the selection and the retention of management staff, as well as their behaviour and performance. A shortage of competent middle-level management and technical staff is often identified as one of the important contributors to the poor performance of the renewable energy sub-sector.

Small- and medium-scale industries, which are predominant in this sub-sector, face specific technological and managerial problems. Common problem areas are the optimal use of scarce resources, the choice and implementation of products and processes, and the organization of efficient production processes.

Organization

Organization of RET projects to ensure rapid development and promotion of the technologies in Eastern and Southern Africa still falls below expectations. Most of the RET projects are disorganized and unfocused, lacking guidance on what technology should be given priority. A typical RET manager in the region has no idea whether to focus on small hydro, solar or wind energy. He is often compelled, therefore, to carry out hurried country reviews and to scatter his efforts and resources by undertaking a wide range of research. Some of the RET projects have no fewer than ten technologies at various levels of development and dissemination. By the time the manager has gained a good understanding of the country's

172

energy needs and identified the most promising technologies, his project is often approaching its end (Karekezi, 1988a).

Although governments can be very influential by establishing guidelines and policies for RET promotion, direct government control is often detrimental to development. According to Walubengo and Kimani (1993), in those countries where RETs have been successfully disseminated, government has played a minor role. In the case of the KCJ cookstove the absence of coherent national energy policy guidelines in the early stages of its development seems to have been a blessing. The energy policy and planning vacuum in which the KCJ project operated permitted the innovative research and initiatives that were instrumental in its success. Now that it has achieved a measure of success, however, policy guidance that would greatly facilitate the expansion of the KCJ to other urban areas in Kenya is required (Karekezi, 1993).

In the long term, experience shows that small-scale, decentralized systems are somewhat easier to manage. Decentralized plants can be controlled by the local community which can provide financing, secure the equipment, select the construction team, supervise the construction process and, above all, control the output from the plant and retain the profits (Sampa and Sichone, 1995). This ensures project sustainability. Experiences in Uganda prove that the management of large-scale biomass briquetting technology is not yet well developed in the region. Small-scale briquetting technology, by contrast, has shown signs of success (Turyahikayo et al., 1995). Other examples of successful projects which can be replicated in the region include decentralized solar PV systems and water heaters in Kenya and biogas in Tanzania, Burundi and Kenya. Decentralized systems, however, require autonomous authority to be successful.

There is a need to establish independent or autonomous agencies that would pursue rural electrification vigorously. The existing power utilities in the region, which should be promoting the use of decentralized renewable energies because of their poor rural electrification performance, have not taken up this challenge. The dispersed and modular nature of renewable energy sources is in many aspects alien to the culture of conventional utilities, which are more comfortable with large-scale centralized projects. The South African utility, ESKOM, which is pursuing an aggressive solar programme, seems to be the only exception.

ESKOM is one of the world's most advanced parastatal electric utilities and one of its major priorities is the introduction of electricity in many areas where it is non-existent. It launches many projects which are aimed at harnessing solar energy for the production of non-grid electricity in remote areas and provides funds for pilot projects under the Reconstruction and Development Programme (RDP). Already it supplies over 90 per cent of the country's electricity. Although it is an autonomous organization, it is responsible to the Ministry of Mineral and Energy Affairs in the final analysis; thus, it is indirectly controlled in a minimal way, by the government. ESKOM's prices are based on recovering its costs without either making profits or sustaining losses.

Independent rural electrification agencies can be designed to cope with small-scale and decentralized RETs that require active collaboration with local manufacturers and end users. Such agencies would be more willing to undertake the management-intensive task of building small, discrete renewable energy projects into large programmes that can be financed by major bilateral and multilateral programmes (Karekezi, 1994).

'New Approaches to Organization and Management of Rural Power Supply', the Stockholm Environment Institute (SEI) research project initiated in 1993 and aimed at organizing village electrification co-operatives in Tanzania, provides one example of an attempt to address the issue (SEI, 1994). The project sees cooperatives as a possible organizational mode for locally managed electricity distribution in Tanzania. Guidelines for their organization and management will be developed. The three phases of the project are: (1) identification of suitable villages for electrification; (2) formation of electrification cooperative; (3) follow-up study and evaluation of the cooperatives. In Urambo the project is in its third phase, while in Mbinga it is still in phase two. Besides the activities in Tanzania, SEI and TANESCO have decided to carry out a survey of international experiences from locally managed power systems. Much more extensive efforts in this direction will be needed if viable village-level remote electrification schemes are to be adopted on a significant scale.

Though integration of energy projects with other socio-economic programmes has some financial benefits, there is a danger of the energy component being relegated to a lower priority. The Busoga Growers Co-operative in Uganda, which produced briquettes with support provided by USAID, had a production level of only 10 per cent of the installed production capacity. The major reason for the poor performance and eventual collapse of the plant was that the briquetting operation was never perceived to be an important cooperative activity. The primary rationale for involvement in briquette production was to deal with the dispersal and fire hazard problem caused by the build-up of coffee husk waste piles (Turyahikayo et al., 1995).

Many RET projects in the region remain stuck at the pilot stage and do not mature into full commercialization. The 'pilot project' approach has been a major drawback in most of the renewable energy initiatives. While this approach is effective in verifying the technical feasibility of particular technologies, it creates an excuse for mainstream engineers to overdesign and fails to nurture the proactive decision making and interventions that would lead to lower costs and economically viable projects (Karekezi, 1989a). Consequently, most pilot projects are overdesigned, increasing overheads and overall costs and thus eliminating the chance of continuity (ibid.).

In some cases, attempts are made to embark on large-scale dissemination

of RETs without undertaking users' needs assessment. Intended beneficiaries are not involved in the planning and implementation of RET
projects and solutions do not take into consideration their social norms.
Three donor-funded biogas projects in Lesotho, for example, did not
require intended beneficiaries to contribute any money towards building
the systems. The predictable result was a lack of commitment to the
projects on the part of the intended beneficiaries (Kanetsi and Phuroe,
1994).

The same problem has been identified in solar cooker programmes
where, too often, users perceive solar cookers as gifts from donor-funded
projects and are unwilling to make the continuous investment in maintenance and replacement that will ensure long term sustainability
(Karekezi, 1994b). The beneficiaries of a project must believe they own
the project and be part of its initiation, planning and management. They
must feel responsible for its success from the beginning. The Taung/
Phamong solar water pumping project, one of the successful RET initiatives in Lesotho, involved the villagers in planning and implementation.
They pay for the systems and have committees responsible for collecting
the payments and paying back the project (Kanetsi and Phuroe, 1994).

The Ampefy small hydro project in Madagascar is an excellent example
of community participation. Initially, the Ampefy community negotiated
for siting land and then provided labour and materials. At the end of the
project, the community took over the operation, maintenance and
management of the mechanical component of the Ampefy hydro-power
facility. Its final role (management of the mechanical equipment) was
crucial to the sustainability of the project since the entire mechanical
operation was expected to be self-financing. Local entrepreneurial
participation in the project was not as robust as envisaged, however, and
this was a major drawback (Karekezi, 1989a). The use of local consultants
to assist the external consultants would have minimized the project's
costs and facilitated technology transfer. Since most of the local engineering consultants were ardent entrepreneurs, their involvement in the
project would have increased the role of local private sector and could
have led to additional local investments in small hydro (Karekezi, 1989a).

There is inadequate appreciation of the importance of active participation by local manufacturers/assemblers and end users in the region's
RET projects. The KCJ stove project demonstrates that end users are an
important source of innovation and modification (Karekezi, 1993b). Too
often, project management involves local actors only in the final stages of
a RET programme, instead of ensuring their active participation from the
initial stage. The Kijito windpump experience in Kenya is a unique case
because a local entrepreneur invested significant amounts of capital to
launch a renewable energy project. He then spared no effort in marketing
the technology to ensure that he could recuperate his initial investment,
thus ensuring the sustainability of the windpump technology in Kenya.

Management

Inadequate planning of RET projects before implementation constitutes a major management problem in the region. In most cases, planning is undertaken on an *ad hoc* basis. It requires prior knowledge of the renewable energy source, the quantities available and the location of the resource.

A lack of documentation and, especially, baseline data has also contributed to the poor location and siting of RET installations, few of which are in sites where maximum utilization can be achieved. Several windpumps in the interior of Burundi are functioning poorly due to poor siting (Katihabwa, 1994). Poor siting also affected four small demonstration biogas digesters in Uganda which were installed at institutions in the remote Karamoja region between 1991 and 1992. While they functioned well during the rainy season, they could not get feedstock (cow dung and water) during the dry season as the inhabitants and their livestock had migrated, and eventually were abandoned (Turyahikayo, 1994). Eight windmills installed in Botswana with German aid as part of water supply programmes in five major villages were sited poorly for want of accurate wind speed information: as a result, they did not deliver sufficient water to justify their use.

There is an imperative need for countries to undertake extensive resource assessments at both national and local levels to document as accurately as possible the types, location, and quantities of the various renewable energy sources available, and to update this information regularly (Bassey, 1992). In Botswana during 1985–7 the Department of Meteorological Services, in collaboration with the Botswana Technology Centre, the Rural Industries Innovation Centre (RIIC) and the Department of Water Affairs installed an array of anemometers throughout the country at a height of ten metres. This was undertaken to provide baseline data on wind speeds and assess the potential for using wind energy to pump water in the country (Mosimanyane *et al.*, 1995). Additional data collection on the subject will enable analysts to select geographical areas that have potential for windpumping systems and indicate the appropriate sizes of such units (*ibid.*). Another goal of the project was to verify an output prediction model so that the performance of windpumps could be predicted under differing conditions of head and flow (*ibid.*). The data would also enable government policy makers to formulate more appropriate policies and assist RET suppliers, manufacturers and potential users in making correct investment decisions (Bassey, 1992).

A number of countries have started collecting data on suitable sites for small hydro installations, solar irradiation levels and wind speeds. The numerous meteorological institutes in the region have been particularly active. In Zambia, studies have been conducted in different provinces to determine sites that are economically viable and technically as well as socially feasible for small hydro development (Sampa and Sichone, 1995).

Table 8.1 A selection of projects which have imported windpumps

Year	Importing organization	No. & type of windpumps	Comments
	NCCK: Windmill for Africa Project	3 Dempsters 8' diameter 5 Dempsters 6' diameter	
	NCCK: Daballa, Fachana	1 Climax 14' diameter	
	NCCK: Dandora, Nairobi	1 Aquva Agencies . 3.5' diam	Water supply. failed due to lack of maintenance and faulty pump installation.
1966	USAID	11 Dempsters	Ministries of Water Development and Agriculture. In Lake Basin, Turkana and Coast. Organizational problems.
1979	Food Security Programme: Merti	Aermotor 12' diameter	Water supply. Still working in 1982
1976	Machakos Rural Industrial Development Centre	Own design 2.7m diameter. At least 10 installed	Danish assistance. Design based on Sparco. No follow-up after windpump installation.
	Catholic Mission	1 Dempster (from Windmills for Africa Project). 8 others	Irrigation. No information on present condition.
1982	Masai Action for Self-Improvement: Olosho Oibok	4 Dempsters 8' diameter 4 Dempsters	In 1982, 3 were not working. 2 had mechanical failures, 1 had subsided foundations. Installed in 1982. No further information.
	Masai Rural Training Centre: Olooseos	1 Dempster (from USAID programme) 3 Dempsters	Leaking piston cup meant unable to pump to required height. Still crated. No one knew how to install.

Source: IT Power, 1987

In Madagascar, the second phase of the Ampefy project focused on hydro-power assessments and the project was extended in order to train the Malagasy personnel on the identification of hydro-power sites and in the use of a computerized model for hydro plant design (Karekezi, 1989a). Basic data on solar radiation in Botswana is being compiled by the Department of Physics at the University of Botswana and will guide solar systems design and sizing (Diphaha and Burton, 1993). In Lesotho, a wind pilot project was undertaken to test a tiny wind machine for electric power generation. It was established that the available wind speeds of 4 km/hour were too low for the wind generators to operate successfully and the effort was abandoned. This saved the cost of going to full commercialization for a project that would not have been viable.

The low level of technology development in most of the countries has affected RET projects adversely. In the absence of a strong local techno-logical base, many RETs which were obviously not appropriate for use in the region were introduced, resulting in a major unfruitful diversion of human and financial resources. It has sometimes been assumed that because a cookstove programme is successful in one country it will automatically do well in another country, without taking into account the peculiarities of the country in question (Sampa and Sichone, 1995). Another example is the performance of windpumps imported into Kenya (Table 8.1). On the other hand, local Kenyan-made Kijito windpumps have performed because of support from local technical expertise and know-how. The presence of a strong technological base thus helps to ensure coherent prioritization of RET research and development.

A number of initiatives have demonstrated that the region has the capability of developing a local technology base. The Botswana Tech-nology Centre has developed a photovoltaic controller which is being manufactured locally. Kenya's Gilgil multi-purpose manufacturing com-plex is manufacturing PV-powered public telephones for installation in rural areas. Studies have demonstrated that the technical research agenda should be focused on modifications and adaptation rather than the development of completely new devices or technologies (Karekezi, 1993a). It is estimated that more than 90 per cent of the value added to a typical windpump results from work done in the region, which demon-strates significant technological capability (Karekezi, 1994d). Bob Harries Engineering Limited has designed windpumps that are adapted to the local conditions.

With regard to research and development of local materials and the fabrication of equipment for developing hydro-power projects, the Tech-nology Development and Advisory Unit (TDAU) in Zambia began work on rural small hydro technologies in 1978 and designed, manufactured and installed crossflow water turbines at a number of sites (Sampa and Sichone, 1994). The construction of the Zimbabwean ethanol plant, using locally available materials, is also a clear indication of regional techno-logical capability. The on-site small hydro Ampefy project management provided in Madagascar was exemplary and resulted in the rapid completion of the civil and mechanical installations (Karekezi, 1989a).

Another major obstacle is identification of the stage at which to adopt commercialization and wide-scale dissemination. Some projects, like the Lesotho stove programme, have gone wide-scale without completing the pilot stage properly. Most RET project managers in the region, it seems, have resorted to rapid country appraisals followed by a minimum of prototype research and development, then launched full-scale field tests. According to Razanajatovo *et al.* (1994), if the technology is still at the prototype stage it should not be disseminated. Only RETs with proven efficiency should be considered for commercialization or dissemination, in order to gain the confidence of users and decision makers. Most wind projects started by various organizations in Kenya in the 1970s, with the goal of building windpumps with locally available material, failed because the windpumps were not built properly and new designs were introduced before they had been refined and tested (Hankins, 1987). The success of the KCJ stove demonstrates the need for extensive pilot testing before launching wide-scale dissemination programmes.

The problem of developing an efficient and less costly RET device is not as difficult as ensuring that it reaches its target population, which in the case of household energy devices is in the millions. Wide-scale dissemination requires stronger marketing skills that are more common in the commercial than in the development field. It also calls for proven technology and adequate needs assessment at the manufacturing and user levels. This is demonstrated in the case of the USAID-funded improved stove project in Lesotho, where the cost of dissemination was over US$1,000 per stove. The establishment of a viable and cost-effective dissemination system that would reach many rural and urban households proved to be a difficult and complex task (Karekezi, 1993a).

The problem of disseminating RETs to the rural majority is not just confined to costs but also includes awareness. The majority of the rural population are not aware of the potential of RETs because of poor information dissemination. This becomes critical if the suppliers are located in the urban areas away from the target group and infrastructure is lacking. In Uganda, no organized marketing strategy and established retail outlets exist for improved household stoves. The commercial household stove manufacturers do not carry out awareness campaigns for their products. The advantages of using these stoves are therefore not clear to the people (Turyahikayo, 1994). The same applies to the dissemination of solar energy technologies in the country. The Ministry of Energy has not been able to fund extension work and demonstrations, hence many people are ignorant of the benefits of using solar energy technologies as well as their availability in the market (Turyahikayo, 1994). Ineffective marketing strategies, such as poor advertising, may have contributed further to poor dissemination in the region (Kafumba, 1994a). In some cases, advertisements are placed in newspapers which usually circulate in the urban areas, whereas the main target group is in the rural areas.

Wide-scale dissemination is also likely to face resistance if the technology involves changes in socio-cultural life patterns. In Lesotho it was proposed that, for better dissemination of solar cookers, a more 'user-friendly' design was to be developed (Kanetsi and Phuroe, 1994). This turned out to be one of the reasons why the project was unsuccessful in most parts of the country. Though they were effective, very few individuals opted to retain the solar cookers because they require major changes in cooking habits and norms (Kanetsi and Phuroe, 1994).

The second strategy is the use of existing systems of production, marketing and information dissemination. By using an existing network, the cost of disseminating RETs is reduced dramatically. This 'piggy-back' principle is particularly effective in rural areas, where the cost of establishing new networks is very high. Often renewable energy dissemination initiatives can be a component of an existing integrated income-generating project, or an environmental or health extension programme. The rural stove component of the Kenya Stove Programme successfully used this strategy, and has managed to disseminate more than 90,000 improved stoves using the existing network of home science extension workers. Attempts to market briquettes in Kenya through the supermarkets rather than the traditional charcoal dealers is one of the reasons for low consumption (Karekezi, Ewagata *et al.*, 1995). Similarly, solar and wind energy technology programmes that have registered encouraging results have relied on existing agricultural extension or marketing networks to provide rapid, low-cost marketing and dissemination (Karekezi, 1994b).

The Zambian government has been involved in organizing seminars and workshops in both rural and urban areas, as well as practical demonstrations, pilot schemes and field days on successful RET applications, to enhance dissemination (Sampa, 1994). The Zambian Environment Education Program (ZEEP) is planning to establish a demonstration biogas digester as a way of developing positive attitudes towards conservation and the use of natural resources. The programme also plans to disseminate other renewable sources of energy (solar, wind) using the educational system in Zambia (Sampa and Sichone, 1995). The Zambian Department of Social Development has an infrastructure of Women's Clubs (1,900 clubs with about 23,000 members) throughout the country. Sampa and Sichone (1995) believe that the Department can play a major role in disseminating RETs such as solar driers, water heaters and biogas digesters in rural areas through the clubs. Whenever there are fairs (on trade and on environment), the Department of Energy (DOE) in Lesotho and its Appropriate Technology Section (ATS) participate and show the RETs they are involved in (Kanetsi and Phuroe, 1994).

Botto-Solar, a company in Kenya involved in producing and selling solar equipment and institutional stoves, is flourishing due to the aggressive marketing it has carried out. The firm attends agricultural shows and exhibits its products. It also makes visits to institutions and hotels to market its products and sends brochures to all schools in the country on RETs and energy conservation measures.

Effective dissemination of RETs has been hampered by the absence of quality control. Some of the technologies disseminated have turned out to be of low quality, undermining consumer confidence. Encouraged by inadequate regulation and driven by the desire for profit maximization, a number of unscrupulous firms are churning out sub-standard RETs in the region. A study undertaken in Kenya reveals that in pursuit of higher profits or under the pressure of fierce competition, a number of stove producers have decreased the amount of vermiculite and cement used in the KCJ, thus affecting its charcoal-saving potential and lifespan. The author believes that if this trend continues, the KCJ could stand to lose a large share of its market to the traditional metal *jiko* (Karekezi, 1988b). Installation of faulty solar water heating systems has affected dissemination of solar systems and has led to the build-up of mistrust of the technologies. Faulty solar water heating systems were installed on an estate of about 1,000 houses in Kenya. The proliferation of one-man operations selling solar energy technologies has encouraged unscrupulous dealers who seldom supply complete and correctly sized solar systems. For example, in Kenya, a third to a half of PV lighting systems were sold without charge controllers (Karekezi, 1994b). Such practices create a lasting bad image of solar systems. In a study conducted in Lesotho, it was established that only 50 per cent of the solar water heaters installed in one of the hospitals was functioning after a period of less than ten years. This is a clear indication of poor installation and inadequate systems maintenance (Phuroe and Mathaha, 1995). Consequently, photovoltaics acquired a bad reputation in Lesotho amongst some consumers.

This problem is likely to be exacerbated by the current wave of economic liberalization sweeping across the region, which has facilitated the importation of products without restriction. Consequently, cheap but poorly designed and untested RETs are entering without scrutiny. This is one of the main problems in the Seychelles, where no regulations restrict the import of electrical appliances with inappropriate ratings and low efficiencies, including inappropriate solar systems (Razanajatovo *et al.*, 1994).

Some level of quality control should be instituted either by the government through the Bureau of Standards or by other agencies with the requisite technical, legal and manpower capability. In Kenya the Bureau of Standards lacked the technical manpower to set standards for the KCJ and there are no quality control measures for solar systems. The only component of the system that undergoes quality checking is the battery. As far as briquetting equipment is concerned, there are no design rules and therefore the final choice of technology depends on careful consideration of a particular application by individuals experienced in the field (Siemons *et al.*, 1989).

Governments in the region, in liaison with relevant groups, should also establish codes of practice, technical specifications and standards, quality control measures and design rules. For a Bureau of Standards to operate effectively, it will need to have personnel qualified in the various RETs.

In Botswana, past problems such as poor installations and inadequate maintenance of solar water heaters have been overcome by the formulation of a code of practice to be followed during solar water heater installations. The code of practice was established by a group of users, manufacturers, government officials and experts in the field (Mosimanyane, 1994). This code will probably be adopted by other SADC countries. In addition, private sector companies and manufacturers have been involved in the improvement of technical standards and delivery systems to consumers (*ibid.*). Lesotho is also in the process of implementing similar policies. South Africa has adopted a voluntary policy which requires that no RET equipment be utilized unless it is thoroughly tested and found to be of the required standard (Buttle, personal communication). In Malawi, one of the main problems in solar water heater technologies is lack of a strict code of conduct and hence no strict adherence to standards (Kafumba, 1994a). An important area of research in the Malawian solar energy programme is the development of appropriate guidelines on battery selection for PV appliances (*ibid.*).

Standards may be set, but if no strict code of conduct exists to enforce them they will not be helpful. In Zambia, in order to enhance dissemination of RETs, policy measures have been proposed such as the establishment of a specialized RET agency. The agency's role would be to evaluate, certify and monitor all new and renewable sources of energy (NRSE) technologies being developed and introduced into the country. This is aimed at ensuring that RETs conform to the required quality, health, safety and environmental standards (Sampa, 1994).

Maintenance

Lack of maintenance is a recurrent problem in all energy sub-sectors of the Eastern and Southern Africa region. The region has to pay dearly in rehabilitating inadequately maintained projects, vividly recorded in the ghostly sights of abandoned and inoperative windpumps, solar installations and biogas plants. In 1989, the DOE in Lesotho made field trips to the 45 digesters that were built by the FAO and discovered that only 20 per cent of them were functioning. This is partly attributed to poor management of personnel: technicians were trained but not employed to continue disseminating and maintaining the installed system (Kanetsi and Phuroe, 1994). This problem also affected all the biogas digesters introduced in

Uganda by the Church of Uganda in the early 1980s. They worked for a number of years before developing problems, mostly due to lack of proper maintenance (Turyahikayo, 1994). Almost all the briquetting plants in Uganda are either operating below capacity or have collapsed, mainly owing to management and maintenance problems. The Black Power project was initially producing five tonnes of charcoal briquettes per month, until machinery started breaking down and production went down drastically. Although Black Power has plans to rehabilitate and modernize its briquetting plant, it lacks the requisite capital (Turyahikayo et al., 1995).

Equipment maintenance requires well-trained technicians and engineers. When equipment is imported and technicians do not have sufficient training, the result is heavy dependence on foreign expertise for maintenance. Less sophisticated and locally manufactured equipment would be more practical. The case of Zimbabwean ethanol production illustrates this very well. Since the equipment was fabricated locally, any problems that arose were easily dealt with. In the Kenyan case, however, the machinery was largely imported and breakdowns were very common (Baraka, 1991).

In Botswana, PV water pumps introduced by aid agencies as demonstration projects fell into repair since no local organization took responsibility for their maintenance when the aid-funded projects were terminated. Those installed later by the Department of Water Affairs at the request of district councils are doing no better because the councils do not always have the necessary technical skills to provide the required maintenance support (Diphaha and Burton, 1993).

The turbine of the Kagando small hydro power station in Uganda is currently in a very poor state of disrepair, having suffered corrosion. The turbine is due for replacement and the de-silting facilities at the power station are to be redesigned to avoid recurrence of the corrosion problems (Turyahikayo et al., 1995).

Since wind technologies are a decentralized option, they are usually scattered in different parts of the country. This causes logistical problems when it comes to maintenance. In Lesotho, windpumps have been used in the country for water pumping by individuals. Most of them stopped functioning, however, owing to lack of maintenance and spare parts in the country (DOE/GTZ, 1988). Approximately half of the windpumps installed in Karamoja, Uganda, are no longer functioning for the same reason (Turyahikayo, 1994). The two producers of windpumps in Kenya are heavily involved in maintenance. A great number of the windpumps installed by projects and NGOs depend on after-sales services from Bob Harries Engineering Limited and Pwani Fabricators. Both producers inspect the installed windpumps in a particular area during regular visits. This is because non-functional installations are considered bad publicity for future sales. Thus detailed manuals designed to facilitate maintenance of the pump cylinder were prepared for Kijito windpumps (IBRD, 1993).

Product quality is a crucial factor in resolving maintenance problems in the region. When RET projects fall behind schedule, the pressure becomes almost irresistible to neglect aspects related to maintenance. There is always the temptation to forgo maintenance when funds are short or when equipment is in heavy use, a temptation which becomes acute in many poor African countries. This is especially true of donor-funded projects. When projects run short of either money or time, one of the first things to be compromised is the effort to institutionalize adequate maintenance procedures.

Manufacturers should be encouraged to provide guarantees for their equipment, and avoid selling equipment without issuing a guarantee. Bob Harries Engineering Ltd offers a one-year guarantee on its wind-pumps during which period the company does all the maintenance and even changes worn-out parts if necessary. The customer is responsible for all the maintenance after the guarantee expires, unless a maintenance contract is signed (Borg and Oden, 1995). The regular visits made by the company to its customers provide feedback which is useful in product development. A survey undertaken in Kenya revealed that the only solar firms which offer guarantees are those which undertake the installation themselves: such a guarantee is limited to one year, and in some cases only applies to the panel (Karekezi, 1994b).

Preventive maintenance reduces the frequency of breakdowns. It has been shown repeatedly that regular and preventive maintenance is cheaper than rehabilitation. The frequency of breakdowns is a function of system fragility and complexity, maintenance, availability and cost of spare parts, and skill levels of the operator and repair personnel. In some cases, the prevalent attitude is that routine maintenance is a luxury to be undertaken at those times of the year when funds are in surplus and equipment utilization is low (Karekezi, 1988). A survey undertaken in Botswana established the causes of windpump breakdowns as lack of preventive maintenance and improper installation due to lack of proper training and knowledge of the technology (Mosimanyane et al., 1995). Spare parts are not locally available in the region, mainly owing to lack of funds or the bureaucratic process involved in importing them. This problem is worse in countries which have not liberalized their economy.

For preventive and regular maintenance to be carried out, adequately equipped workshops with tools must be available. In the case of wind-pumps, maintenance suffers when tools are missing or the correct type of lubrication fluid is unavailable. The poorly equipped workshops in the region have meant that the requisite tools to do the maintenance are not readily available. About 85 per cent of pump owners interviewed in Botswana indicated that repair of windpumps required special tools and spares (Mosimanyane et al., 1995).

Most of the windpump distributors in Botswana are concentrated in the capital, Gaborone (except the RIIC, which is about 120 km from the capital), in a country with a large territory and dispersed settlements

---

Box 8.1
Pwani windpump maintenance programme – Mombasa, Kenya

---
*

Pwani windpumps are sold only to customers within reach of their factory. Their coverage is limited to the coastal strip from Mombasa to Lamu with a maximum width of 150 kilometres. Free maintenance is given for the first five years, after which the owner has to pay for maintenance of the pump. Since the air is salty and the towers cannot be galvanized, rust is a problem. Pwani offers to paint the windpumps free of charge each year; the owner only has to pay for the paint. Painting can be done within two days by one man. Maintenance costs are kept down when the farmers provide transport for the technicians.

Source: Kruger Consult, 1993

(*ibid.*). About 57 per cent of those interviewed were dissatisfied with RIIC's response time (Mosimanyane *et al.*, 1995). After-sales service and replacement of redesigned parts is very expensive, especially when it involves scattered installations. In Zimbabwe, the PV companies are mainly centred in Harare, the capital, and again this partly explains unsatisfactory back-up services. Users whose systems break down are hundreds of kilometres from the nearest technicians and response times suffer (Hankins, 1993).

To achieve cost-effectiveness in inspection and maintenance, clustering RET installations in the same vicinity is of paramount importance. This reduces maintenance costs since technicians do not have to travel long distances. In Kenya, Kijito windpumps are widely scattered, leading to high maintenance costs since technicians have to travel on a light aircraft to maintain them. Windpump density is still insufficient to ensure an adequate level of maintenance support. (In contrast see Box 8.1 on the Pwani windpump maintenance programme.) The phenomenal growth in the home solar systems market in Kenya is to a large extent due to the demonstration effect within villages where PV systems are often found in clusters (*ibid.*).

The frequency of breakdowns is also a function of how well repair work is done. The recurrence of a problem is unlikely if repairs are done properly the first time, and the ability of repair crews to fix and maintain equipment is directly related to their skill level, training and supervision. One of the factors that militated against the effectiveness of dissemination of solar water heaters in Malawi in the late 1960s was lack of in-country expertise and experience with SWHs, which resulted in very poor installations and malfunction problems that could not be resolved in the absence of a comprehensive back-up spare capacity and technical maintenance programmes (Kafumba, 1994a). As the users of solar technology in Kenya continue to increase, the shortage of skilled technicians, particularly in the remote areas, becomes a major constraint on the industry (Karekezi, 1988). In Seychelles, a PV refrigerator failed because there was insufficient expertise to repair and refill the refrigerator with ammonia.

A small hydro plant erected in the Thaba Tseka district, Lesotho, fell into disuse in the early 1980s because it was kept running by expatriate workers who left no one with the skills and interest to keep it going (Kanetsi and Phuroe, 1994). This also applies to most small hydro plants in Uganda, such as Maziba and Kikagati. The lack of skilled maintenance mechanics in the country, particularly in the remote areas where the Kijito windpumps are installed, is still a major problem.

As far as skills and human resources are concerned, the firms or organizations that supply the applications should also have in their teams qualified technicians to service and maintain the applications. Most windpump suppliers in Botswana do not provide operator training. Windpump owners and operators learn to maintain and repair windpumps by themselves (Mosimanyane *et al.*, 1995). The Botswana country case study report recommended that RETs should be purchased only from suppliers who have local support structures and can render technical back-up support in the form of installation, repair, spare parts, training of users/operators and local technicians. In this way, the repair and maintenance infrastructure will be enhanced (*ibid.*). Bob Harries Engineering Ltd often provides advice on how to organize the operation, maintenance and management of the windpump. It also provides basic education for the windpump operators as part of the sale price. There is, however, a need for user commitment to the sustainability of the windpump for the education to be effective (Borg and Oden, 1995).

The import factor also complicates effective maintenance of RETs in the region. PVs in Kenya are made largely from imported components and consequently maintenance skills are not widely available. As a result, many PV systems face severe maintenance constraints. Often the problems are of a simple nature and could be resolved by a technician with rudimentary knowledge of how PV systems work. But because it is a relatively new technology and is usually installed in rural areas, provision of maintenance back-up is not always feasible.

Some technologies such as stoves, biogas systems, windmills, ethanol plants, SWHs and solar cookers can be made locally, which facilitates maintenance. The hydro-power technology used in the Ampefy project has very low maintenance requirements because local manufacture and assembly of the components means that low-cost, knowledgeable and skilled maintenance service is only a phone call away (Karekezi, 1989a).

Even when initial capital is available to establish a plant, operation and maintenance for some RETs may still present insurmountable barriers. One of the major drawbacks of donor funding is that the recipient country inherits, and cannot meet, the long-term operating and maintenance costs of projects. The region should embark only on projects that are sustainable and likely to generate funds for their operation and maintenance.

Table 8.2 Organizational, management and maintenance incentives for RET dissemination and promotion in the region (see ranking procedure in Appendix 5)

Country	Rank	Organization, management, and maintenance
Kenya	110	Adoption of a semi-commercial approach in the Maendeleo stove project whereby the commercial production centres produced the liners while various organizations with extension programmes at grassroots level disseminated them.
Botswana	107	Code of practice for domestic solar water heating systems. One year guarantee on all RIIC windpumps (covers materials and workmanship). Group of consultants studied the potential of windpumps under a government scheme.
Zimbabwe	106	Solar PV system awareness promotion campaign by government. Establishment of local solar systems manufacturers.
Uganda	104	Technical assistance for SHP plants by church missions. Rehabilitation by the Ministry of Energy of SHP plants in disuse as part of government's Economic Rehabilitation Programme, e.g. Kikagati SHP scheme.
Zambia	104	NCSR has demonstrated use of biogas in their pilot project. It made a local adaptation of designs of floating dome digester, gas stoves and lanterns. Department of Energy has prepared a manual on charcoal production.
Malawi	103	ETHCO, in collaboration with polytechnic, Chancellor University and Halls Garage, involved in R&D on optional funding and development of 100% ethanol engines and stoves.
Sudan	103	The Energy Research Council and Biomass Technology Group provide technical, management and marketing assistance for briquette production.
Mauritius	102	Information and literature on co-generation was provided by the on-line computer centre at the University of Mauritius.
Tanzania	102	Biogas demonstration units set up.
Swaziland	102	Village Technology Unit Centre offers demonstrations for solar devices.
Seychelles	102	Solar companies offer after-sales service for systems installed.
Burundi*	102	Maintenance of SHP plants as part of government policy.

* Civil war may have disrupted organization, management and maintenance initiatives.

9

Human Resource Development
and Retention

Human resources is a broad term that encompasses manpower, knowledge and experience in a nation's inhabitants, and not just those who possess professional skills. Also included are the non-professionals who have had little or no formal training on a specific subject, such as clerks, typists and craftsmen. The introduction of unfamiliar technologies requires the development of skills (Thomsen, 1994). The importance of engineers, technologists and trained technicians in the better utilization of energy resources to bring about economic development has been recognized in the region, but in spite of efforts by governments there is a continuing shortage of qualified personnel (Baguant and Manrakhan, 1994).

A cursory glance at the region's general manpower rating demonstrates the seriousness of the situation. Global technical manpower reviews consistently show that sub-Saharan African countries face monumental manpower shortages in crucial areas such as engineering. This region has the lowest number of scientists and engineers per million of population in the world. While Africa has only 53 engineers per million population, Japan and USA have 3,548 and 2,685, respectively. This acute shortage of skilled manpower is exacerbated by a persistent external brain drain and falling expenditure on education (Karekezi, 1994c). The external brain drain is compounded by what experts increasingly refer to as 'internal brain drain', which refers to wasteful or incoherent placement of highly qualified manpower in inappropriate positions (*ibid*.). Two reasons given for the shortage of trained policy makers, engineers, and technicians are the inappropriate education systems inherited from the colonial period and the lack of flexibility in modifying these systems. The education systems in African universities were adopted from resource-rich European or American systems (Baguant and Manrakhan, 1994).

The performance of some of the trained personnel in the actual implementation of the projects has not been satisfactory. One energy expert attributes it to the fact that students are not given training in business management procedures such as book-keeping, establishing business plans or maintaining spare part inventories. The findings of most of the researchers have also been incompatible with the realities in the field and therefore cannot be implemented. He recommends the creation of a training framework that produces a 'field engineer', who combines the theoretical knowledge of the technologically trained engineer with the practical, hands-on capability of a technician. Field engineers can also provide training opportunities for end users in technologies that require the adaptive capability that rural conditions frequently need (Hirsch, 1994).

The basic purpose of human resource development in RETs is to build, over the long term, a critical mass of professional African policy analysts, economic managers and engineers who will be able to manage all aspects of the RET development process, and to ensure effective utilization of already trained African analysts and managers (World Bank, 1991). Trained manpower capable of developing and manufacturing renewable energy technologies is a prerequisite for their successful dissemination.

This chapter discusses human resource development for RETs with emphasis on the formal academic system and more informal mechanisms. The chapter assesses the development of human resources in learning institutions through the existing education system; refresher courses; on-the-job training; informal training on an *ad hoc* basis (usually at the grassroots level to impart useful skills for RET utilization); and the retention of human resources – which basically means ways of motivating and making use of existing human resources and skills.

RET human resource development in the region

The problems mentioned above have not spared the renewable energy sector. This is especially true in government ministries and departments which have not been able to retain qualified personnel. In Kenya, for example, there is a lack of general expertise in all aspects of windpumps in the relevant ministries and NGOs. There is a small number of trained staff in the Ministry of Energy (MOE), however, who have been involved in the Special Energy Programme (SEP) (IT Power, 1987). The situation is worse in Zambia where only one engineer is responsible for coordinating all new and renewable energy activities of the government (Sampa and Sichone, 1995). This deficit is largely responsible for the generally underdeveloped research and technological capability and the poor management of renewable energy programmes. A British-financed project to map out the wind regime in the Seychelles was unsuccessful in the absence of trained personnel (Razanajatovo *et al.*, 1994).

These shortages have to some extent been responsible for the increased reliance on expatriates, but their eventual departure on expiry of their contracts often leads to the demise of RET projects. This is exemplified by a case in Kenya where an expatriate developed a low-cost, locally made control unit for PV lighting systems; on his departure, production stopped and has not been resumed since (Karekezi and Masakhwe, 1991). Expatriates are also costly and their allowances end up taking the bulk of the project budget. For instance, the total cost of solar water heaters used to test their effectiveness as alternatives to electrical water heaters in a hotel in the Seychelles escalated from US$38,000 to US$42,000 to cater for the engineers who had to be flown into the country to install the system (Razanajatovo *et al.*, 1994).

Excessive reliance on external technical expertise is demonstrated by the numerous disused small hydro plants in the region, many of them set up in the pre-independence period. A study carried out in Uganda identified the lack of locally trained and skilled manpower as the main factor hindering the dissemination of small hydro-power in the country. Design and installation of all the small hydro systems, even including basic steps such as feasibility studies, have relied on external support (Turyahikayo *et al.*, 1995). In Uganda, the installations were undertaken by foreign experts and fell into disuse immediately upon their departure (Turyahikayo *et al.*, 1995). A small hydro-power project in Lesotho fell into disuse in the early 1980s mainly because the plant was kept running by expatriate workers who did not train interested locals to keep it going (Kanetsi and Phuroe, 1994).

Expatriates who come in on this basis should be discouraged and/or replaced with local researchers. According to Karekezi and Masakhwe (1991), local researchers are an asset in that they provide a long-term and reliable source of technical expertise often referred to as 'institutional memory'. Lack of involvement of local personnel occurred in the expatriate-run biogas plants in eastern Uganda. This led to the malfunctioning of six digesters which negatively affected the further dissemination of biogas plants in the country because there were no trained technicians to offer proper maintenance (Turyahikayo, 1994). In Zimbabwe, a local expert team was used on an ethanol project thus minimizing reliance on the foreign (German) team. The availability of a local team facilitates replication of the technology, which supports the further dissemination of RETs (Scurlock *et al.*, 1991b).

Development in the academic system

To develop a comprehensive and sustainable human resource base in RETs requires that this potential resource be sensitized from an early stage. This calls for the inclusion of important energy issues in the existing school curricula, preferably from primary level up to the tertiary stages. The presentation of the subject should centre on local energy resources, with a special emphasis on RETs. The school curriculum has been modified in some countries to incorporate RET education at the basic level. The government of Zimbabwe is considering the introduction of renewable energy concepts at the kindergarten level (Asian Institute of Technology, 1994). There is a 'Cooking To Conserve' programme in Kenyan schools designed by the Bellerive Foundation and implemented by the Ministry of Education: it was incorporated in the Home Economics courses, a vital means of information dissemination at an early stage.

The primary responsibility for initiating and supporting appropriate training programmes in RETs rests with the institutions of higher learning and other middle-level training institutions. Conventional higher education systems in the region have not yet included renewable energy in their syllabi. NRSE is not included in the curriculum of technical colleges in Lesotho: as a result, technicians (as well as their teachers) who graduate from the colleges do not have any knowledge of RET technologies (Kanetsi and Phuroe, 1994).

Where universities and colleges have made attempts to include renewables in their curriculum, they are only referred to as important sources of energy (Karekezi, 1994). The subject is taught as part of other courses such as engineering and agriculture. The Faculty of Mechanical Engineering at the University of Nairobi provides a core course on solar energy (Nairobi University, 1992; Karekezi, Turyareeba and Ewagata, 1994). Most energy-related course materials concentrate on conventional energy systems such as thermal generation and large-scale power. Little attention is paid to renewable and traditional energy resources. Walubengo and Kimani (1993) point out that in Kenya there are only two charcoal experts teaching at the four public universities, despite charcoal being used by at least 30 per cent of the population.

The above information reveals that there has been reluctance in the development of a programme to cater for education on NRSE in the region. To overcome the lack of interest in RETs at African institutions of higher learning, centres of appropriate technology such as the Appropriate Technology Centre (ATC) at Kenyatta University and the Development Technology Centre (DTC) at the University of Zimbabwe have been established. The ATC undertakes various renewable energy programmes while offering a Bachelor of Science and Master of Science in Appropriate Technology (ATC, 1992; Karekezi, Turyareeba and Ewagata, 1994; Kimani and Naumann, 1993). Almost all these centres are underfunded and understaffed, and are housed in some of the worst university premises (Walubengo and Kimani, 1993). As has been mentioned, the ATC has to date not been able to mobilize the funding that would allow it to provide testing and research facilities on a continuous basis (Karekezi and Masakhwe, 1991). High regard for renewable energy subjects within the scientific community and funding of the respective research and development by governments can make this field attractive to young scientists and engineers. Despite their shortcomings, the role played by these centres in the development of NRSE human resources is of vital importance to the region.

Other governments in the region have also realized the importance of skilled manpower in the development of RETs and have started initiatives to address the deficit (see Box 9.2). The Physics Department in the University of Zambia started a renewable energy programme for both undergraduate and postgraduate students in the academic year 1994/5. To address the shortage of skilled PV technicians, the Botswana

Technology Centre is now assisting the Botswana Polytechnic to establish a technical course on PV theory, installation and maintenance which is expected to provide a steady supply of adequately qualified PV personnel (Diphaha and Burton, 1993). Kenyatta University in Nairobi has initiated a Bachelor of Environmental Studies degree which has several modules on renewable energy. Similarly, the Kenya Polytechnic has a diploma course in Environmental Science (Kimani and Naumann, 1993). In Tanzania, a research unit exists at the University of Dar es Salaam that deals with anaerobic digestion. These initiatives should be emulated by other institutions of higher learning in the region.

Additional funds are required for the successful implementation of energy and renewable energy courses. Funds can be sought from private companies, utilities and donor agencies. For instance, Ghana utilizes the petroleum fund for human resource development. Another way to make the training cost-effective is to initiate regional training centres on RETs. This means that the countries could share the cost of setting up the centres and equipping them. The Harare-based Africa Capacity Building Foundation, which is managing a US$100 million trust for capacity building in Africa, may be interested in providing capacity building support in other sectors of the economy such as RET policy analysis.

An attempt is being made to include RETs in the training programmes of technical and vocational schools in Lesotho. About eight teachers from technical and vocational schools and two energy officers from government departments dealing with NRSE were scheduled to attend a training programme in the US funded by Renewable Energy for African Development (REFAD). The programme will emphasize the practical installation and maintenance of RETs (Kanetsi and Phuroe, 1994). Other postgraduate-level training courses offered in colleges outside the region are made possible through sponsorships to develop the region's capacity in RETs. Venues include the University of Oldenburg in Germany; the University of Twente in the Netherlands; the International Development Technologies Centre in the Faculty of Engineering, University of Melbourne, Australia; Loughborough University of Technology in the UK; and the International Energy Foundation in Tripoli, Libya (Asian Institute of Technology, 1994). The design and scope of the course offered at the University of Oldenburg is described in Box 9.1.

Refresher courses

The demand for trained personnel to run RETs projects is crucial. It is not necessary to wait for a new generation of experts with all the required qualifications in this field (Naumann, 1993). One strategy to overcome the current deficit of trained manpower is to develop short-term training courses for project staff members in the field of RETs. Civil engineers

Box 9.1
The renewable energy education programme at the University of Oldenburg

———————————— * ————————————

The postgraduate course
This one-year MSc course has been running since 1987. It is aimed at students with an academic education of at least four years in engineering or natural sciences who intend to apply their knowledge of renewable energies in their future occupational work. From 1987 to 1993 a total of 72 engineers from all over the world participated in the course.

Course objectives
- Scientific principles of renewable energies;
- Technical feasibility of renewable energy systems;
- Economic theory of energy resources;
- Components of small-scale energy supply systems (laboratory);
- Analysis, simulation and design of energy systems;
- Case studies;
- Thesis on a subject related to the participant's future occupation; and
- Eight weeks' external practice training with enterprises and institutions concerned with energy systems.

Topics of the syllabus
- Photovoltaics;
- Solar thermal conversion;
- Wind energy conversion;
- (Micro) hydro power;
- Energy from biomass; and
- Storage components (electric and thermal).

The scientific level of the lectures, seminars and laboratory classes is such that the theoretical background is profound enough not only to apply but to understand renewable energy systems, their positive impacts and their limitations. On the other hand, the application of RETs should be matched by the practical problems in the field.

Curriculum guidelines and materials for pre-university education
The five years' experience of offering the Postgraduate Course in Renewable Energies was used to prepare curriculum guidelines and materials aimed at introducing RE into the undergraduate and postgraduate education of universities in developing countries. For this purpose, the Renewable Energy Group was contracted by GTZ in 1992 to develop curriculum guidelines within the frame of a Supra-Regional Programme on New Energy Technologies of the German Ministry of Economic and Development Cooperation (BMZ). The materials have been available to all interested universities since June 1993.

Box 9.1 contd

To apply, evaluate and improve this approach, a corresponding project was to be launched at the University of Zimbabwe, starting January 1994. Based on the materials developed in Oldenburg, a German expert will assist in creating a Renewable Energy Centre in the Faculty of Engineering, conducting RE education, research and dissemination in Zimbabwe.

Summer schools on solar and wind technologies conducted by the Renewable Energy Group
Apart from the postgraduate course the Renewable Energy Group started a summer school programme in 1992. This is aimed at specialists from partner institutions working on Renewable Energy Dissemination Programmes of the German government in developing countries. Such programmes include the Photovoltaic Pumping Programme (PVP), Sonne 2 and Wind, which are part of the Eldorado Programme funded by Germany's Ministry for Research and Technology.

For further information please contact: The Course Director, Renewable Energies, University of Oldenburgh, Postfach 25 03, D-W-2900 Oldenburg, Germany, Tel. +49 441 798 3544, Fax +49 441 798 3326. Telex 25 655 unol d

Source: Naumann, 1993

should be trained to handle small dam construction, for example (Gullberg, 1994).

The GEF large-scale biogas project in Tanzania has realized the importance of training as an ingredient of project development and has incorporated it into the programme. This involves not only the plant manager and technical staff, but also other cooperating groups such as the applied microbiology unit at the University of Dar es Salaam (who will act as advisers); the City Council; the Directorate of Environment in the Ministry of Environment; and the Department of Renewable Energy in the Ministry of Energy, Water and Mineral Resources. Training will be given both in Tanzania and abroad. The project also includes an educational programme to educate people from other areas where the biogas technology can be replicated (GEF, 1993).

In Lesotho, none of the institutions of higher learning offer professional degrees such as engineering. The Energy Conservation Division, which is one of the institutions involved in RETs, has recruited new graduates in science from the National University of Lesotho and trained them internally for a few years before sending them outside the country for further training with the assistance of international agencies. The Division has to contend with competition from parastatal organizations and the Republic of South Africa, which provides better remuneration for newly qualified staff (Phuroe and Mathaha, 1995).

Box 9.2
South African Development Community (SADC) training programmes on rural energy planning and environmental management (1994–7)

---
*

The SADC energy ministers' strategy for woodfuel has placed high priority on rural energy planning and strengthening of local institutional capabilities to plan, implement, monitor and evaluate woodfuel projects effectively. SADC/TAU has therefore contracted Eastern and Southern Africa Management Institute (ESAMI) to execute a three-year project on the above topic. Under this contract, ESAMI shall design and conduct both policy analysis seminars and specialist technical courses on rural energy planning and environmental management. A total of 12 training programmes will be conducted each year for the next three years of which four will be technical in nature. Two of the programmes are policy-level seminars targeting Ministers of Energy, Permanent Secretaries and other senior policy advisers. There is also a course on training of trainers whereas the rest are management training courses in various aspects of related subjects. The target audiences for the training programmes vary depending on the specific programme being offered. However, all participants will come from economic sectors which have direct links to energy and environment.

Source: SADC training programmes brochure

Lesotho is one of the countries in the region where there have been a number of initiatives to train skilled RET personnel. The United Nations Food and Agricultural Organization (FAO) funded a project from 1982 to 1984 with the aim of training professionals in biogas technology. In the process it sent technicians to China and Nepal for training whilst for other technicians it provided on-the-job training. A total of 25 technicians were trained. More than ten technicians and science graduates received on-the-job training in biogas technology, design, construction, maintenance and feeding through a UNESCO-funded project. Technicians were also trained in bio-digester technology under the auspices of a project funded by the Government of China and the Kingdom of Lesotho. Despite such an aggressive training programme, none of the project technicians were absorbed to continue these activities in any of the projects (Kanetsi and Phuroe, 1994).

Formal training of interested energy experts should be available at a small fee, as in the Solar Energy International's 1995 Renewable Energy Education Programme, where training is given in the practical use of solar, wind and water power.

Table 9.1 Summary of RWEPA's annual training courses

Year	No. of persons trained	Countries represented
1988	8	Kenya, Madagascar, Uganda, Ethiopia, Burundi, India.
1989	13	Sudan, Uganda, Zambia, Tanzania, Kenya.
1990	11	Kenya, Sudan, Rwanda, Angola, Tanzania, Zambia.
1991	11	Kenya, Uganda, Zaire, Angola, Zimbabwe, Ethiopia, Botswana, Tanzania.
1992	11	Kenya, Zambia, Tanzania, Sierra Leone, Malawi, Namibia, Nigeria, Mozambique, Uganda, Ethiopia.
1993	30	Ethiopia, Kenya, Tanzania, Uganda, Ghana.
Total	84	

Source: Karekezi et al., 1994.

Workshops and seminars

One of the approaches adopted in the training of engineers, technologists, technicians and extension officers in various aspects of RETs has been the development of workshops with the assistance of several international agencies. The aim is to help participants to understand the basic concepts of renewable energy production, storage, distribution and consumption. In addition, it is expected that through practical work and hands-on experience participants will be able to adapt the new technologies to suit national needs (Baguant, 1994). For instance, REFAD is working with a consortium of universities and colleges in the US and their African counterparts to organize hands-on training workshops that enable African educators to create their own renewable energy courses.

The Regional Wood Energy Programme for Africa (RWEPA) of the Kenya Energy and Environment Organization (KENGO) – a programme that is no longer functional because of limited financial resources – used to organize annual 'tailor-made' training courses to address specific needs: the International Biomass Courses, for example, and the Regional Solar Awareness Workshop. A few courses were also organized for participants interested in improved stove production and dissemination. Before the programme was discontinued, RWEPA had trained a total of 320 renewable energy project managers, entrepreneurs and technicians. These courses were designed to raise or improve the awareness of the participants in RETs and to provide a forum for information exchange among professionals from different countries (Rabar, 1992). A breakdown of the number of people trained (1988–93) is shown in Table 9.1.

In 1992, the Appropriate Technology Centre, Kenya (ATC) organized a two-week solar energy workshop for 15 participants who were drawn from universities, government ministries, and NGOs. The workshop provided a practical view of solar energy technologies, with emphasis on specifications, installations, maintenance and troubleshooting for solar water heaters and photovoltaics. Other solar technologies were also covered briefly (ATC, 1992). In November 1993, the Kagera Development Authority in Tanzania conducted its first practical PV training course at a newly established solar energy centre (Hankins, 1994). In Kenya, the African Centre for Technology Studies (ACTS) solar box dissemination project has been training the end users in making their own solar box cookers (Mwove, 1994). The Energy Society of Botswana promotes solar energy utilization and organizes seminars from time to time to disseminate information (Mosimanyane, 1994)

Past attempts to train through workshops have faced some difficulties. Baguant (1994) identifies some of the drawbacks of the workshop approach to training:

1   Disparities in the backgrounds of the participants have hampered effective running of the workshops and the appropriateness and adequacy of the training material, primarily because of the absence of a systematic participant recruitment procedure in the region.
2   The resource persons responsible for organizing and running these courses have been recruited from developed countries, and often have limited prior knowledge of the experience in the region.
3   Follow-up on the outcome of the workshops has been neglected.
4   The necessary infrastructure has not been available at the national level for participants to implement skills and knowledge acquired during the workshop.
5   Insufficient incentives were provided to participants, since the workshops did not lead to recognized diplomas or certificates.

These impediments have to be addressed before workshops can become an effective training tool.

Informal training and apprenticeship

Informal training is an important factor in capacity building not only in the near future but also in the long run. Usually conducted at the grassroots level, it engages the end users of RETs directly. In Uganda, JEEP provides training on stove production and dissemination, mainly targeting rural farmers who are directly involved in energy production at grassroots level (Turyahikayo, 1994). Community Management and Training Services provides grassroots training in wood energy technologies in Kiserian, Kenya (Community Management and Training brochure, 1995). The role of trained extension workers has proved to be of great significance. In one region in Lesotho, the dissemination of the stone *paola* improved stove was mainly attributed to an active extension worker who was interested in energy conservation (Gay *et al.*, 1993) and who had received some limited training.

Some emerging RET companies in Kenya have realized the importance of human resource development and have begun training women's groups and *jua kali* (informal sector) artisans to meet the high demand for woodfuel technologies. Training is mainly in stove and kiln construction. Another common way of training, especially for small-scale entrepreneurs, is through apprenticeship. This approach is more cost-effective and practical than formal training. In Kenya, the stove producers at Shauri Moyo are trained on the job.

Short courses have been organized by KENGO and the Ministry of Energy at the ministry's energy centres. SEP has technicians who offer technical support to end users of PV systems. These technicians are given in-house training when they are attached temporarily to the agency (Mbuuri, 1993; Karekezi, Turyareeba and Ewagata, 1994). The GTZ-SEP has five energy centres based in Nairobi, Kisii, Kakamega, Kikambala and Nyeri (Kenya) which offer in-house training programmes through seminars and workshops (Mbuuri 1993; Karekezi, Turyareeba and Ewagata, 1994). The Appropriate Technology Section (ATS) has offices in all ten districts of Lesotho which are responsible for disseminating RETs and training local people in how to produce these technologies.

Retention

Human resources have to be motivated, informed and placed where they can be most effective. Improved terms of service for researchers enhance the research environment (Gullberg, 1994). The sponsorship of research projects in developing countries – by the Swedish Agency for Research Cooperation with Developing Countries (SAREC), for example, or the World Bank – tends to give the employees a sense of job security. They are more likely to settle in their jobs than if the project was not funded by a reputable donor (World Bank, 1991).

The exodus of qualified personnel, either from the public sector to the more lucrative private sector, or from the region to the developed countries, has affected the promotion of RETs adversely. It has led to understaffing of RET technical units in the region, hindering the development of the technologies in Uganda, for example (Turyahikayo, 1994). Lesotho has been a victim of the migration of its qualified personnel to the neighbouring Republic of South Africa which offers better remuneration. The Appropriate Technology Section (ATS) in the country, like all institutions created out of externally funded projects, has experienced difficulty in retaining trained senior staff. None of the five senior staff employed by ATS during the project phase are still with the section, which has had four heads since its inception in 1984: inevitably, the continuity of its work has been affected (Phuroe and Mathaha, 1995). A UNESCO-funded

Table 9.2 Human resource development and retention incentives for RET dissemination and promotion in the region (see ranking procedure in Appendix 5)

Country	Rank	Human resource development and retention
Kenya	108	Training of Maendeleo stove producers on the manufacture, business management and marketing of the stove. Inclusion of solar energy in the National Educational syllabus in the late 1980s. Training of wind pump end users by Bob Harries Engineering Ltd at no cost save for accommodation expenses. Ministry of Energy's Special Programme launched training course for biogas plant builders with instructions provided by GTZ.
Lesotho	107	Training of LEC staff on SHP. REFAD training programme in the USA. Government sends people to be trained there.
Zimbabwe	103	Government has incorporated renewable energy as part of the education curricula from primary school upwards.
Botswana	103	Technician course on PV theory instruction and maintenance by BTC and Botswana Polytechnic.
Uganda	102	JEEP, IUCN, and YWCA are carrying out awareness programmes to teach end users how to produce their own stoves.
Zambia	102	In the Zambia charcoal project, artisans were trained in the making of improved stoves. Women's groups were also trained on how to use improved stoves properly.
Malawi	102	Department of Energy has been carrying out several workshops.
Seychelles	101	TSSD with the assistance of two French experts organized a regional training programme on biomass gasification principles and operation of gasifiers on one island.
Tanzania	101	Personnel are being trained in subjects related to biogas at the applied microbiology unit, University of Dar es Salaam.

project on the development of solar energy and biogas production, conducted by the Physics Department at the University of Lesotho, currently has only one lecturer pursuing research in the field of solar energy. The other lecturers who were involved have either retired or left the University for other assignments (Kanetsi and Phuroe, 1994).

Few of the region's institutions and departments can provide adequate support required by their researchers and development workers. This is attributable to the meagre financial resources available in the renewable energy development sector. Mbewe (1990) recommends the introduction of incentives in the form of consultancy fees to encourage research scientists. These fees can be derived from sources such as the 'petroleum fund' in Ghana (Wereko-Brobby, 1993). It is ironic that the consequence of the exodus is the hiring of expatriates at very high remuneration rates. The governments in the region should instead offer incentives to the local personnel at a small fraction of the amount offered to the expatriates.

Forced transfers, retirements and resignations influenced by political and personal considerations have also led to staff attrition and are likely to have affected manpower for PV technology development in the Ministry of Energy in Kenya (Nyoike and Okech, 1993; Karekezi, Turyareeba and Ewagata, 1994). Shortages of skilled manpower are also due to the 'internal brain drain' mentioned earlier, a process in which highly qualified personnel are placed in inappropriate positions (Mohapeloa and Lebesa, 1989; Karekezi, 1994e). For example, a renewable energy expert in the Ministry of Energy can be transferred to a management position in the Ministry of Labour. Minimization of arbitrary transfers and political interference in staff deployment would assist in ensuring the retention of scarce RET expertise in the region.

10

Equity

Rapid urbanization of the Eastern and Southern African countries is one of the most significant demographic changes taking place in the region. The urban population in Africa is expected to double in the next 12 to 15 years. This demographic shift is strengthening the historical bias of channelling development resources to urban areas and has continued to push rural energy issues into the background. Consequently, mobilizing support for developing and implementing technology options for rural areas has been and will continue to be an uphill task (Karekezi, 1992b). Renewable energy technologies can play a significant role in reducing the gap between the energy services available in rural as compared with urban areas and low-income as compared with high-income households. RETs reduce dependence on foreign energy resources and technologies, thus reducing the energy inequity between industrialized countries and oil-importing developing countries.

Oil crisis

None of the countries in the region except Angola and Sudan is endowed with (or has discovered) substantial petroleum fuel reserves. Most countries within Eastern and Southern Africa rely on petroleum imports from outside the region. The importation of this vital commodity takes a huge share of scarce foreign exchange (over 30 per cent in some countries in the region: see Table 10.1).

The second problem that the region faces is its vulnerability to oil price manipulations by oil-exporting countries and multinationals, and unexpected disruptions in supply: the three oil crises that have occurred in the past demonstrate the problem well. In the first oil crisis, oil prices rose in real terms by a factor of three. The region's oil import bill jumped from an average of 10 per cent of total export earnings to over 20 per cent. Most countries resorted to external borrowing to pay their rapidly rising energy import bills. Their difficulties were compounded by the low prices that the region's export commodities fetched in the international market, further reducing export earnings.

The second oil crisis in the late 1970s found the region no better prepared than before. Oil import bills jumped from an average of 20 per

Table 10.1 GNP *per capita,* debt service as a percentage of exports and energy imports as a percentage of merchandise exports for selected countries in Eastern Africa, 1992

Country	GNP/capita (US$)	Debt service as % of exports[a] (US$)	Energy imports as % of merchandise exports
Seychelles	5,460	–	90[b]
Mauritius	2,700	8	12
Kenya	310	27	19
Rwanda	250	23	53[b]
Burundi	210	35	22
Uganda	170	40	73
Tanzania	110	32	40
Ethiopia	110	14	47
Sudan	–	5	41

[a]Exports refer to goods and services
[b]Figures quoted are for 1987
– Data not available
Source: World Bank, 1989; 1994

cent of export earnings to over 50 per cent for a number of low-income countries. The resultant heavy import bill and the continued price collapse of raw material exports increased the region's debt load. Many countries failed to meet their external loan repayment obligations and were forced into rescheduling, which increased their debt servicing load. The same process was repeated in the early 1990s, during the Gulf War.

Renewable sources of energy can help alleviate this recurring crisis and provide a degree of security against external shocks. The Zimbabwean ethanol programme has made a substantial contribution to the security of the economy by reducing annual gasoline imports by 40 million litres (Scurlock, Rosenschein and Hall, 1991). Malawi's ETHCO has a capacity of 60,000 litres/day and 17 million litres/year, and has helped to reduce foreign exchange spending by a substantial amount. The demand for petroleum has also dropped by more than 10 per cent per annum (Kafumba, 1994). A study carried out in Kenya indicates that a typical windpump which replaces a diesel pump could save 2,200 litres of diesel per year (IBRD, 1993).

Most hydro-power schemes replace diesel generators and therefore save foreign exchange. In Ethiopia, small hydro is considered to be the best option compared with grid extension and diesel generators. Ethiopia's power utility cannot cover its costs because of inefficient performance when utilizing diesel to generate electricity in remote areas where this method costs about three times as much as small hydro (Ranganathan, 1992).

Socio-economic and rural development

In Eastern and Southern Africa, access to energy services has been determined by a skewed urban–rural distribution of income. The bulk of investment in the energy sector has gone to modern energy carriers for transport and electricity that cater for urban residents (FNI, 1994).

Table 10.2 Electrification of households in selected countries in the region

Country	Percentage of households connected		
	Urban	Rural	Total
Angola	17.28	0.00	4.84
Botswana	26.48	2.09	7.95
Lesotho	14.00	4.00	5.60
Malawi	11.00	0.32	1.38
Mozambique	17.05	0.66	2.79
Namibia	26.00	5.00	9.83
Swaziland	42.00	2.00	11.60
Tanzania	13.00	1.00	3.76
Zambia	17.85	1.39	8.31
Zimbabwe	64.72	0.60	15.35
Average	24.93	1.70	7.14

Source: Bogach et al., 1992.

Loans acquired by governments to build electricity generating facilities are repaid by all the citizens (with or without electricity) in the form of taxes, whereas only a very small percentage of the population receives electricity services. Rural cash-crop farmers pay taxes and levies which go into the repayment of these loans, while most of the farmers are found in the rural areas and have no access to electricity. As shown in Table 10.2, electricity is largely confined to urban and industrial centres.

Electricity generation from decentralized wind installations, for example, is more equitable since those who benefit from the wind plant are also the ones responsible for its construction and maintenance. In South Africa, ESKOM has been using PVs to provide electricity to households that were left out (in part as a result of the policies of the apartheid regime) of the electrification programme. Apart from the ESKOM initiative, utility involvement in solar energy technologies has been very limited (Gregory, 1994).

In Kenya, there are more rural households using solar PV lighting systems than there are connections to the official rural electrification programme (Van der Plas, 1994). By 1995, the number of households using solar energy PV systems was more than 40,000 compared with 17,000 connected to the grid through the rural electrification programme (Karekezi, 1995). According to Diphaha and Burton (1993), to provide electricity to all the scattered communities of rural Botswana by means of grid extension is not practical. PV, however, can provide cost-effective and reliable power for lighting, radio, television and some cottage industries that can generate income. They provide examples of areas where PV power could be used to replace animate or diesel-driven power. Standard rechargeable power tools could be used in a small workshop and small household grinders could be used to grind maize in family-sized amounts instead of taking maize to a centralized diesel-powered mill. Since such applications require applied technology and research, they envisage that, once PV becomes accepted as a normal source of energy at village level, innovations will start to come from that level. It has been shown in Kenya that a PV-powered electric sewing machine (modified to run on a car windscreen wiper motor powered by PV) can raise the profits of a tailor sufficiently to pay for the PV system required (*ibid.*).

RETs are ideal for the decentralized energy demand of rural areas in Eastern and Southern Africa where conventional grid electrification would be too costly to implement. Access to wind energy services can stimulate economic development in these areas. Wind generators and pumps offer employment opportunities which, in the long run, could help curb rural–urban migration. Small hydro-power development promotes rural industrial growth and improvement in the general welfare of rural inhabitants. Biomass resources can also provide economic development and employment opportunities.

Charcoal production provides employment to producers, transporters, wholesalers and retailers. In Zambia over 45,000 people are employed in the charcoal industry, of whom 90 per cent are in charcoal production (Hibajene, 1994). Charcoal production also provides indirect employment to stove producers in urban areas. The manufacture and installation of improved stoves has played a major role in income and employment generation. The ethanol plant in Kenya has about 200 employees and has generated additional indirect employment for about 1,000 people (Baraka, 1991).

The availability of modest quantities of energy, particularly electricity, could contribute substantially to meeting essential rural health needs and improving the quality of rural life by providing light, television (for education and entertainment), telecommunications, water pumping, and refrigerators for vaccines and medicines. It would also provide a means to generate income through small-scale industries. For people not connected to the grid, a few hours of electricity in their homes each day can transform their lives.

For communities in remote areas, RETs can provide a reliable water supply essential for survival. Throughout the rural areas in Ethiopia, the procurement of water for household use is undertaken manually, frequently with hardship and after heavy input of human energy. Electricity supplied by decentralized small hydro-power can replace these tedious methods. Most of the Kijito water pumps have been installed in the arid and semi-arid parts of the region, thereby supplying residents with a reliable water supply.

In the Ampefy small hydro project in Madagascar, the installation of the agro-processing facility has, to a great extent, resolved the difficulties of processing rice and other agricultural crops by eliminating the need for imported petroleum fuels and minimizing the need for imported lubricants and spare parts. It also provides low-cost and dependable power that opens the way for local producers of rice to realize greater added value by selling milled rice instead of paddy (Karekezi, 1989).

As shown in stove projects in Kenya, improved stoves are an important stimulus for the emancipation and general development of women. A housewife who adopts an improved stove is often more amenable to other development projects and more proactive in enhancing her living conditions. The time absorbed by woodfuel collection is also reduced, particularly benefiting rural women whose onerous household and family responsibilities leave them with little time. The shortage of time is particularly acute for households headed by women (often the spouses move to urban areas in search of work). In Kenya, it is estimated that between one-third and two-thirds of rural households are headed by women. The time freed by improved cookstoves can be used to undertake recreational or income-generating activities (Karekezi, 1993b).

The introduction of RETs is not in itself sufficient to address the question of equity. In certain cases, they can widen gaps rather than narrow them. The biogas programme in India is said to have made it more difficult for the rural poor to have access to cattle dung for use as fuel and fertilizer because of the competing demands of the rural middle class, who now use cattle dung as biogas feedstock. Equity is not only an issue at the field implementation level of rural energy technology. It is also of increasing concern at the level of research and development (Karekezi, 1992a). Hoffman (in Barnett *et al.*, 1982) explains that

> a massive inequality is being built up in the international distribution of capabilities relevant for the exploitation of alternative energy technologies. The pattern of R&D expenditures indicates that substantial research and development capabilities are being accumulated in a handful of industrialized economies, and that their scale far outweighs those being accumulated in the whole of the Third World.... In short, this scenario will need little development or elaboration before it looks remarkably similar to the present-day costly state of affairs with respect to conventional energy technology.

11

Environment

All energy systems – whether energy is being produced, converted or used – have adverse as well as beneficial impacts on the environment. They vary in quality and quantity, in time and in space. While the global consensus on the link between energy and the environment is growing, the situation in sub-Saharan Africa is not clear. The region's consumption of modern energy is the lowest in the world. The use of coal, the fuel associated with numerous environmental problems, is still embryonic in most of the region. Consequently, African energy planners and experts have accorded low priority to environmental issues in energy development up to the present. Recent developments, however, have demonstrated the inadequacy of this approach as environmental problems begin to emerge. Renewable energy sources can play a very important role in addressing energy-related environmental problems.

Deforestation

Biomass is often referred to as a 'conditionally renewable' source of energy. This is because it is not renewable if exploitation exceeds regeneration. Recent estimates indicate that biomass energy is the fourth most important source of energy in the world (Scurlock and Hall, 1990). It is also the dominant fuel in many sub-Saharan African countries. For example, biomass accounts for over 83 per cent of the national energy supply in Ethiopia (World Bank, 1996) and about 80 per cent of the total energy supply in the SADC region (Kaale, 1991). Demand for biomass in urban areas is increasing while supply is diminishing in many rural areas.

The rate of land degradation and deforestation is alarming in the region. Although the felling of trees for construction and the clearing of land for agricultural activities, rather than the increasing demand for energy, have proved to be the major causes of deforestation, the role played by the production of charcoal and the supply of firewood cannot be underestimated. Available evidence indicates that charcoal demand in Lusaka, the capital city of Zambia, is a major cause of deforestation.

The Beijer Institute study in Kenya (1984) suggested that wood and charcoal met over 50 per cent of institutional energy needs (Joseph and

Walubengo, 1988). Currently in Kenya, total consumption of fuelwood is approximately 700,000 tonnes per year. There is strong evidence to show, however, that the increased prices of petroleum fuels and their frequent unavailability are causing institutions to switch to wood and charcoal (*ibid*.). Institutional fuelwood consumption varies from 10 to 60 tonnes per month, with an average of 50–60 kilograms per person per month. An institution using 30 tonnes of wood per month clears about 3 hectares of forest cover per year; if these trees are not replaced, the impact on the local environment could be devastating (*ibid*.).

Other industries making intensive use of biomass energy, such as tea and tobacco, have also contributed to deforestation. As the use of biomass energy in the regional economy (primarily in the household sector) increases, related environmental problems will become more serious. For instance, an increasing proportion of households in the region depend on low-quality fuels such as agricultural residues, a practice that may lower crop yields and increase indoor air pollution.

Over half of the population in the region, and especially in the rural areas, rely on various forms of biomass (wood, agricultural and animal wastes) to satisfy most of their energy needs, which mainly consist of cooking and some space and water heating. The exposure to carbon monoxide is higher for charcoal users than any other fuel (Ellegard, 1990). Most of the time, the biomass is burnt in open fires inside the dwellings, resulting in a major health risk to the household, mainly the women and children. In many cases, the smoke produced as a result of combustion is not vented out of the cooking space. These emissions contain pollutants that can affect health adversely.

Indoor air pollution from smoke is considered to be a major contributor to respiratory diseases, a major cause of death in the region. Unfortunately, in most cases the traditional cookstoves used in the region are inefficient, physically hazardous, unhealthy and inconvenient. Smoke fumes from traditional cookstoves are increasingly perceived to be a major contributor to the high incidence of respiratory disease. Improved stoves fitted with chimneys could help to reduce this hazard (Karekezi, 1993b).

A number of options for addressing the growing deforestation problem exist: one is to address the problem of inefficient charcoal production kilns. Improved kilns in use in the region include the half-orange kiln in Malawi; the Mark V and Katugo in Uganda and the Oil Drum in Kenya. The second option is the introduction of improved cookstoves. The KCJ improved stove programme is a notable success. As has been mentioned, more than 700,000 stoves have so far been disseminated in Kenya. The other successful example is the Maendeleo stove, with a heat utilization efficiency of 30 per cent and a fuelwood saving of 50 per cent (Karekezi, Ewagata *et al.*, 1995). As has been noted earlier, survey results reveal that to cook the same type of food, a traditional institutional stove consumes 528 kg of firewood, whereas the improved stove requires only 92kg of wood (Wickramagamage, 1992). Direct combustion can be improved by the use of more efficient furnaces and pertinent accessories in biomass-intensive industries such as tea and tobacco.

Greenhouse gases and climate change

The energy sector is one of the main sources of greenhouse gas (GHG) emissions in the region. The sector directly contributes GHGs to the atmosphere in the course of production, conversion and use (Okoth-Ogendo and Ojwang, 1995). The transport sector is the leading consumer of petroleum products in the region. The use of fossil fuel in transportation and power generation is an important contributor to urban pollution and has been linked to acid rain, especially in South Africa.

Though the increase in the carbon dioxide level in the atmosphere could also mean an increase in precipitation and a subsequent increase in biomass productivity, the UNEP global environmental monitoring system reports that in the Sudan-Sahel region an increase in temperature of between 1°c and 3°c may lead to an increase in precipitation of about 5 per cent and a decrease of soil moisture of about 10 per cent. This means that the increase in temperature could result in high evaporation and consequently low soil moisture which acts as an impediment to increased crop production. Increased incidence of disease may be experienced. Diseases that prevail under hotter and humid conditions, especially water- and air-borne diseases, could be on the increase. These include hepatitis B, meningitis, measles and tetanus. Diseases spread by vectors, such as dysentery, typhoid and malaria, are also expected to spread to new areas as the new conditions open up new host environments for the vectors. Incidence of cardiovascular diseases may also increase with increasing temperature (Karekezi and Majoro, 1994).

The predicted impact of these processes will affect the region's economic growth adversely (Karekezi and Majoro, 1994). Since energy consumption activities are indispensable in the economic development process, the challenge is how to provide energy to a growing population while at the same time minimizing GHG emissions. Use of fossil fuels can be decreased with an increase in the use of alternative sources of energy (solar, wind, hydro and biomass). Renewable energy use does not lead to a build-up of carbon dioxide and the other greenhouse emissions that contribute to global warming. If grown properly, the use of biomass fuels will not contribute to global warming because the carbon dioxide released when biomass is burned equals the amount absorbed by plants as they are grown for biomass fuel (Johansson et al., 1993). The general impact of electricity generation from wind energy to the grid is a significant saving in fossil fuels not used at the power station (Thomsen, 1994). Renewable energy technologies provide an attractive abatement option because of their dual benefits of increasing the supply of modern energy while reducing GHG emissions.

Another option is the use of bio-fuel resources as a substitute for fossil fuel, especially in the transport sector. Combustion of ethanol produces less carbon dioxide than fossil fuels and also enables the use of lower octane gasoline, avoiding the use of lead additives. Initiatives in the use of ethanol are already operational in Kenya, Zimbabwe and Malawi. There are studies, however, which are sceptical of the potential role of ethanol as a GHG abatement option. Eriksen (1995) contends that energy is consumed and GHGs are emitted during the growing, harvesting and processing of bio-fuels, in their transportation and in disposing of their residues. He shows estimates that gasohol reduces carbon monoxide concentration by 25 per cent, but increases nitrogen dioxide emissions by 8 per cent to 15 per cent, volatile organic compounds by 50 per cent and ozone by 6 per cent. In addition, he asserts that contradictory findings are provided by a study undertaken in Zimbabwe showing that twice as much energy is produced in the form of ethanol than is taken up in its production. Greater research is required to resolve the contentious debate over the potential of ethanol to mitigate GHGs.

Charcoal production is still a major cause of pollution. Production through the use of earth and pit kilns generates toxic substances in solid, liquid and gaseous form. Traditional charcoal kilns generate large amounts of carbon monoxide, carbon dioxide and methane, which are important GHGs, but there is still no solid evidence to prove that charcoal kilns contribute to global warming.

Municipal waste pollution

The urban centres in the region are growing at a rapid pace. Urban authorities are unable to provide adequate sanitation and waste disposal services. As a result, most urban authorities are faced with an escalating problem of waste disposal. Solid waste management, therefore, has become a serious problem in urban areas throughout the region. Solid wastes cause air and water pollution and spread diseases.

The use of biogas from urban waste should be encouraged. This is considered to be an ideal, environmentally benign energy technology that not only provides household energy at affordable prices but also reduces GHG emissions and produces an enhanced organic fertilizer (sludge) that is ideal for agriculture. In addition, the fermentation process that takes place in biogas plants helps to reduce harmful organisms in the sludge. These organisms can be a major source of disease, particularly in developing countries (Karekezi and Karottki, 1989). The municipal waste disposal problem can be alleviated through an integrated programme, as in multi-purpose large-scale biogas projects. This will not only improve the sanitary conditions of the urban centres, but also generate electricity and create employment. Electricity generation by this means will also reduce GHG emissions since it will be a substitute for generation based on fossil fuels. Large-scale biogas projects from municipal wastes is an established technology and Tanzania is setting up a similar plant under the auspices of the GEF. Other countries in the region should seek ways to replicate this technology. It is estimated that there is potential for at least 50 financially viable large-scale biogas plants in Tanzania. If these plants existed, they would each cause an annual reduction in CH_4 emissions of 36.91 million cubic metres and eliminate 679,800 tons of carbon dioxide from fossil fuels (GEF, 1993).

Environmental drawbacks of renewables

The development of large-scale hydro-power can result in major eco-logical and hydrological disruption, damaging local ecosystems and affecting local communities adversely. Large-scale hydro often leads to flooding of large tracts of land, some of which may be arable. It increases incidence of water-borne diseases, decreases fish stocks and sometimes inundates forests and natural woodlands, further reducing the world's biodiversity. Poorly planned large-scale hydro-power plants can trigger mass displacement of indigenous communities which sets the stage for long-term social problems. Small-scale hydro-power is considered to be more environmentally favourable, however, because it does not require the construction of large dams (Karekezi and Karottki, 1989).

Small hydro-power does not lead to air pollution or waste disposal (Inversin, 1986). Small hydro installations on rivers populated by migrating fish species, however, are potentially harmful (Gullberg, 1994). When building small hydro plants on such rivers, care should be taken not to interfere with the fishes' migratory routes. This especially applies during the civil works construction of the hydro scheme. The river banks or any canals that are to be dug may be vulnerable to erosion as a result of the small hydro project (Gullberg, 1994) and this may lead to sedimentation of the river. Surface-mounted penstocks and transmission cables may interfere with the paths and tracks used by the local people, or with farmers' fields (*ibid.*).

An environmental examination or environmental impact assessment of a small hydro project should be a prerequisite. In Madagascar, according to the Initial Environmental Examination (IEE), the river on which a hydro-power station was built carried a very low silt load: very little if any siltation was expected. The only concern raised by the IEE was the possible restriction of eel fishing and the passage of river fauna. To ensure a systematic review of the impact of the station on eel fishing and river fauna, the IEE recommended that there should be bi-annual site environmental reviews and that a comprehensive environmental evaluation be carried out at the end of two years to assess the overall effect of the sub-project civil construction on the ecology of the river and its environs (Karekezi, 1989a).

Other environmental problems include noise pollution and siting constraints. The nuisance caused by wind turbine noise is one of the important limitations on siting wind turbines close to inhabited areas. The acceptable noise level strongly depends on local regulations (Thomsen, 1994). For example, in Denmark, the legal minimum distance from a wind turbine to a dwelling is 200 metres (Johansson *et al*, 1993). The visual impact of the turbines, although of a rather subjective nature, is a realistic planning restriction, particularly for areas of outstanding natural beauty such as wildlife parks (Beurskens and Jensen, 1994).

Birds can also be victims of collisions against wind turbine towers or blades, and breeding or resting birds can be disturbed in the turbine vicinity. Though this is an issue in developed countries such as the USA and the Netherlands, it is yet to be of concern in Eastern and Southern Africa where very few wind generators have been installed (Thomsen, 1994).

To collect large amounts of energy from the wind, turbines must be spread over a wide area and positioned so as not to interfere with one another. Spacing is particularly important in large wind farms where the turbines are typically separated by distances of five to ten rotor diameters (Johansson *et al*, 1993). Despite this, wind plants use only a small portion of the land they occupy, typically less than fifteen per cent, and the rest can be used for grazing or farming (Gipe, 1993).

With the current low level of economic development and energy use, environmental issues might not be a major priority in the region. A survey undertaken in Botswana found that the respondents did not complain of negative environmental impacts associated with the use of windpumps. Instead, the majority of the respondents believed that windmills improve the immediate scenery and they are perceived as safe to operate. Even the noise is not considered a nuisance by the people within the homesteads owning the windmill (Mosimanyane *et al.*, 1995).

As many countries in the region are signatories to the international conventions dealing with the environment, and with donor agencies

Table 11.1 Environmental impacts of renewable energy technologies

Solar	Land-use requirements, use of solvents during cell manufacture, toxic materials hazards during production and disposal (PVs)
Wind	Land-use requirements; visual impact; electro-magnetic interference
Biomass	Land-use requirements, use of fertilizers, atmospheric emissions during conversion

increasingly advocating that these issues be part of projects they finance, gradually environmental issues are being incorporated into national development programmes. If the countries were to start accounting for the social and environmental costs linked to conventional energy, renewables would certainly be more competitive.

Part 4

Policy Recommendations

12

Policy Recommendations

Although Eastern and Southern Africa have an abundance of renewable energy resources, limited exploitation has bedevilled efforts to transform the promise of renewable energy into reality. Expanded exploitation will require several fundamental changes and policy interventions.

Although oil prices have declined in the last decade, RETs still have an important role to play in the energy sector of the region and should not be left out of national energy plans. Government planners and the RET community should not wait for another oil crisis to prompt a policy of aggressive RET development. Hasty decisions in times of crisis can be costly, as past hurried RET dissemination efforts have demonstrated. RET planners and technologists, for their part, should be ahead of the policy makers, ready to provide a range of policy and technology options when the need is recognized.

In the past, much of the RET research effort was focused on the science and basic engineering of RETs in the universities and research institutes. Most of the RETs are now mature and the challenge is how to shift from the research stage and transfer the know-how from research centres and laboratories to commercial firms and end users. Past attempts at promoting RETs often focused on a specific technology for generating energy, whether it be a biogas plant or a windpump. Identified technologies were perceived as stand-alone options that excluded other conventional and traditional energy options. Institutional and cultural considerations were often underestimated. Consequently, potentially attractive opportunities were not fully exploited for expanded use of dual renewable/fossil fuel or dual conventional/traditional energy systems; nor was sufficient emphasis placed on harnessing the latent capability of local institutions and cultural relationships.

Some of the measures that would encourage large-scale dissemination of renewable energy technologies in the region are presented below.

Renewable energy policy programmes

RET policy programmes should be aggressive, long-term, policy-oriented, and aimed at senior decision makers in both government and the private sector. These programmes should demonstrate the economic and environmental benefits of RETs, and propose short- and medium-term policy initiatives to engender large-scale dissemination. Priority should be given to highlighting the real and tangible economic benefits (such as job creation and income generation) that renewable energy programmes can deliver to the region at both micro and macro levels. RETs are generally more labour-intensive than conventional and centralized energy projects and can help address problems of unemployment.

Of particular interest to policy makers would be revenue-neutral policy and institutional measures. For example, it is possible to make the case that the loss of revenue associated with the removal of duties and taxes on RETs can be recouped from the long-term savings in imports of petroleum fuels that require access to convertible currencies.

Institutional

At the institutional level, countries in the region need to realize that the centralized energy model is becoming increasingly obsolete in developed countries where independent power producers, riding on the back of the privatization wave, are registering rapid progress. Rather than continue to expand their centralized power systems, countries in Eastern and Southern Africa should begin to develop a decentralized energy structure which would better match the region's current capital resources and management capability, as well as position it well to adapt to future energy technologies and systems.

In 1989, the World Bank estimated that sub-Saharan Africa would need US$28 billion over the next decade in order to satisfy a 5 per cent growth in energy demand. This projection was based largely on conventional energy options. The modular nature of RETs allows even the poorest of sub-Saharan countries to begin a phased energy investment programme that would not strain its national investment programme or draw investment funds away from other pressing needs such as basic nutrition, health, education and shelter. The existing power utilities in the region should be actively involved in the development of RETs. ESKOM, the South African utility, is already involved in solar power development. The Zimbabwe Electricity Supply Authority (ZESA) is also currently participating in a UNDP rural electrification project using solar energy.

In spite of some high-profile and dramatic setbacks, the increasing number of democratic transformations have ushered in new and proactive administrations willing to adopt imaginative energy policies and innovative institutional changes that combine supply-oriented investments with demand-side and decentralized RET programmes.

Through organizations such as the African Energy Policy Research Network (AFREPREN/FWD), the African Development Bank (ADB), the Common Market for Eastern and Southern Africa (COMESA), the Inter-

Governmental Agency for Desertification and Development (IGADD) and the Southern African Development Community (SADC), there is a growing high-level support for sustainable energy strategies that include a significant RET component. In addition, growing national and regional links are being forged by energy institutions, especially in the non-governmental sector, leading to better networking and information exchange. This can provide an important avenue for rapid diffusion of information on RETs.

Coordination

All institutions and agencies involved should work more closely to integrate the support they provide in the development of RETs. Networking agencies such as AFREPREN should be strengthened to encourage the exchange of experiences and the sharing of research findings and of training and dissemination capabilities. Since RETs have an important role to play in the attainment of sustainable energy goals, they should be integrated into various programmes such as health, agriculture and water supply.

Regional cooperation in energy resource assessment, development and distribution should be promoted. This will create larger markets, encourage standardization, reduce costs and strengthen regional infrastructure. It would also attract local and foreign investment and thus facilitate cost-effective exploitation of the region's vast renewable energy resources. Maximum use should be made of the existing regional trading blocs such as COMESA and the SADC (including the recently launched Southern African Power Pool – SAPP) to promote RETs.

Efforts to integrate analytical expertise within the energy sector with that of other key actors in the development process – such as centres of expertise within the banking, social/community development and public sectors – should be promoted. This is crucial to understanding not only the renewable energy resources and technologies available, but the institutional settings through which they may be adopted and the needs and interests of the target communities.

Since the private sector is an integral part of the promotion process, its participation in RET research, information, evaluation and analysis is vital. Finally, numerous energy agencies in both the government and non-governmental sectors have emerged. In a number of sub-Saharan African countries, the rapid institutional development is beginning to be matched by the development of a critical mass of local energy expertise willing to face the challenge of formulating and implementing effective large-scale RETs programmes.

Innovative dissemination strategies

New strategies for RET dissemination that have demonstrated encouraging signs of success should be applied more widely. Many of these strategies revolve around the ideas of participation, income generation, and small-scale enterprise development. The rationale is that if producers and distributors can make attractive income from the manufacture and marketing of renewable energy equipment, and if users are fully involved in the dissemination process, then the issue of sustainability is resolved in a much more cost-effective fashion.

The second important innovation is the idea of using existing systems of production, marketing, and information dissemination. By using an existing network system, the cost of disseminating renewable energy technologies is dramatically reduced. This 'piggy-back' principle is particularly effective in rural areas, where the cost of establishing new marketing and distribution networks is particularly high. RET dissemination initiatives can be a component of an existing integrated income-generating project, environment programme or health extension exercise.

Increased emphasis on the production-oriented functions (battery charging, rural industries) and entrepreneurial approaches rather than the service functions (lighting, provision of water) and the welfare dimension of RET programmes would create a stronger impetus for investment in RETs. This would create employment in rural areas and ensure a stronger base for sustainable RET development.

New and flexible financing mechanisms

Innovative and sustainable financing programmes for renewable energy technologies should be instituted. Such programmes could include the creation of a national fund for RET projects financed by a modest tax on fossil fuels, credit schemes specifically aimed at developing RET industries, or endowment funding of RET agencies. In Ghana, a national energy fund (replenished by levies on conventional energy) has been utilized successfully to finance RET projects on a sustainable basis. An important challenge is the bundling of discrete renewable energy projects into large programmes that can be financed by major bilateral and multilateral donor and financing agencies. The FINESSE (Financing Energy Services for Small-Scale Energy Users) initiative of the World Bank's Asia Alternative Energy Unit provides a model in this area. Local financial and credit institutions are best placed to administer the relatively modest financing packages that RETs require. Involvement of local financing agencies is an absolute prerequisite for the future success of RET financing schemes in Eastern and Southern Africa.

Resource assessment and statistical databases

Limited access to information on the region's resource base is a major barrier to wider use of RETs and a major cause of contradictory and inconsistent information on RETs. The existing meteorological departments and research institutes with the requisite capability, such as those in universities, should be encouraged to carry out studies to document the types, locations and quantities of the various forms of regional renewable energy resources. In addition, information on the potential RET market, consumer behaviour and economic analysis data, should be readily available to the RET planner. Agencies such as the National Chamber of Commerce and the National Associations of Manufacturers can be of assistance in collecting market-related data.

Institutions such as AFREPREN, the ADB and the Economic Commission for Africa (ECA) should establish a regional data bank for RETs to enable international comparability and projections. This information should be made readily available to the RET industry and regularly updated. The capacity to monitor and undertake requisite exploratory activities to identify and determine the nature and characteristics of renewable energy resources available in the region should be developed. Using the critical mass theory of either number of disseminated RETs or number of local manufacturers and/or assemblers, attempts should be made to establish the point at which the particular RET industry is on a self-sustaining growth path, at which point financial support and subsidies can be withdrawn gradually.

Training and capacity-building initiatives

Long-term RET training programmes, designed to develop a critical mass of locally trained personnel with the requisite technical, economic and social-cultural skills, should be initiated. Many of the engineering and technical courses that are taught at sub-Saharan Universities provide little exposure to energy technologies. Modest changes in the curricula of colleges and universities could increase significantly the supply of skilled RET engineers and technicians. Programmes such as the SADC Technical Assessment Unit/ESAMI project 'Training Programme on Rural Energy Planning and Environmental Management', the REFAD courses and the planned AFREPREN-FWD/SEI training courses should be expanded.

There should be maximum use of local researchers and consultants. Local analytical expertise should be utilized fully in comprehensive evaluations of available renewable energy resources. Non-partisan groups such as NGOs and independent research institutes and networks are well placed to undertake such studies.

Technological leapfrogging

Many experts in the South have recognized the importance of technological leapfrogging in countries where infrastructures are still embryonic. There are, however, several obstacles, notably the general competition for scarce capital. Because the up-front capital requirements of adopting large-scale RET technologies are in general higher than those for older, less environmentally sound energy technologies, the solution to the investment equation differs depending upon whether one optimizes for the short-term objective of meeting pressing demand or for the long-term objective of meeting demand at least economic and environmental cost.

The fast track is to import outdated technology. Private Western industrial interests have encouraged such practices, thereby creating markets for technologies no longer saleable at home. In addition, the funding convention practised by aid agencies of favouring, if not requiring, the adoption of technologies that are well established in the West increases the difficulty of financing investments in advanced RET technologies.

A paradigm shift is needed in development aid towards supporting technological innovation rather than proven conventional energy technologies. Aid agencies can make a significant contribution to the implementation of technological leapfrogging by not only switching their support to advanced RETs, but also assuming some of the risk associated with making cutting-edge investments in RETs. The need to adapt both new and conventional technologies to local settings should be recognized as part of this paradigm shift and the cost of doing so should be incorporated as a prerequisite of support for sustainable RET sector development.

In this context, local manufacture and assembly initiatives such as the Kijito windpump in Kenya should be encouraged with the requisite financial and institutional incentives. The focus should be on low-cost manufacturing techniques through maximum utilization of local manufacturing capability.

Quality control

Quality control is important in ensuring that RETs provide the desired services. The absence of standards for a number of RETs makes it difficult to ensure the desired quality. This is particularly difficult with the increasing number of agencies involved in RET dissemination and marketing. Codes or standards should therefore be formulated by energy and commerce ministries in conjunction with the Bureau of Standards to ensure that end users (who often are unfamiliar with the technologies) are provided with products of acceptable quality. The weak infrastructure for maintenance of RETs in the region should be strengthened through the production of the requisite spare parts and the clustering of remote RET installations to minimize associated maintenance costs.

Bibliography

Abasaed, A., 1989. 'Cotton Stalks a Useful Waste', *Boiling Point*, Special Edition, p.9.

Abusam, A.A., 1990. 'A Realistic View of Improved Stoves Prospects in Sudan', *Boiling Point*, No. 21, ITDG/GTZ, April, p. 36.

Acker, R.H. and Kammen, D.M., 1994. *The Quiet (Energy) Revolution: Analyzing the Dissemination of Photovoltaic Power Systems in Kenya*, University of Chicago, Illinois and Princeton University, New Jersey.

Ackerman, F. and de Almeida, P.E.F., 1990. *Iron and Charcoal: The Industrial Woodfuel Crisis in Minas Gerais*, SEI report, p. 2.

Ahmed, A.I., 1988. *Options for Power Generation in Somalia*, Energy Planning Unit of Ministry of National Planning and Jubba Valley Development, Mogadishu, Somalia, p. 3.

Ahmed, K., 1994. *Renewable Energy Technologies: A Review of the Status and Costs of Selected Technologies*, The World Bank, Washington, DC, pp. 31, 34-36 and 121.

Ahring, B.K., 1993. *Status of the Technology for Large and Medium Size Biogas Plants*, Danish Technological Institute, Tastrup.

Al-Karaghouli, A.A., Minasian, A.N. and Hasan, M., 1990. 'A Wick-Basin Solar Still', *Energy and the Environment Into the 1990s*, Vol. 2, Pergamon Press, Oxford, pp. 1309–14.

Alemayehu, T., 1993. 'News From Ethiopia – The Laketch', *RWEPA News*, No. 12, May, p. 1.

Ali, G.E.F., 1992. *Introduction to Biomass Energy*, Course Proceedings 1991, Regional Training Course on Biomass Energy Development, Management of Community Biomass Energy Programmes, Muiruri, J.K. (ed.), KENGO, Nairobi, p. 20.

Ali, G.E.F. and Hood, A.H., 1992. 'Household Energy in Sudan', KENGO Wood Energy Programme for Africa, KENGO and MOTIF Creative Arts, Nairobi, Kenya, pp. 7, 8, 10.

Alward, R., Eisenbart, S. and Volkman, J., 1979. *Micro Hydro Power: Reviewing an Old Concept*, National Centre for Appropriate Technology, Montana, Canada, p. 18.

Annan, B. and Rice, V., 1991. *Solar Electric Applications and Directory of the US Photovoltaic Industry*, Solar Energy Industries Association, Washington, DC, p. 3.

Arafa, S., 1987. 'Integrated Rural Energy Systems and Community Development: Basaisa Village Integrated Field Project', *Proceedings of Investing in Development Conference*, The US Department of Energy, Louisiana, pp. IV-25–IV-50.

Ashforth, J.H. and Neuendorffer, J.W., 1980. *Matching Renewable Energy Systems*

221

to *Village Level Energy Needs*, Solar Energy Research Institute, Colorado, USA, June, p. 22.

Ashley, C. and Young, P., undated. *Stoves for Sale: Practical Hints for Commercial Dissemination of Improved Stoves*, ITDG, UK, p. 4.

Asian Institute of Technology, 1994. *Abstracts prepared for the 4th International Symposium on Renewable Energy Education*, Bangkok, Thailand on 12–14 December.

ATAC, 1987. *Ceramic Stove Production*.

ATC, 1992. *Report on a Solar Energy Training Workshop*, Appropriate Technology Centre, Kenyatta University, p. 4.

Awori, F., 1995. 'Alcohol Firm Cries Foul', *East African Standard Business and Finance*, 6 June, Nairobi, p. 5.

Babut, R., 1990. 'Low-Energy Multi-storey Residential Building WE-110 in Warsaw', *Abstracts of the International Solar Energy Society Solar World Congress*, Hungarian Solar Energy Society, Budapest, Hungary, p. 597.

Bachou, S.A., 1990. *Key Factors for the Dissemination of Renewable Energy Technologies: Cookstoves and Briquettes in Uganda*, Paper prepared for the fourth AFREPREN Workshop, 10–16 August, 1990, pp. 26–9.

Bachou S. and Otiti, T., 1994. *Dissemination of Photovoltaic Technology in Uganda*, AFREPREN, Nairobi, p. 20.

Baguant, J., 1990. *The Case Of Mauritius*, AFREPREN, Nairobi, Kenya.

Baguant, J., 1992. 'Energy Management in Electricity Generation: The Case of Mauritius', *Energy Management in Africa*, Bhagavan, M.R. and Karekezi, S. (eds), ZED Books in association with AFREPREN, London, pp. 131, 142.

Baguant, J., 1994. 'Human Resources Development and Training in the African Energy Sector', *Science in Africa – Energy for Development Beyond 2000*, American Association for the Advancement of Science, Washington DC, USA, p. 57.

Baguant, J. and Manrakhan, J., 1994. *Issues in Energy for the African Region: A Higher Education Training With Particular Reference to Mauritius*, AFREPREN, Nairobi, Kenya, p. 1.

Baraka, M.L., 1991. 'The Kenya Experience with Ethanol', *Driving New Directions: Transportation Experiences and Options in Developing Countries*, Birk, M.L. and Bleuiss, D.L. (eds), IIEC, Bangkok.

Barlow, R., McNeils, B. and Derrick, A., 1993. *Solar Pumping: An Introduction and Update on the Technology, Performance, Costs, and Economics*, Intermediate Technology Publications, London, p. 69.

Barnard, G., 1987. 'Woodfuel in developing countries', *Biomass: Regenerable Energy*, Hall, D.O. and Overend, R.P. (eds), John Wiley and Sons, p. 357.

Barnard, G. and Kristoferson, L.A., 1985. *Agricultural Residues as Fuel in the Third World*, Technical Report No. 4, IIED, p. 29, 39.

Barnes, D.F., Openshaw, K., Smith, K.R. and van der Plas, R., 1993. 'The Design and Diffusion of Improved Cooking Stoves', *The World Bank Research Observer*, Vol 8, No. 2, IBRD/World Bank, July, pp. 119, 120–1, 124, 130.

Barnett, H., Bell, M. and Hoffman, K., 1982. *Rural Energy and the Third World – A Review of Social Science Research and Technology Policy Problems*, Pergamon Press, Oxford.

Barnett, A., Pyle, L. and Subramanian, S.K., 1978. *Biogas Technology in the Third World: A Multi-Disciplinary Review*, International Development Research Centre, Ottawa.

Bassey, M.W., 1992. 'Renewable Energy Research And Development in West and Central Africa', *Energy For Rural Development*, Baghavan, M.R. and Karekezi, S. (eds), Zed Books in association with AFREPREN, London. pp. 30, 96, 98, 102–3.

Beeharry, R.P.and Baguant, J., 1995. *Bagasse Gasification for Electricity Generation in Mauritius*. University of Mauritius, Reduit.

Bellerive Foundation, 1992. 'Landmark Installation', *Environmental Impact Bulletin*, Bellerive Foundation, Ruiru, Kenya, p. 6.

Bellerive Foundation, 1993. *Specifiers Guide to Fuel Efficient Cooking Systems Designed and Manufactured by Bellerive Foundation*, Bellerive Foundation, Ruiru, Kenya.

Bellerive Foundation, 1994. *Bellerive Bulletin*, No. 9, Bellerive Foundation, Nairobi, Kenya.

Bennet, K., 1989. 'The Future of Fuel Briquetting', *Boiling Point*, Special Edition, ITDG/GTZ, pp. 2-3.

Bernard, M.P., 1990. 'Improved Efficiency of Biomass Usage in Malawi', *Energy and Environment*, Vol.3, Sayigh, A.A.M. (ed.), Pergamon Press.

Berndt, G.W.P., 1993. '50 DOMUS Solar Homes in Different Regions of Germany', *Abstracts of the International Solar Energy Society Solar World Congress*, Hungarian Solar Energy Society, Budapest, Hungary, p. 588.

Best, G., 1992. 'The Role of Renewable Energy Technologies in Rural Development', *Energy for Rural Development*, Bhagavan, M.R. and Karekezi, S. (eds), Zed Books in association with AFREPREN, London.

Beurskens, H.J.M. and Jensen, H.P., 1994. *Wind Energy Systems: Environmental Aspects*, Paper presented in the WEC Work Group 4C Workshop, 26–28 November, Naivasha, Kenya, p. 2.

Bhagavan, M. and Karekezi, S. (eds), 1992. *Energy Management in Africa*, Zed Books in association with AFREPREN, London, pp. 1, 17.

Bhatia, R., 1988. *Wind Energy Utilization in India: Performance Evaluation and Economic Analysis*, Institute of Economic Growth, New Delhi, India, p. 1.

Biomass Users Network, 1989. *Network News*, Vol.3. BUN Regional Office for Asia: Energy Research and Training Centre, Chulalongkorn University Bangkok.

Bogach, S., Peters, R. and Sellers, P., 1992. *Assessment of Applications and Markets for Solar Photovoltaic Systems in the SADCC Region*, Southern African Development Coordination Conference, Luanda, Angola.

Boiling Point, 1991. 'More Charcoal by Traditional Methods', *Boiling Point*, No. 24, Reproduced from ODA Newsletter No. 10, pp.10–11. Also see 'Biomass Briquetting', pp. 11–12.

Boiling Point, 1992. 'Casamance Kiln: Best for Charcoal Burning', *Boiling Point*, No. 29, p. 27.

Bokalders, V. (ed.), 1989. *Renewable Energy for Development*, No.3, The Beijer Institute, Stockholm, p. 5.

Borg, C. and Oden, H., 1995. 'The Kijito Windpump: A Private Initiative In Kenyan Rural Water Supply', *A Study of Renewable Energy Technology Diffusion in the Third World*, Chalmers University of Technology, Department of Industrial Marketing, pp. 44, 50, 55, 62, 84.

Box, de la Rive J., 1990. *CWD Market Reconnaissance Study*, CWD, Netherlands. pp. 4, 29.

BP Shell, 1991. *BP Shell Statistical Review of World Energy, 1991*. The British Petroleum Company, UK.

BP Shell, 1992. *BP Shell Statistical Review of World Energy, 1992.* The British Petroleum Company, UK.

BP Solar, 1993. *BP Solar: Putting the Sun to Work,* BP Solar Ltd, UK.

Branco, G.M. and Szwarc, A., 1992. *Ethanol: Energy Source for a Sustainable Society,* Sao Paulo State Environment Protection Agency, Brazil, pp. 18.

Brandt, H., 1989. 'Densification of Biomass', *Boiling Point,* Special Issue, p. 17.

Brenndorfer, B., Kennedy. L., Bateman, C.O.O., Trim, D.S., Mrema, G.C. and Wereko-Brobby, C., 1985. *Solar Dryers – Their Role in Post-Harvest Processing,* Commonwealth Science Council, London, foreword.

Brew-Hammond, A., 1994. 'Finance and Market For Electric Power In Ghana', *Science In Africa: Energy For Beyond 2000,* American Association For The Advancement Of Science, Washington, DC.

BTC (Botswana Technology Centre), 1992. 'Casamance Kiln Best for Charcoal Burning', *Boiling Point,* No. 29, ITDG/GTZ, December, p. 27.

BUN (Biomass Users Network), 1995a. 'Crop Waste Briquetting a Success', Biomass News, Vol. 1, No. 1, Causeway, Zimbabwe, p. 7.

BUN, 1995b. 'Community Biogas Project for Small Scale Dairy Farmers', Biomass News, Vol. 1, No. 1, Causeway, Zimbabwe, p. 6.

Buttle, personal communication, 1995.

Cabraal, A., Delasanta, D., Rosen, J., Nolfi, J. and Ulmer, R., 1981. *Market Assessment of Photovoltaic Power Systems for Agricultural Applications Worldwide,* NASA, Ohio and US Department of Energy, Washington, D.C., pp. 3-5, 5-1, 5-3, 5-4, 5-5 and B6–8.

Chitauro, 1993. 'Consequences of the Final Report of UNCED for the African Continent', *Energy in Africa Economic and Political Applications of Renewable Energies in Developing Countries,* Ponte Press.

Christensen, J.M. and McCall, M.K., 1994. *AFREPREN – African Energy Policy Research Network: An Evaluation,* SAREC, Stockholm.

Christensen, J.M, Allen, M.R. and Karekezi S., undated. *The New Energy Agenda: The Role of New and Renewable Sources of Energy,* United Nations Environment Program (UNEP), Nairobi, Kenya, p. 12.

COGEN, 1994a. 'Pre-Investment Studies: Indonesia, Philipines, Singapore, Thailand and Malaysia', *COGEN,* Special Issue, November, p. 4.

COGEN, 1994b. 'Energy from Wood: Malaysia', *COGEN,* Special Issue, September, p. 2.

Community Management and Training brochure, 1995.

CORECT/AID, 1988. *Renewable Energy for Agriculture and Health,* United States Agency for International Development (USAID), USA, p. 18.

Cowan, W.D., 1992. 'PV Power for Rural Areas of Southern Africa: Costs, Constraints and Opportunities for Institutional Support', *Journal of Energy R & D in Southern Africa,* February, p. 12.

Davey, C., 1988. 'Bellerive Foundation, Kenya (UNEP), Institutional Programme', *Boiling Point* No. 15, ITDG, Rugby, UK, p. 11.

Davidson, O. and Karekezi, S., 1993. 'A New Environmentally Sound Energy Strategy for the Development of Sub-Sahara Africa', *Energy Options for Africa – Environmentally Sustainable Alternatives,* eds Karekezi, S. and Mackenzie, G.A., ZED Books, London, pp. 12, 18.

Davidson, O., 1993. 'Opportunities for Efficiency in the Transport Sector', *Energy Options for Africa – Environmentally Sustainable Alternatives,* eds Karekezi, S. and Mackenzie, G.A., ZED Books, London.

Dayal, M., 1989. *Renewable Energy: Environment and Development*, Konark Publishers PVT Ltd., Delhi, pp. 90, 107, 113, 130 and 133.

De Laquil, P., Kearney, D., Geyer, M. and Diver, M., 1993. 'Solar Thermal Electric Technology', *Renewable Energy Sources for Fuels and Electricity*, eds Johansonn, T.B., Kelly, H., Reddy, A.K.N., Williams, R.H. and Burnham, L., Island Press, Washington, DC, pp. 214, 221–3 and 265–8.

Derrick, A., 1993. Solar Energy and Health: Economic and Environmental Considerations, Paper prepared for World solar Summit, July 1993, UNESCO, Paris. IT Power Ltd., Eversley, p. 2, 5, 6, 7.

Derrick, A., Barlow, R.W. and Dicko, M., 1994. 'Solar Power, the Power Guide: An International Catalogue of Small-Scale Energy Equipment', Hulscher, W. and Fraenkel, P. (eds), IT Publications, London pp. 23, 123–36.

Derrick, A., Barlow, R.W., McNeils, B. and Gregory, J.A., 1993. *Photovoltaics: A Market Overview*, James & James Science Publishers Ltd., London, pp. 6, 8, 10 and 13–15.

Derrick, A., Francis, C. and Bokalders, V. 1989. *Solar Photovoltaics Products*, Intermediate Technology Publications, London.

Derrick, A., Francis, C. and Bokalders, V., 1991. *Solar Photovoltaic Products: A Guide for Development Workers*, Intermediate Technology Publications, London, pp. 2, 11–12, 69.

Diab, R.D., 1988. 'The Wind Energy Resource in Southern Africa', *Renewable Energy Resources and Technology Development in South Africa*, Eberhard, A.A. (ed.), Elan Press, Cape Town, p. 167.

Diphaha, J. and Burton, R., 1993. 'Photovoltaics and Solar Water Heaters in Botswana', *Energy Options for Africa – Environmentally Sustainable Alternatives*, eds Karekezi, S. and Mackenzie, G.A., ZED Books, London, pp. 139–53.

DNV (Det Norskeveritas Industri Norge AS), 1992. *Renewable Energy Sources in Developing Countries: State of Art*, DNV, Norway, July, pp. 14, 30.

DOE/GTZ (Department of Energy, Lesotho/Deutsche Gesellschaft fur Technische Zusammenarbeit), 1988. Lesotho Energy Master Plan, Department of Energy, Lesotho.

Durand, M., 1987. 'Photovoltaic Refrigerators – The Zaire Experience', *Proceedings of Investing in Development Conference*, US Department of Energy, Louisiana, pp. VI-5 to VI-6.

Dutt, G.S. and Ravindranath, N.H., 1993. 'Bioenergy: Direct Applications in Cooking', *Renewable Energy: Sources for Fuels and Electricity*, eds Johansonn, T.B., Kelly, H., Reddy, A.K.N., Williams, R.H. and Burnham, L., Island Press, Washington, DC.

East African Standard, 1995. 'Business and Finance', Kenya.

Eberhard, A.A., 1982. 'Technological Change and Rural Development: A Case Study of Lesotho', Ph.D. thesis, University of Edinburgh.

Eberhard, A.A., 1988. 'The Potential of Renewable Energy Technologies in South Africa', *Renewable Energy Resources and Technology Development in Southern Africa*, eds Eberhard, A.A. and Williams, A., Energy Research Institute, University of Cape Town, South Africa, p. 17.

Eberhard, A.A. and Trollip, H., undated. *Background on the South African Energy System*, Energy for Development Research Centre, University of Cape Town, South Africa, p. 28.

Eckholm, E., 1975. *The Other Energy Crisis: Firewood*, Worldwatch Paper 1, Worldwatch Institute, Washington, DC.

EDI (Energy/Development International), 1986. *Improved Cookstoves in Kenya: Experiences of the Kenya Renewable Energy Development Project*, EDI, Washington, DC, August.

EIC (Energy Information Centre), undated. *Energy Information File: Solar Energy*, EIC, Victoria, p. 2.

Ellegard, A., 1990. 'Biogas', *Bioenergy and the Environment*, eds Janos Pasztor and Lars A. Kristoferson, Westview Press, San Francisco, pp. 164–6.

ERC (Energy Research Council), 1990. 'Introduction of Improved Stoves in Gezira Area', *Report of the Proceedings of the International Biomass Course*, KENGO, Nairobi, Kenya, June, p. 34.

Eriksen, S. H., 1995. 'Transport and GHG emissions', *A Climate for Development*, eds Okoth-Ogendo, H.W.O. and Ojwang, J.B., ACTS Press, Nairobi, pp. 134, 213.

ESKOM, 1992. *ESKOM In Perspective*, ESKOM, Johannesburg.

ESMAP (Energy Sector Management Assistance Programme), 1991. *SADC Regional Sector: Regional Capacity-Building Programme for Energy Surveys and Policy Analysis*, World Bank, Washington, DC.

Exell, R.H.B., 1990. 'Solar Timber Seasoning in Asia', *Energy and the Environment Into the 1990s*, Volume 2, International Solar Energy Society, Washington, DC, pp. 983–4.

FAO (Food and Agriculture Organization), 1990. *The Briquetting of Agricultural Waste for Fuel*, FAO, Roma, Italy.

Flavin, C. and Lenssen, N., 1990. *Beyond the Petroleum Age: Designing A Solar Economy*, World Watch Paper 100, Worldwatch Institute, Washington, DC, December.

FNI, 1994. *Final Report: Energy and Environmental Challenges in Southern Africa -Towards a Policy Research Agenda*, AFREPREN and FNI, Norway, p. 57.

Foley, Gerald, 1993. 'Renewable Energy in Third World Development Assistance – Learning From Experience', *Renewable Energy – Prospects For Implementation*, ed. Jackson, T., Butterworth-Heinemann, UK.

Forest Department, 1992. *Study on Pitsawing, Charcoal Production and Fuelwood Cutting*, Uganda Forest Department Report.

Fraenkel, P., Crick, F., Derrick, A. and Bokalders, V., 1993. *Windpumps – A Guide for Development Workers*, Stockholm Environment Institute (SEI), Stockholm, Sweden, pp.15, 21–2, 28, 44.

Fraenkel, P., Paish, O., Bokalders, V., Harvey, A., Brown, A. and Edwards, R., 1991. *Micro Hydro Power: A Guide to Development Workers*, IT Publications and SEI, London, pp. 4, 13, 54, 74–5, 79, 82–3, 86–7, 112.

Frandsen, S., 1991. *Wind Energy Development in the Light of Danish Experiences*, Riso National Laboratory, Roskilde, Denmark, pp.1, 2, 14.

FWD (Foundation for Woodstove Dissemination), 1992. Household Energy: Annual Report of the FWD (1990–1), Stove Note 7. FWD, Nairobi.

Gamser, M.S., 1987. *Briquetting and the Poor*, ITDG, November, pp. 1–3.

Garg, H.P., 1990. 'Status and Prospects of Solar Crop Drying', *Energy and the Environment Into the 1990s*, Vol. 2., Pergamon Press, Oxford, pp. 618–32.

Gate, 1984. *Charcoal: Small Scale Production and Use*, German Appropriate Technology Exchange in GTZ, Eschborn, Federal Republic of Germany.

Gay, J., Green, T. and Hall, D.O., 1993. *Renewable and Conservation Energy Technology in the Kingdom of Lesotho: A Socioeconomic Study of Constraints to Wider Adoption by Households and in Residential Buildings*, report prepared for the Department of Energy, Ministry of Water, Energy and Mining, Government of Lesotho, Sechaba Consultants, May, pp. 22–3, 25, 35, 37–8, 41.

GEF (Global Environmental Facility), 1993. Report by the Chairman to the May 1993 Participants' Meeting, GEF, Washington, DC, pp. 30–2.

Getta, M.O., 1990. *Household Energy in Ethiopia*, prepared for IGADD, August, p. 47.

Gielink, M.I., 1991. *Energy Profile: Malawi*, National Energy Council, Pretoria, South Africa.

Gielink, M.I. and Dutkiewicz, R.K., 1992. *Energy Profile: Mozambique*, National Energy Council, Pretoria, South Africa, p. 12.

Gipe, P., 1993. 'Wind Energy – Experience from California and Denmark', *Renewable Energy – Prospects for Implementation*, ed. Jackson, T., Stockholm Environment Institute, Sweden, pp. 75, 83.

Gitau, T., 1991. Personal communication.

Global Coalition for Africa, 1992. *African Social and Economic Trends: 1992 Annual Report*, Global Coalition for Africa Washington, DC, p. 6.

Glow, 1990. 'Charcoal in Japan', *Glow*, Vol 2, p. 11.

Glow, 1991. 'A Charcoal Tour: The Japanese Way, *Glow*, Vol 1, June, p. 7.

Goldemberg, J., Monaco, L.C. and Macedo, I.C., 1994. 'The Brazilian Alcohol Programme', *Renewable Energy: Sources for Fuels and Electricity*, eds Johansonn, T.B., Kelly, H., Reddy, A.K.N., Williams, R.H. and Burnham, L., Island Press, Washington, DC, pp. 842–62.

Gregory, J., 1994. 'Financing Mechanisms for Solar Energy Technologies', paper prepared for the first Renewable Energy Technologies in Eastern and Southern Africa Workshop, 30 May–1 June 1994, Naivasha, Kenya, AFREPREN/FWD-SEI, Nairobi, pp. 7, 11–12, 17, 19, 35.

Gregory, J. and McNeils, B., 1993. 'The Growing Role of Solar Electric Power Production in Developing Countries', paper prepared for Power Generation Technology, IT Power Ltd, London, p. 1.

GTZ, 1991. Rural Energy Supply, GTZ, Energy Division, Eschborn.

GTZ, 1994. *Micro and Macro-economic Benefits of Household Energy Conservation Measures in Rural Areas of Kenya*, GTZ, Eschborn, July, p. 9.

GTZ, undated. *Renewable Energy: Solar Home Systems*, GTZ, Eschborn, p. 5.

GTZ/SEP (Deutsche Gesellschaft fur Technische Zusammenarbeit/ Special Energy Programme), 1987. *Dissemination of Biogas Plants In the Rural Areas of Kenya*, SEP, Kenya.

Guichard, A., 1994. 'Tests in Antarctic Conditions', *RERIC News*, Vol. 17, No. 4, RERIC, Bangkok, Thailand, p.3.

Gullberg, M., 1994. *Human Resource Development and Retention in the Context of Renewable Energy Technologies*, AFREPREN, Nairobi, Kenya, pp. 20–1, 24, 25.

Guymont, F., 1988. *The Ampefy Hydropower for Agroprocessing Project – An Energy for Africa Sub-Project*, USA, pp. 22, 31, 59, 71, 74.

Haile L. Tebicke and Hailu G. Mariam, 1990. 'A Case Study of Small Hydro and Grid Extension for Rural Electrification Alternatives and Complementarities', *African Energy: Issues in Planning and Practice*, AFREPREN in association with Zed Books, London, pp. 57–63.

Hall, D.O., 1993a. ' Biomass Energy', *Renewable Energy: Prospects for Implementation*, ed. Jackson, T., Stockholm Environment Institute, Stockholm.

Hall, D.O., 1993b. 'Appraisal of Effectiveness of Recent Activities on Renewable

Energy Technologies in sub-Saharan Africa', *Recent Experiences in Research and Development and Dissemination of Renewable Energy Technologies in Sub-Saharan Africa*, eds Kimani, M.J. and E. Naumann, KENGO, Nairobi, p. 13.

Hall, D.O. and de Groot, 1987. *Biomass for Fuel and Food – A Parallel Necessity*, Plenum Press, USA.

Hall, D.O., Rosillo-Cale, F., Williams, R. H. and Woods, J., 1993. 'Biomass for Energy, Supply Prospects', *Renewable Energy Sources for Fuels and Electricity*, eds Johansonn, T.B., Kelly, H., Reddy, A.K.N., Williams, R.H. and Burnham, L., Island Press, Washington, DC.

Halliday, D., 1987. 'Photovoltaics and Universal Child Immunization', *Presentations of the Photovoltaics: Investing in Development Conference*, pp. VI, 35–8.

Hangzhou International Centre on Small Hydro Power (HIC), 1995. *Special issue of International Network on Small Hydro Power (IN-SHP)*, Hangzhou Regional Centre for Small Hydro Power, p. 15.

Hankins, M.J., 1987. *Renewable Energy In Kenya*, Motif Creative Arts Ltd, Nairobi, Kenya, pp. 7, 40, 42, 61, 84–6, 90–1, 98, 104–6.

Hankins, M.J., 1989. *Renewable Energy in Kenya*. Motif Creative Arts Ltd, Nairobi.

Hankins M.J., 1992. 'A Profile of the Kenya Solar Electric Industry', *Proceedings of the Regional Solar Electric Training and Awareness Workshop*, ed. M.J. Kimani, African Development Foundation, Nairobi, pp. 91–8.

Hankins, M.J., 1993. *Solar Rural Electrification in the Developing World*, Solar Electric Light Fund, Washington, DC, pp. 17, 33, 37, 42, 64–5, 67–8, 70.

Hankins, M.J., 1994. *Solar Rural Electrification in the Developing Countries. Case Study: Kenya*, Solar Electric Light Fund, Washington, DC, p. 37.

Hankins, M.J., 1995. *Solar Electric Systems for Africa: A Guide for Planning and Installing Solar Electric Systems In Rural Africa*, Agrotech and Commonwealth Science Council.

Hankins, M.J., personal communication.

Hankins, M.J. and Bess, 1993. *Photovoltaic Sector. Status and Policy Review in Kenya*. World Bank, Kenya.

Hassan, W., 1992. 'Sudan National Energy Research Council and Renewable Energy Technologies', *Energy For Rural Development*, eds Bhagavan, M.R. and Karekezi, S., AFREPREN in association with Zed Books, London, pp. 119–21.

Heber, G., Schafer, G. and Teplitz, W., 1985. *Biofuels for Developing Countries: Promising Strategy or Dead End?*, Deutsche Gesellschaft fur Zusammenarbeit (GTZ), Eschborn.

Hibajene, S.H., 1994. *Assessment of Earth Kiln Charcoal Production Technology*, Republic of Zambia, Ministry of Energy and Water Development, Department of Energy, SEI Energy, Environment and Development Series No. 39, SEI and SIDA, pp. i, 1, 4, 14–24, 27.

Hibajene, S.H., 1995. 'The Zambia Charcoal Industry', *Boiling Point*, No. 35 , ITDG/GTZ, January, pp. 7–8.

Hibajene, S.H. and Chidumayo, E.N., 1993. *Charcoal Industry Workshop, Policy and Management: Challenges for the Future*, Ministry of Energy and Water Development SEI and SIDA, pp. 15, 30, 36.

Himberg, H.A., 1987. 'Financing Overseas Photovoltaic Investments in Developing Countries', *Presentations of the Photovoltaic Investing in Development Conference*, US Department of Energy, New Orleans, p. VIII-29.

Hirsch, S., 1994. 'Commentary on Human Resources Development and Training in the African Energy Sector', *Science in Africa – Energy for the Advancement of Science*, Washington DC, p. 69.

Holland, R., 1986. *Micro Hydro Electric Power: Technical Papers 1*, ITDG, Rugby, pp. v, 10.

Hollingdale, A.C., Krishna, R. and Robinson, A.P., 1991. *Charcoal Production: A Handbook*, Commonwealth Science Council, Natural Resources Institute, Energy Programme, Technical Paper No. 268, pp. 16, 32–3, 44.

Home Power Magazine, 1993. 'A Kitchen in the Sun', *Home Power*, No. 37, October/November, Home Power, Inc., Ashland, p. 22.

Hong, C.J., 1995. 'Air Pollution and its Challenge in China: Response Options for the Household Energy Sector', Shangai Medical University, Shangai – paper prepared for the Indoor Air Pollution Preparatory Meeting, 25 February–1 March 1995, Naivasha, Kenya, pp. 17–18.

Hos, J.J. and Groeneveld, M.J., 1987. 'Biomass Gasification', *Biomass: Regenerable Energy*, eds Hall, D.O. and Overend, R.P., John Wiley & Sons, Chichester, p. 237.

Hosier, R., 1993. 'Charcoal Production and Environmental Degradation', *Energy Policy Special Issue: Urban Energy and Environment in Africa*, Vol 21, No. 5, eds Hosier, R., Mwandosya, M.I., Luhanga, M.L., May, p. 491.

Hydronet, 1994. 'Micro Hydropower Network', *Hydronet*, 2/94, 3/94.

IBRD (International Bank of Reconstruction and Development), 1993. *The Wind Energy Sector in Kenya Study Report*, Kruger Consult, September, pp. 2, 12–14.

IFSC (International Forest Science Consultancy), 1986. *The Use of Wood by the Tobacco Industry in Kenya*, IFSC, p.1.

IIED (International Institute for Environment and Development), 1981. *14 Sources of New and Renewable Energy*, IIED, London, p. 5.

INforSE (International Network for Sustainable Energy), 1994. 'Wind Energy in Cape Verde: Promising Prospects', *Sustainable Energy News*, No. 5, INforSE, Denmark, p. 13.

Inversin, A.R., 1986. *Micro Hydro Power Source Book: A Practical Guide to Design and Implementation in Developing Countries*, NRECA, Washington, DC, pp. 1–3, 225–6, 248.

ISES (International Solar Energy Society), 1994. 'An Ecological Country Club', *Sun World*, Vol. 18, No. 3, September, ISES, Victoria, pp. 16–17.

IT Power, 1987. *Global Wind Pump Evaluation Programme – Kenya*, IT Power Ltd, Rugby, executive summary, pp. 74, 97–9.

IT Power, 1988. *Global Wind Pump Evaluation Programme – Botswana*, IT Power Ltd, Rugby.

ITDG/GTZ (Intermediate Technology and Development Group/Deutsche Gesellschaft fur Technische Zusammenarbeit), 1992. 'Stove Profile: Maendeleo', *Boiling Point*, No. 28 , ITDG/GTZ, August, p. 37.

ITDG, 1994. *The Power Guide – An International Catalogue of Small Scale Energy Equipment*, ITDG and University of Twente, London, p. 80.

Jackson, T., ed. 1993. *Renewable Energy: Prospects for Implementation*, SEI, Oxford, p. 95.

Jihrad, 1990. *Power Sector Innovation in Developing Countries: Implementing Multi-faceted Solutions*, Annual Review Inc. California.

Jimoh, Y.A., 1986. 'Solar Water Distillation Plant', *Renewable Energy Development in Africa*, Vol. 2, Commonwealth Science Council, London, pp. 168–9.

Johansson, T.B., Kelly, H., Reddy, A.K.N., Williams, R.H. and Burnham, L., eds, 1993. *Renewable Energy: Sources for Fuel and Electricity,* Island Press, Washington DC, pp. 4, 73, 83–4, 86–7, 121, 172–4.

Joseph, S. and Walubengo, D. 1988. *Wood Energy in Kenya Institutions – A Summary of Result Findings,* KENGO, Nairobi.

Kaale, B.K., 1990. 'Traditional Fuels', Bioenergy and the Environment, Pasztor J. and L.A. Kristoferson (eds.), Westview Press, San Francisco, p. 33.

Kaale, B.K., 1991. 'SADCC Traditional Fuel Data', *SADCC Energy Bulletin,* Vol. VIII, No. 23, TAU/SADCC Energy, Luanda.

Kafumba, C.R., 1994a. 'The Status of Renewable Energy Technologies In Malawi', paper presented during the first Regional AFREPREN Workshop On Renewable Energy Technology Dissemination, Naivasha, Kenya, 30 May–1 June, AFREPREN, Nairobi, pp. 20, 34–5, 41–2, 49, 51, 60.

Kafumba, C.R, 1994b. Personal communication.

Kammen, D.N., 1995. 'Cookstoves for the Developing World', *Scientific American,* July, USA, p. 73.

Kammen, D. M. and Kammen, A., 1993. 'Energy Food Preparation and Health Care in Africa: The Role of Technology, Education and Resource Management', *African Technology Forum,* February/March.

Kammen D. M., Smith, K. R., Nditu, M. and Joshi. V., 1994. *Energy, Health Management and Environmental Policy: Case Studies from Sub-Saharan Africa.*

Kanetsi, B. and Phuroe, T., 1994. *Renewable Energy Technologies Dissemination in Lesotho,* AFREPREN, Nairobi, pp. 8, 16–24, Appendix A.

Karekezi, S., 1987. 'Burundi Improved Charcoal Stoves', *Boiling Point,* No. 13, ITDG/GTZ, August, pp. 20–21.

Karekezi, S., 1988a. *Renewable Energy Technologies In Africa,* AFREPREN Working Paper Series, AFREPREN, Nairobi, pp. 51, 56, 58.

Karekezi, S., 1988b. *Review of Mature Renewable Energy Technologies in Sub-Saharan Africa,* SAREC/IDRC Research Report, p. 24.

Karekezi, S., 1988c. *Tackling the Wood Energy Challenge in Somalia,* KENGO Wood Energy Series, KENGO and Motif Creative Arts, Nairobi, Kenya.

Karekezi, S., 1988d. *Surviving the Wood Energy Crisis in Lesotho.* Kenya Energy and Environment Organizations, Nairobi, Kenya.

Karekezi, S., 1989a. *The Ampefy Hydropower for Agro Processing Project: An Energy Initiative for Africa (EIA),* Sub-Project 698-0424, REDSO/ ESA, Madagascar.

Karekezi, S., 1989b. *Project Assistance Completion Report (PACR) of Madagascar Sub-Project,* US Government Memorandum, USA, p. 1.

Karekezi, S. 1990. Using Surveys to Monitor Stove Programmes. *Stove Notes 1,* FWD and ACTS Press, Nairobi.

Karekezi, S., 1991. *The Role of a Stove Information Network in Addressing Indoor Air Pollution – An African Perspective.*

Karekezi, S., 1992a. 'African Energy Research Networks: Impact on Policy Formulation and Implementation', *International Experience in Energy Policy Research and Planning,* eds Eberhard, A. and Theron, P., Elan Press and Energy Research Institute, University of Cape Town, pp. 92–120.

Karekezi, S., 1992b. 'Energy Technology Options For Rural and Agricultural Development: The Major Issues', *Energy for Rural Development,* eds Bhagavan, M. R. and Karekezi S., Zed Books, London, pp. 48, 52, 58.

Karekezi, S., 1993a. 'Rural and Decentralized Options – Moving to Wider Scale

Dissemination', *Recent Experiences in Research, Development and Dissemination of Renewable Energy Technologies in Sub- Saharan Africa*, eds Kimani, M.J. and Naumann, E., seminar proceedings, KENGO International Outreach Department and Renewable Energy Group, University of Oldenburg, pp. 47–8.

Karekezi, S., 1993b. 'Improved Charcoal Production And Fuel Efficient Stoves', *Stove Notes*, 8, FWD and Motif Creative Arts, Nairobi, Kenya, pp. 11, 18, 27–9, 32, 34, 37, 52–3, 58–9.

Karekezi, S., 1994a. 'Organization and Management: Small Scale Biomass Energy Technologies in Eastern and Southern Africa', paper presented during the first Regional AFREPREN Workshop On Renewable Energy Technology Dissemination, Naivasha, 30 May–1 June, AFREPREN, Nairobi, pp. 409, 411, 415.

Karekezi, S., 1994b. *Photovoltaics and Solar Water Heaters in Kenya*, AFREPREN RETs Research Project Final Report, AFREPREN, Nairobi, pp. 14, 17, 59, 85, 88, 90, 92–6.

Karekezi, S., 1994c. *Networks as Mechanisms for Capacity Building: A Comparative Assessment of Regional Energy Networks in sub-Saharan Africa*, SEI-AFREPREN/FWD, Nairobi, Kenya, March, p. 6.

Karekezi, S., 1994d. 'Dissemination of Renewable Energy Technologies In sub-Saharan Africa', *Annual Review Energy Environment*, pp. 393, 398, 409, 411, 413.

Karekezi, S., 1994e. 'Generic Skills of Management and Organization: The Energy Sector in Africa as a Case Study', paper prepared for the International Seminar on Development Aid Policy Approaches to New Generic Technologies, Hasselbacken, Stockholm, 20–21 April.

Karekezi, S., 1994f. 'Household Energy Initiative for a Sustainable Energy Future', *Stove Notes*, 10, FWD, Nairobi.

Karekezi, S. 1995. *Photovoltaics and Solar Water Heaters in Kenya*. Working Paper No. 50, Nairobi.

Karekezi, S. 1996. *Solar Energy for Development in Sub-Saharan Africa*, AFREPREN/FWD, Nairobi.

Karekezi, S. and Karottki, R., 1989. *A Contribution to the Draft Paper on the Role of New & Renewable Sources of Energy from the Perspective of the Environmental Problems Associated with Current Patterns of Energy Use and Consumption*, United Nations Environment Programme, Nairobi, Kenya, July, pp. 13, 15.

Karekezi, S. and Mackenzie, G.A., eds, 1993. *Energy Options for Africa: Environmentally Sustainable Alternatives*, Zed Books, Riso, Denmark, p. 87.

Karekezi, S. and Majoro, L., 1994. *Energy-related Climate Change Responses In The Transport Sector of Eastern Africa: Eastern Africa Regional Report*, Climate and Africa Project, SEI/ACTS, Nairobi.

Karekezi, S. and Masakhwe, K., 1991. *Key Factors for the Successful Dissemination of Renewable Energy Technologies*, AFREPREN, Nairobi, pp. 31–2, 44–5, 47, 49, 51.

Karekezi, S. and Murimi, N., 1994a. *Institutional Stove: A Global Guide*, FWD Working Paper No. 22, pp. 5–7.

Karekezi, S. and Murimi, N., 1994b. *Wood and Charcoal: Household Fuels for Developing Countries*, FAO/FWD Document on Household Energy, 3rd Draft, September, p. 14.

Karekezi, S. and Turyareeba, P., 1994. 'Woodstove Dissemination in East Africa: A Review', *Energy for Sustainable Development Journal*, pp. 5–6, 10.

Karekezi, S. and Turyareeba, P., 1995. *Renewable Energy Technologies: Mini and*

Micro Hydro Power in Eastern and Southern Africa, AFREPREN, Nairobi, Kenya, pp. 2, 6–8.

Karekezi, S. and Walubengo, D., 1989. *Household Stoves in Kenya – the Case of the Ceramic Jiko,* KENGO, Nairobi, Kenya.

Karekezi, S., Ewagata E., Bii, S. and Kibua, K. 1995. *Renewable Energy Technologies In Kenya: A Study on The Maendeleo Stoves and Ethanol Plant,* SEI/AFREPREN, Nairobi.

Karekezi, S., Majoro, L. and Ewagata, E., 1994. 'Renewable Energy Technologies in Kenya', paper prepared for the first Regional RETs Workshop, 30 May–1 June 1994, Naivasha, Kenya, SEI-AFREPREN/FWD, Nairobi, pp. 7–11, 16, 18, 23.

Karekezi, S., Majoro, L. and Ranja, T., 1994. *Renewable Energy Technologies Dissemination in Burundi,* AFREPREN, Nairobi, p. 8.

Karekezi, S., Turyareeba, P. and Ewagata, E., 1994. *Renewable Energy Training in Kenya: The Case of Solar Photovoltaics,* AFREPREN, Nairobi, p. 8.

Karekezi, S., Turyareeba P. and Mbuuri, M., 1994. *Photovoltaic and solar water heaters in Kenya,* AFREPREN, Nairobi, Kenya, pp. 75–80, 85, 92–6.

Karekezi, S., Turyareeba, P. and Musumba, C., 1995. 'Household Energy, Indoor Air Pollution and the Impact on Health in Africa', paper prepared for the Preparatory Meeting on Indoor Air Pollution, 26 February–1 March, Naivasha, Kenya, AFREPREN, Nairobi, Kenya, pp. 2, 5–7, 44.

Katihabwa, J., 1993. *The Socioeconomic and Environmental Implications of Diffusion of Photovoltaic Technology and Improved Cookstoves in Burundi,* AFREPREN, Renewable Energy Technologies (RETs) Group Interim Report, Nairobi, Kenya.

Katihabwa, J., 1994. 'Renewable Energy Technologies Dissemination in Burundi', paper prepared for the first Regional RETs Workshop, 30 May–1 June 1994, Naivasha, Kenya, SEI-AFREPREN/FWD, Nairobi, pp. 8, 24, 28.

Katus, T., 1987. 'Existing Public Sector Financing Mechanisms', *Proceedings of Investing in Development Conference,* US Department of Energy, Louisiana, pp. VIII-41–VIII-46.

Katyega, M.J.J., 1994. Personal communication.

KENGO (Kenya Energy and Environment Organization), 1987. *A Summary of Briquettes as a Household Fuel,* results of a survey carried out by KENGO in Nakuru, Kenya, June–July, pp. 1–2.

KENGO, 1991. *How to Make and Use the KCJ,* KENGO/Regional Wood Energy Programme for Africa (RWEPA), Nairobi.

Kenya Engineer, 1994. 'Two Wind Turbines Installed at Ngong', *Kenya Engineer,* Nairobi, p. 13.

Kimani, M.J., 1993. *Field Visit Report: Securicor Solar Services Ltd,* AFREPREN/FWD, Nairobi.

Kimani, M. J. and Naumann, E., eds, 1993. *Recent Experiences in Research, Development and Dissemination of Renewable Energy Technologies in Sub-Saharan Africa,* seminar proceedings, International Outreach Department and Renewable Energy Group, University of Oldenburg, pp.15–16, 60.

Kioko, J.M., 1993. 'Photovoltaic Technology: The Case of Kenya', *Recent Experiences in Research, Development and Dissemination of Renewable Energy Technologies in Sub-Saharan Africa,* eds Kimani M.J. and E. Naumann, KENGO, pp. 84–7.

Kismul, H. et al., 1990. *Mid-Term Evaluation Report: Fuel Efficient Stove Project – PN 16,* Care International, Sudan.

Kjellström, B., 1990. 'Producer Gas', *Bioenergy and the Environment*, eds Pasztor, J. and Kristoferson, L.A., Westview Press, San Francisco.

Kjellström, B., 1994. 'Institutional Development for Large Scale Biomass Energy Technologies: The Swedish Experience and Its Relevance to Africa', paper presented during the first Regional AFREPREN Workshop On Renewable Energy Technology Dissemination, Naivasha, Kenya, May 30–1 June, 1994, AFREPREN, Nairobi, pp. 9, 11.

Klingshirn, A., 1992. *Improved Cookstove as a Focal Point for Development Process*, abbreviated version of an impact study of the Women and Energy Project Kenya, Eschborn, GTZ/GATE.

Knyazeva, V.V., 1990. 'Wind Energy Activities of The Soviet Union', *Windirections*, Vol. X, No. 1, European Wind Energy Associations, United Kingdom, p. 12.

Kozloff, K., (undated). *Achieving The Potential for Achieving Renewable Electricity*, World Resource Institute, Washington, DC.

Kozloff, K. and Shobowale, O., 1994. *Rethinking Development Assistance for Renewable Electricity*, World Resource Institute, Washington, DC, p. 37.

Kristoferson, L.A. and Bokalders, V., 1987. *Renewable Energy Technologies: Their Applications in Developing Countries*, Pergamon Press, Oxford, pp. 88–100.

Kristoferson, L.A., Bokalders, V. and Newham, M., 1984. *Renewable Energy for Developing Countries: A Review, Vol. D: Solar, Wind, Hydro, etc.*, Beijer Institute, Stockholm, May, p. 103.

Kruger Consult, 1993. *The Wind Energy Sector in Kenya*, study report, International Bank for Reconstruction and Development (IBRD), USA.

Krugmann, H., 1987. *Review of Issues and Research Relating to Improved Cookstoves*, International Development Research Centre (IDRC), Ottawa.

Kuhnke, K., Reuber, M. and Schwefel, D., 1990. *Solar Cookers in the Developing World*, Friedr. Viewef & Sohn, Braunschweig, pp. 38, 46, 55, 60 and 116.

Kumar, S.K. and Hotchkiss D., 1988. 'Fuel Collection and Nutrition in Nepal', *Boiling Point*, No. 27, ITDG, Rugby.

Kyalo, J.M., 1992. 'Firm's Efforts Praised', *Daily Nation*, Nairobi.

Larson, E. 1987. *Wind Resources in Botswana* (Draft Final Report). Ministry of Mineral Resources and Water Affairs.

Larson, E. 1991. *A Developing Country Oriented Overview of Technologies and Costs of Converting Biomass Feedstocks into Gases, Liquids and Electricity*, Princeton University Centre for Energy and Environment Studies, Report No. 266, Princeton University.

Le Houerou *et al.*, 1993. *Agro-Bioclimatic Classifications of Africa*, FAO Agrometeorology Series, Working Paper No. 6. FAO, Rome.

Liebard, A. and Amado, D., 1993. '11 Years Experience in Photovoltaic Pumping – India, Nepal, Mali – Social and Economic Results', *Energy in Africa: Economic and Political Initiatives for Application of Renewable Energies in Developing Countries*, Ponte Press, Bochum, p. 127.

Linden, E., 1993. *Namibia's Energy Sector – A Country Review*, Namibia's Economic Policy Research Unit (NEPRU), Namibia, pp. 17, 19.

Little, R.G., 1987. 'Financing of Photovoltaic Investments', *Presentations of the Photovoltaic: Investing in Development Conference*, US Department of Energy, New Orleans, p. VIII-2.

Little, R.G., 1993. *Petroleum Market Structure and Pricing Study*. Ministry of Energy, Kenya.

Lopes, H. and Macamo, S., 1994. 'RETs Dissemination in Mozambique', paper presented during the first Regional AFREPREN Workshop On Renewable Energy Technology Dissemination, Naivasha, Kenya, 30 May–1 June 1994, AFREPREN, Nairobi, p. 15.

Makau, D. and Obura, B., 1991. 'Briquetting of Biomass Wastes', *Proceedings of the 1990 International Biomass Course,* ed. Susan Matindi, KENGO, Nairobi.

Manawanyika, G., 1992. 'Biogas Application for Rural Development in Zimbabwe', *Proceedings of 2nd World Renewable Energy Congress,* September, Reading, pp. 13–18.

Mandishona, G., 1994. 'The Zimbabwe UNDP-GEF PV Solar Project', paper presented at the Workshop on The Implementation of Rural Decentralized Electrification Programmes, Paris, 19–22 September, p. 1.

Martinez, M., 1992. 'What's New Under the Sun', *Ceres – The FAO Review,* No. 133 (Vol. 24, No.1) January–February, FAO, Rome., pp. 33–7.

Masakhwe, J.K., 1993. 'The Private Sector In The Solar Industry: The Case Of Kenya', *Recent Experiences in Renewable Energy Technologies in Sub-Sahara Africa,* eds Kimani, M.J. and Naumann E., KENGO, Nairobi, pp. 65–6, 69.

Matete, K., 1994. Personal communication.

Mbewe, D.J., 1990. 'Effectiveness of Research and Policy on Rural Energy Technology and Applications', *Africa Energy Policies: Issues in Planning and Practice,* AFREPREN in association with Zed Books, London, pp. 8, 34.

Mbewe, D.J., 1994. *Research on the Economic and Environmental Implication of Diffusion of the Photovoltaics Technology in the Households and Agriculture,* Ministry of Energy and Water Development, Lusaka, pp. 22, 27–8.

Mbewe, A., Mariam, G.H., Ramasedi, B., Khalema, L. and Ahmed, I.A., 1992. *Rural Electrification in Africa,* ed. Ranganathan, V., AFREPREN in association with Zed Books, Gaborone and London, pp. 72, 78, 82, 86, 104, 108, 138, 173.

Mbuuri, M., 1993. *GTZ Special Energy Programme: Field Report,* AFREPREN, Nairobi.

McGraw-Hill, 1984, *Energy Data Conversion Handbook. How to Combine and Compare International Energy Data.* Macmillan, London, p. 47.

McChesney, I., 1989. 'Briquettes – Potential Impact on Urban Poor', *Boiling Point,* Special Edition, pp. 5–6.

Meel, J. van and Smulders, P., 1989. *Wind Pumping – A Handbook,* IBRD/World Bank, Washington, DC, pp. 25, 27.

Meicherczyk, R., 1992. 'Advantages of Small Scale Charcoal Production', *Gate Topics,* 1/92, pp. 8–9.

Ministry of Water, Energy, and Minerals, 1993. *Statement by the Principal Secretary, Ministry of Water Energy and Minerals, Tanzania,* presented at the Conference on Medium and Large Biogas Plants, 29 November–4 December.

Mohapeloa, L. and Lebesa, M. 1989. *The Effectiveness of Foreign Technical Assistance in Manpower Development in Lesotho's Energy Projects,* AFREPREN, Nairobi, p. 5.

Moreira, J.R. and Poole, A.D., 1993. 'Co-generation Technologies in Brazil: Potential and Limitations', paper prepared for the Second Colloquium on Renewable Energies for Environment and Development, Castel Gandolfo, Italy, p. 1.

Moshi, B.E., 1993. *Statement Prepared for the Conference on Medium and Large Scale Biogas Plants,* Ministry of Water, Energy and Minerals.

Mosimanyane, M.T., 1994. 'Renewable Energy Technologies in Botswana', paper presented during the first Regional AFREPREN Workshop On Renewable Energy Technology Dissemination, Naivasha, Kenya, 30 May–1 June,

AFREPREN, Nairobi, pp. 8, 13–14, 16, 36.

Mosimanyane, M.T., Zhou, P.P and Kgathi, D.L., 1995. *Renewable Energy Technologies in Botswana – The Case of Wind Energy for Water Pumping,* SEI/AFREPREN/FWD, Draft Report, pp. 2, 12, 15–16, 24, 26–8, 31.

Murgel, G., 1992. *Ethanol,* Sao Paulo Environmental Protection Agency.

Muriithi, J., 1995. 'Women and Energy Project – Kenya An Impact Study', *Boiling Point,* No. 35 , ITDG/GTZ, January, pp. 7–8.

Muruli, B.I., 1992. 'Facts and Figures', *Standard* newspaper, Nairobi.

Musa, 1993. 'The Role of the African Development Bank In Energy Development' *Energy Options for Africa,* eds Karekezi, S. and Mackenzie, G., Zed Books, London.

Mwandosya, M.J., 1990. *Energy: Research, Development and Extension Projects in Tanzania,* IDRC, Canada, p. 78.

Mwandosya, M.J. and Luhanga, M.L.P., 1983. *Energy Resources Flow and End Use in Tanzania,* Dar es Salaam University Press, Tanzania, pp. 67, 109–12.

Mwandosya, M.J. and Luhanga, M.L.P., 1993. *Stockholm Environment Institute Special Issue Urban Energy and Environment,* SEI, Stockholm, Sweden, p.449.

Mwangi, S., 1993. *Renewable Sources of Energy in Kenya, A Meteorological Overview,* Kenya Meteorological Department, Nairobi, Kenya.

Mwove, N. M., 1994. *Renewable Energy Technologies and Development Policies in Kenya,* ACTS, Nairobi, Kenya (no pagination).

Nachula, S.R., 1989. 'The Zambia Charcoal Stove Project', *Report of the Proceedings of the International Biomass Course,* KENGO, Nairobi, Kenya, June, p. 16.

Nairobi University, 1992. *Syllabus for B.Sc. Mechanical Engineering 1992/93,* Department of Mechanical Engineering, University of Nairobi, pp. 46–7.

Naumann, E., 1993. 'The Renewable Energy Education Programme in Oldenburg', *The Dissemination of Renewable Energy Technologies in Sub-Saharan Africa,* eds Muiruri, K. and Naumann, E., Nairobi, pp. 121–4, 128.

Ndyakira, A., 1992. 'Charcoal Briquettes Output Starts', *New Vision,* December, Kampala, p. 10.

New Energy Foundation, 1981. *Solar Heating, Cooling and Hot Water Supply Systems,* Three 'I' Publications Ltd., Tokyo, p. 13.

News at Seven, 1994. *Cities: Exploring Financing Options for Improvements,* Energy Efficiency Centre, Prague, p. 1.

Nieuwenhout, F.D.J., 1991. *Status and Potential of Photovoltaic (PV) Systems in Rwanda,* Energy Research Foundation, Petten, pp. 6–7.

Ntholi, M., 1991. *Renewable Energy Technologies (RETs) Research Project: Improved Cookstoves and Biogas in Lesotho,* AFREPREN RETs Theme Group Interim Report, pp. 14–15.

Nuclear Forum, 1992. 'Wind Power: An Expensive Deal', *RERIC News,* Vol. 15, No. 3, RERIC, Bangkok, p. 7.

Nyoike, P.M. and Okech, B.A, 1992. 'Energy Management In Manufacturing Industry – The Case of Kenya', *Energy Management In Africa,* eds Bhagavan M.R. and Karekezi S., AFREPREN in association with Zed Books, London, p. 118.

Nyoike, P. and Okech, B., 1993. *A Study of Appropriate and Performance of Energy Sector Institutions in Kenya,* Interim Report, AFREPREN, pp. 40, 58.

O'Keefe, P, Raskin, P. and Bernow, S., 1984. *Energy, Environment and Development in Africa 1 – Energy and Development in Kenya: Opportunities and Constraints,* Beijer Institute and the Scandinavian Institute, Sweden.

ODA (Overseas Development Agency), 1991. 'More Charcoal by Traditional

Methods', *Boiling Point*, No. 24, ITDG/GTZ, April, pp. 10–11.

Oguya, Caleb, 1995. Personal Communication, Technical Manager, ACFC, Muhoroni, Kenya.

Okoth-Ogendo, H. and Ojwang, J.B., eds, 1995. *A Climate For Development: Climate Change Options for Africa*, ACTS, Nairobi.

Okwatch, D., 1994. 'Molasses Put to Good Use', *Standard* newspaper, Nairobi.

Omondi, R., 1991. 'Molasses – Major Raw Material', *Kenya Times*, Nairobi.

Onaji, P.B. and Siemons, R.V., 1993. 'Production of Charcoal Briquettes from Cotton Stalk in Malawi: Methodology for Feasibility Study using Experiences in Sudan', *Biomass and Bioenergy*, Vol. 4, No. 3, eds Coombs, J. Hall,D.O., Overend, R.P. and Smith, W.H., p. 199.

Open University, 1994. *T521 Renewable Energy File 1 A Resource Pack for Tertiary Education*, Open University, pp. 6-4–6-30.

Othieno, H., 1992. 'Alternative Energy Resources: A Kenyan Perspective', *Energy Sources*, Vol. 14, Taylor and Francis, UK, p. 409.

Othieno, H., 1993. 'Research And Development In Renewable Energy Technology In Sub-Saharan Africa', *Recent Experiences in Research and Development and Dissemination of Renewable Energy Technologies in Sub-Saharan Africa*, eds Kimani, M.J. and E. Naumann, KENGO, Nairobi, pp. 5–6.

Otiti, T., 1991. 'Improved Stoves in Tanzania', *Stoves Notes*, 6, FWD and ACTS Press, Nairobi, Kenya.

Otiti, T., 1992. 'Tanzanian Stoves', *Boiling Point*, No. 29, ITDG/GTZ, December, p. 8.

Otiti, T., 1993. 'Renewable Energy Technologies in Use in Sub-Saharan Africa: The Case of Uganda', paper prepared for the African Regional Energy and Environment Policy Seminar, 17–18 March, Nairobi, Kenya.

Pandey, M.R., Boleij, J.S.M., Smith, K.R., Wafula, E.M., 1989. 'Indoor Air Pollution in Developing Countries and Acute Respiratory Infection in Children', *Lancet*, 25 February.

Pasztor, J. and Kristoferson, L.A., 1990. 'Bioenergy and the Environment – The Challenge', *Bioenergy and the Environment*, Westview Press, San Francisco, p. 17.

Peters, R. and Kijek, F., 1992. *Study on the NRSE Pricing in the SADCC Region*, Southern African Development Coordination Conference, Luanda, pp. 10, 14, 19, 34, 39, 44, 46.

Phuroe, T. and Mathaha, P., 1995. *Draft Renewable Energy Technologies Dissemination in Lesotho*, AFREPREN, Lesotho, pp. 8, 15–16, 19–20, 24.

Plas, R., 1993. *Identification of Household and Renewable Energy Activities – Proposed Energy I Project*, World Bank Aid Memoirs, Annex 4.

Power Guide, 1994. *An International Catalogue of Small Scale Energy*, IT Publications, pp. 123–4, 126, 131–2, 173.

Prasad, K.K., 1985. 'Stove Design for Improved Dissemination', *Woodstove Dissemination – Proceedings of the Conference*, Wolfheze, The Netherlands, ed. R. Clarke, IT Publications, London, p. 59.

Prasad, K.K. and Verhaart, P. 1983. *Wood Heat for Cooking*, Indian Academy of Sciences, Bangalore.

Rabar, J.A., 1992. *Biomass Energy Technologies for Small Industries and Institutions*, Regional Training Course on Biomass Energy Development – Training Guide 8 to 20, KENGO/RWEPA, Nairobi and Nakuru, pp. 1–3.

Ramachandra, T.V., 1994. 'Getting into Hot, Hot Water', *Glow*, Vol. 14, December,

p. 9.

Ramakrishna, J., 1995a. *Indoor Air Pollution – Challenges and Research Activities In India – Response Options for the Household Energy Sector*, paper prepared for the Indoor Air Pollution Preparatory Meeting, 25 February–1 March, Naivasha, Kenya, p. 7.

Ramakrishna, J., 1995b. Personal communication.

Ramasedi, B.R., 1992. 'Rural Electrification in Botswana', *Rural Electrification in Africa*, ed. Ranganathan, V., AFREPREN in association with Zed Books, London, p. 139.

Ranganathan V., ed., 1992. *Rural Electrification in Africa*, AFREPREN in association with Zed Books, London.

Razanajatovo, M., Juliette, Y. and Jean-Louis, A., 1994. *Renewable Energy Technologies Dissemination in Seychelles*, AFREPREN/FWD, Nairobi, Kenya, pp. 7–8, 10, 13–14, 20.

RERIC News, 1993a. 'Largest Solar Water Heating System in India', *RERIC News,* Vol. 16, No. 4, December, Regional Energy Resources Information Centre, Bangkok, p. 2.

RERIC News, 1993b. 'Solar Bizz in Malawi', *RERIC News,* Vol. 16, No. 1, March, Regional Energy Resources Information Centre, Bangkok, pp. 2, 4–5.

Ribot, J.C., 1993. 'Forestry Policy and Charcoal Production in Senegal', *Energy Policy Special Issue: Urban Energy and Environment in Africa,* Vol. 21, No. 5, eds Hosier, R., Mwandosya, M.I., Luhanga, M.L., May, pp. 561, 563, 578.

Roos, W. and Rojczyk, U., 1984. 'Construction of Simple Kiln Systems', Gate/GTZ, Vieweg, Eschborn, pp. 4–5.

RTE (Rural Technology Enterprises), undated. *Renewable Energy for Sustainable Development,* RTE, Nairobi, pp. 2–3.

Rubindamayugi, M.S.T. and Kivaisi, A.K., 1993. 'Application of Anaerobic Digestion-Biogas Technology in Africa', paper presented at the International Conference on Medium and Large Scale Biogas Plants in Developing Countries, 29 November–4 December, Arusha, Tanzania.

SADC (Southern African Development Community), 1992. *1990 Energy Statistics Year Book,* SADC, Luanda.

Sampa, R.C., 1994. 'Renewable Energy Technologies Dissemination in Zambia', paper prepared for the first Regional RETs Workshop, 31 May–1 June 1994, Naivasha, Kenya, SEI-AFREPREN/FWD, Nairobi, pp. 14-15.

Sampa, R.C. and Sichone, E.C., 1995. *Mini and Micro-Hydro Power In Zambia: A Draft Study Report On Dissemination Of Renewable Energy Technologies,* AFREPREN, Nairobi, executive summary, pp. 7, 9, 12, 15, 18–19, 21–25, 27, 36–39, 45, 49, 54.

Sattar, M.A., 1990. 'Rural Application of Solar Energy – Timber Drying', *Energy and the Environment Into the 1990s,* Volume 2, International Solar Energy Society, Washington, DC, p. 599.

Sawe, E.N., 1990. *Issues In New and Renewable Sources of Energy (NRSE) Activities And Policy Formulation in Tanzania,* Ministry of Water, Energy and Minerals, Dar es Salaam, Tanzania, p. 14.

Schaeffer, L., 1993. 'Large Scale Financing for Renewable Projects', paper prepared for Solar Energy Forum – SOLTECH 93, 28 April, Washington, DC, p. 4.

Scheffler, T.B., undated. *Solar Energy in Southern Africa,* University of Pretoria, Pretoria, p. 4.

Scurlock, J.M.O. and Hall, D.O., 1990. 'The Contribution of Biomass to Global

Energy Use (1987)', *Biomass Journal*, Vol. 21, No. 1., eds Coombs, J., Hall, D.O and Smith, W.H., Elsevier Science Publishers Ltd., Essex.

Scurlock, J.M.O., Hall, D.O. and Bolhar-Nordenkampf, H.R., 1991a. *Photosynthesis and Production in a Changing Environment – A Field and Laboratory Manual*, p. 78.

Scurlock, J.M.O., Rosenschein, A. and Hall, D.O., 1991b. *Fuelling the Future: Power Alcohol in Zimbabwe*, ACTs, Nairobi, p. 16.

Sebbowa, F.B., 1987. 'Solar Energy for Crop Drying in Kenya', *Solar Drying in Africa*, International Development Research Centre, Ottawa, pp. 60–74.

SEI (Stockholm Environment Institute), 1990. *Renewable Energy for Development*, No. 4., SEI, Stockholm, pp. 14–17.

SEI, 1991. *Renewable Energy for Development*, Vol. 4, No. 2, SEI, Stockholm, Sweden, pp. 10–11, 19.

SEI, 1993. *Energy, Environment and Developemt Programme: Quarterly Progress Report*, SEI, Stockholm.

SEI, 1994. *Community Electrification, Improved Customer Service and Demand-side Management – A Note to SIDA*, SEI, Stockholm.

SEIA (Solar Energy Industry Association), 1991. *Solar Industrial Journal*, Second Quarter, Vol. 2, No 2, SEIA, pp. 15, 17, 22.

SEP/GTZ (Special Energy Programme/Deutsche Gesellschaft fur Technische Zusammenarbeit), 1987. *Dissemination of Biogas Plants in the Rural Areas of Kenya*, SEP, GTZ, Nairobi, p. 32.

SEP, 1993. *GTZ SEP News*, Vol. 1, No. 3, July/September, Nairobi, p. 8.

SERI (Solar Energy Research Institute), 1980. *Fuel from Farms*, SERI, Washington, DC.

Shea, C.P., 1988. *Renewable Energy: Today's Contribution, Tomorrow's Promise*, Worldwatch Paper 81, Worldwatch Institute, Washington, DC, p. 33.

Shepperd, W.L. and Richards, E.H., 1993. *Solar Photovoltaic for Development Applications*, Sandia Laboratories, New York.

SHP News, 1994. 'Hangzhou Regional Centre for Small Hydro Power', *SHP News*, No. 2, pp. 6–7, 23; No. 3, pp. 3–4, 13–14, 25, 36.

Siemons, R.V., Ahmed and Hood, H., 1989. 'Cotton Stalk Charcoal Agglomeration in the Sudan', *Boiling Point*, Special Edition, pp. 11–15.

Singh, P., 1991. 'Rural Solar Electric Power – A Case of Kenya', *Energy Sources*, Vol. 13, pp. 67–75.

Smith, K.R., 1989. 'Dialectics of Improved Stoves', *Economic and Political Weekly*, 11 March.

Smith, K.R., 1993. 'Fuel Combustion, Air Pollution Exposure, and Health: The Situation in Developing Countries', *Annual Review of Energy Environment*, Vol. 18.

Smulders, P.T., 1992. 'A New Solution To An Old Problem In Wind Pumping', *RERIC News*, Vol. 15, No. 3, RERIC, Bangkok, p. 2.

Sorensen, Bent, 1995. 'History of, and Recent Progress in, Wind Energy Utilization', *Annual Review, Energy and Environment*, 20, pp. 387–424.

Standard, 1991. 'Stop Power Alcohol Usage', *Standard* newspaper, 23 January, Nairobi, p. 8.

STAP/GEF, 1996. *The Outlook of Renewable Energy Technologies and Roles for the GEF*, executive summary, GEF/UNEP.

STARS World Tables, 1995. *World Bank Data on Diskette: 1995 User's Guide*, International Economics Department, World Bank, Washington, DC.

Stassen, 1986. *Die Regering se rol in die ontwikkeling en implementering van alter-natiewe hernubare energiebronne in Suid-Afrika*, M. Phil. thesis, Rand Afrikaans University, Johannesburg.

Strehler, A., 1990. 'The Modern Combustion of Dry Biomass', *Bioenergy and the Environment*, eds Pasztor, J. and Kristoferson, L.A., Westview Press, San Francisco, pp. 207–8.

Thomsen, N.J., 1994. *Equity and Environment: Wind Energy Technologies The Danish Experience and it's Relevance to Africa*, Riso National Laboratory, May, pp. 11, 14, 17, 24, 28.

Thondhala, B., 1994. 'Zimbabwe Taps Energy From the Sun', *Choices*, Vol. 3, No. 1, UNDP, New York, pp. 8–10.

Tillman, D.O., 1987. 'Biomass Combustion', *Biomass: Regenerable Energy*, eds Hall, D.O. and Overend, R.P., John Wiley & Sons, Chichester, pp. 203–7.

Tinker, I., 1993. 'Women and Community Forestry in Nepal: Expectations and Realities', *Society and Natural Resources*, Vol. 17, pp. 368, 373.

Traore, S.A., 1984. 'Report of Burkina Faso to Conference', *Proceedings of International Conference on Biogas Technology, Transfer and Diffusion*, 17–24 November, Cairo, p. 605.

Turyahikayo, G., 1994. 'Renewable Energy Technologies in Uganda', paper presented during the first Regional AFREPREN Workshop On Renewable Energy Technology Dissemination, Naivasha, Kenya, 30 May–1 June, AFREPREN, Nairobi, pp. 1, 13–15, 19, 24, 26.

Turyahikayo, G.R., Hatanga, E.S., Otiti, T. and Kebirungi, P., 1995. *Renewable Energy Technologies Dissemination: Case Study on Uganda*, AFREPREN, Uganda, March, executive summary, pp. 8, 15, 17, 19, 23–30, 38–9, 43.

Turyareeba, P., 1990. 'The Performance of Four Woodburning Cookstoves and The Relationship Between Wood Properties and the Performance of Two Woodburning Cookstoves', M. Phil. thesis, Aberdeen University, pp. 20–1, 27, 40, 49, 50, 92.

Turyareeba, P.J., 1991a. *Ethiopia Visit Report*, KENGO Regional Wood Energy Programme for Africa, December.

Turyareeba, P.J., 1991b. 'Improved Charcoal Production in Uganda, A Case Study', paper presented at the Regional Training Course on Biomass Energy held in Nairobi and Nakuru, Kenya, June.

Turyareeba, P.J., 1992. 'Uganda Institutional Stoves', *Boiling Point*, No. 29, ITDG/GTZ, December.

Turyareeba, P.J., 1993a. *Stoves and Household Energy Programme of the Development Through Conservation Project Area*, Kabale, field visit report, CARE (Uganda).

Turyareeba, P., 1993b. 'Mobilizing Local Financial Resources – The Case of Uganda', *Energy Options for Africa – Environmentally Sustainable Alternatives*, eds Karekezi, S. and Mackenzie, G.A., ZED Books, London, p. 9.

UNDP (United Nations Development Programme), 1994. *Human Development Report*. Oxford University Press, Oxford.

UNDP/World Bank, 1982. *Rwanda: Issues and Options in the Energy Sector*, Washington, DC.

UNDP/World Bank, 1986. *Agricultural Residues Briquetting Pilot Projects for Substitute Household and Industrial Fuels – Ethiopia*, World Bank, Washington, DC.

UNDP/World Bank, 1991. *Rwanda: Commercialization of Improved Charcoal*

Stoves and Carbonization Techniques, ESMAP mid-term progress report No. 141/91.

UNESCO/VITA (UN Educational, Social and Cultural Organization/ Volunteers In Technical Assistance), undated. *Extending Renewable Energy Technologies in the Developing World*, VITA, Virginia, USA, pp. 8, 10.

UNIDO (UN Industrial Development Organization), 1994. *Biomass Energy for Industrial Development in Africa: Preparatory Assistance*, UNIDO Project Document No. US/REF/94/080.

US Department of Energy, 1987. *Presentations of the Photovoltaics: Investing in Development Conference*, US Department of Energy, New Orleans.

Van Horen, C., 1994. *Financing and Economic Implications of Household Energy Policies*, Energy for Development Research Centre/University of Cape Town, Cape Town.

Van der Plas, R. 1994. 'Solar Energy Answer to Rural Power in Africa', *FDP Note*, No. 6, April, World Bank, Washington, DC, pp. 1 and 3.

Van Lierop, W. D., 1982. *Wind Energy Development in Kenya*, Steering Committee, Wind Energy Developing Countries, Netherlands, p. 14.

Wade, H.A., 1991. *Photovoltaic Rural Electrification Projects in the Pacific Region and Lessons Learned*, South Pacific Institute for Renewable Energy, Tahiti, p. 1.

Wade, H.A., undated. *Rural Power Utilities and the Role of Photovoltaics*, South Pacific Institute for Renewable Energy, Mahina, p. 41.

Wade, H.A., undated. *The Socio-Economic Benefit of PV Applications in the Pacific*, United Nations Pacific Energy Development Programme, Suva, p. VII-13.

Walubengo, D., 1986. 'Institutional Stoves in Kenya: The Present and Future', *Boiling Point*, No. 10, August, pp. 4–13.

Walubengo, J., 1988. *Wood Energy in Kenya Institutions*, KENGO, Nairobi.

Walubengo, D., 1990a. 'Improved Stoves Programmes in East and Southern Africa', *Report of the Proceedings of the International Biomass Course*, KENGO, Nairobi, Kenya, June, pp. 13–14.

Walubengo, D., 1990b. 'Briquetting of Biomass Waste', *Report of the Proceedings of the International Biomass Course*, KENGO, Nairobi, Kenya, June, pp. 26, 28.

Walubengo, D., 1991. 'Charcoal Creeps into Zimbabwe', *RWEPA News*, No. 5 KENGO, Nairobi, Kenya, January, pp. 1–3.

Walubengo, D. and Joseph, S., 1988. *Wood Energy in Kenyan Institutions*, KENGO, Nairobi.

Walubengo, D. and Kimani, M.J., 1991. 'Technical Issues: Dissemination of RETs in Africa', *Regional Training Course on Biomass Energy Development: Management of Community Biomass Energy Programmes 1991 Course Proceedings*, KENGO/RWEPA, Nairobi, Kenya, pp. 2–3.

Walubengo, D. and Kimani, M.J., 1993. 'The Successful Dissemination Of Renewable Energy Technologies In Sub-Sahara Africa', *Renewable Energy Technologies In Sub-Saharan Africa*, eds Muiruri, J.K. and Naumann, E., KENGO, Nairobi, pp. 55, 59–60.

Ward, R.F., 1982. 'Digesters in the Third World', *Anaerobic Digestion*, eds Hughes, D.E. *et al.*, Elsevier, Amsterdam.

Ward, M., Ashworth, J.H. and Burrill, G., 1984. *Renewable Energy Technologies in Africa: An Assessment of Field Experience and Future Directions*, Bureau for Africa/Agency for International Development, Washington, DC, p. B-3.

Wardi, H., 1992. 'Sudan National Energy Research Council and Renewable Energy Technologies', *Energy For Rural Development*, eds Bhagavan. M.R. and Karekezi, S, AFREPREN in association with Zed Books, London, p. 120.

Wauthelet, M., Rolot, D., Naveau, H.P., Nyns, E.J., Nditabiriye, D., Ndayizeye, A., Ndayishimiye, J., Harimenshi, R. and Mbesherubusa, D., 1989. 'État de Techniques de Biomethemisation en Burundi – Le Projet Belgo-Burundais', *MIRCEN Journal*, pp. 5, 283–95.

WEC (World Energy Council), 1992. *Energy for Tomorrow's World – the Realities, the Real Options, and the Agenda for Achievement*, Draft Summary-Global Report, 15th WEC Congress, September 1992, Madrid, Spain.

WEC (World Energy Council), 1992. *World Energy Council Journal*, WEC, London.

Wenmann, C., 1985. 'The Production and Use of Fuel Ethanol in Zimbabwe', *Energy from Biomass*, eds Coombs, J., Hall, D.O., Elsevier Applied Science Publishers, London.

Wereko-Brobby, C., 1993. 'Innovative Energy Policy Investments and Institutional Reform – The Case of Ghana', *Energy Options for Africa*, eds Karekezi, S. and Mackenzie, G.A., Zed Books, London.

Wickramagamage, P., 1991. *Improved Biomass Cookstove Programmes: A Global Evaluation*, Country Studies, No. 5, EPI-EWC, ESMAP/WB and UNDP.

Wickramagamage, P., 1992. 'Improved Cookstove Programmes in East and Central Africa', *Boiling Point*, No. 29, December 1992, Intermediate Technology Development Group, Rugby.

Williams, R.H. and Larson, E.D., 1993. 'Advanced Gasification Based Biomass Power in Generation', *Renewable Energy: Sources for Fuels and Electricity*, eds Johansonn, T.B., Kelly, H., Reddy, A.K.N., Williams, R.H. and Burnham, L., Island Press, Washington, DC, p. 736.

Williams R.H. and Terzian, G, 1993. *A Benefit/Cost Analysis of Accelerated Development of Photovoltaic Technology*. *Centre for Energy and Environmental Studies*, Princeton University.

Williams, R.H., Karekezi, S., Parikh, Jyoti and Watanabe Chihiro, 1996. *The Outlook of Renewable Energy Technologies*, STAP/GEF Report.

Wood, J. and Hall, D.O, 1993. *Biofuels as a Sustainable Substitute for Fossil Fuels: Their Potential for CO_2 Emissions Reduction*, FAO, p. 29.

World Bank, 1980. *A Survey of the Future Role of Hydro-electric Power in 100 Developing Countries*, Energy Department Paper No. 17, Washington, DC.

World Bank, 1986. *Agricultural Residue Briquetting Pilot Projects for Substitute Household and Industrial Fuels – Ethiopia, Vol. 1: Technical Report*, UNDP/World Bank/ESMAP, report No. 062A/86, Washington, DC.

World Bank, 1989. *Sub-Saharan Africa: From Crisis to Sustainable Growth – A Long Term Perspective Study*, World Bank, Washington, DC.

World Bank, 1991. *The African Capacity Building Initiative: Toward Improved Policy Analysis and Development Management*, Washington, DC.

World Bank, 1992. *Database, 1991/92*, Washington, DC..

World Bank, 1993. *Database, 1992/93*, Washington, DC.

World Bank, 1994. *World Development Report 1994: Infrastructure for Development*, World Bank, Washington, DC.

World Bank, 1995. 'Energy Issues', *FPD Energy Note*, No. 1, World Bank Energy Practice Management Office, Washington, DC.

World Bank 1996. *Ethiopia: Energy Assessment. Report No. 179/96*. Report of the Joint United Nations Development Programme/World Bank Energy Sector Assessment Programme, Washington, DC.

World Bank/ESMAP (Energy Sector Management Assistance Programme), 1990. *Zambia Household Energy Strategy Report*, Washington, DC.

World Resources Institute (WRI), 1994. *World Resources 1994-95: A Guide to Global Environment,* Oxford University Press, New York, p. 178.

Young, P., 1987. *Sawdust Briquettes and Stoves,* ITDG, November, pp. 5–9.

Zandbergen, P. and Moreira, J.R., 1993. 'Biogas in Brazil', paper prepared for the International Conference on Medium and Large Scale Biogas Plants in Developing Countries, 29 November–4 December, Arusha, Tanzania, p. 1.

Appendices

Appendix 1 Diagrams of solar thermal technologies

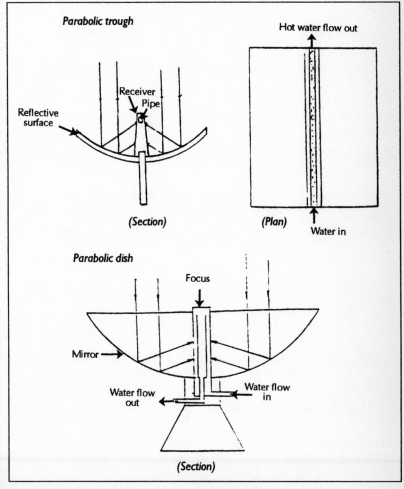

Parabolic trough

Receiver Pipe

Reflective surface

(Section)

Hot water flow out

(Plan)

Water in

Parabolic dish

Focus

Mirror

Water flow out

Water flow in

(Section)

Source: *Adapted from de Laquil et al, 1993.*

Appendix 2 Groups of impulse and reaction turbines

Turbine Type	Head		
	High	Medium	Low
Impulse	Pelton Turgo Multi-jet pelton	Crossflow Turgo Multi-jet pelton	Crossflow
Reaction		Francis	Propeller Kaplan

Source: Fraenkel *et al*, 1991.

Appendix 3 Examples of renewable energy research and development institutions in Eastern and Southern Africa

Country	Institution	Research field
Botswana	Botswana Technology Centre	Solar
	EECG Consultants	Delivery systems and environmental impacts
Burundi	Centre for Alternative Energies Studies	Alternative energy sources
	University Research Centre for the Utilization of Alternative Energies	New renewable energy
Ethiopia	Ethiopian Energy Studies and Research Centre	Biogas, solar, mini hydro, briquetting and industrial energy conservation
	Addis Ababa University	Photovoltaic systems
Kenya	Foundation for Woodstove Dissemination/Africa Energy Policy Research Network	Energy policy
	Appropriate Technology Centre, Kenyatta University	Biogas digesters, briquetting, wind generators, solar water heaters, crop dryers and cookers, hydro rams
Malawi	Ministry of Energy and Mining	Renewable energy systems
	Energy Studies Unit	Wood- and charcoal-based energy-efficient devices
Mozambique	Agro-alfa	Windmills
	Eduardo Mondlane University, Engineering Faculty	Biomass

Appendix 3 cont.

Country	Institution	Research field
Seychelles	Environment Resources Oceans	Environment, including energy sector, transport and climate change
	Technological Support Services Division	RETs
South Africa	Energy for Development Research Centre	Photovoltaics, Remote Area Power Supply (RAPS), Biomass
	ESKOM	Stand-alone RETs
	University of Pretoria, Physics Department	Solar box cookers, solar water heaters, solar desalination and solar thermal electric
Sudan	Energy Research Council	Photovoltaic systems, solar thermal, wind and biomass, solar stills
Tanzania	University of Dar es Salaam	Solar thermal materials, photovoltaic systems
	Itili Women's Training Centre	Improved stoves
	Tanzania Traditional Energy Development Organization	Potential RETs for local applications
Uganda	Institute of Environmental Protection and Natural Resources, Makerere University	Energy requirements and sources, both renewable and non-renewable
	Makerere University, Physics Department	Solar energy and improved stoves
	Senior Women's Advisory Group	Biogas
Zambia	University of Zambia, Department of Physics	Solar
Zimbabwe	Institute of Agricultural Engineering	Agricultural engineering
	Environment Development Activities – Zimbabwe	Wood biomass use patterns
	University of Zimbabwe	Photovoltaic systems (solar water heaters are manufactured locally)
	Faculty of Agriculture and Natural Resources, African University	Natural resources

Source: SEI/AFREPREN Directory, 1995; Othieno, 1994; Mosimanyane et al., 1995; Katihabwa, 1994.

Appendix 4
Major development funding sources for renewable energy projects

THE WORLD BANK AND RELATED MULTILATERAL DEVELOPMENT BANKS:

World Bank
Energy Development Division
1818 H Street, N.W., Washington D.C. 20433, USA
Phone 202-473-3266/477-1234 Fax: 202-477-6391
The United Nations created the World Bank by founding the International Bank for Reconstruction and Development (IBRD) in 1945; this was joined by another special UN agency, the International Development Association (IDA) in the mid-1950s. The World Bank works closely with the UN Development Programme to finance infrastructure projects in developing countries, and has spawned a number of related programmes/projects.

United Nations Development Program (UNDP)
1 United Nations Plaza,
New York, NY 10017, USA
Phone 212-906-5000 Fax 212-906-5364
UNDP provides financial and technical support to projects in energy, agriculture, education and other development-related areas, and helped establish the Global Environmental Facility.

Global Environmental Facility (GEF)
(see the World Bank)
The GEF was established by the World Bank in 1990 to support energy efficiency and new and renewable energy activities that developing countries would otherwise have too little incentive to undertake. It is a cooperative venture between the World Bank, the United Nations Development Program (UNDP), the United Nations Environmental Program (UNEP), and national governments.

Energy Sector Management Assistance Program (ESMAP)
(see the World Bank)
Established in 1983 as a joint programme of the World Bank and the UNDP. Provides technical assistance on a range of energy issues to recipients of World Bank loans.

Financing Renewable Energy for Small-Scale Energy Users (FINESSE)
(see the World Bank)
The FINESSE project was created by the World Bank's Energy Sector Management Assistance Program (ESMAP) to provide workable approaches to address the financing and infrastructural problems that hinder the spread of the renewable technologies.

International Fund for Agricultural Development (IFAD)
107 Via del Serafico
00142 Rome, Italy
Phone 39-6-545-91 Fax 39-6-504-34-63
Since 1974, IFAD (a specialized agency of the United Nations) has made low-interest loans available directly to poor, small-scale farmers, and to small- and medium-scale agricultural development projects. IFAD goals include promotion of food-based rather than export-driven agriculture, and to improve living conditions in rural areas.

International Finance Corporation (IFC)
(see the World Bank)
A World Bank private sector affiliate.

Inter-American Development Bank (IDB)
1300 New York Avenue,
N.W. Energy Division, Washington, D.C. 20577, USA
Phone 202-623-1963 Fax: 202-623-3096
A regional branch of the World Bank.

African Development Bank
01 B.P. No. 1387
Abidjan 01, Ivory Coast
Phone 225-32-07-11
A regional branch of the World Bank.

BILATERAL ASSISTANCE AGENCIES & PROGRAMMES:

United States Agency for International Development (USAID)
Office Energy Washington, D.C. 20523, USA
Phone 703-875-4203 Fax 703-875-4053

United States Committee on Renewable Energy (CORECT)
1000 Independence Avenue S.W.,
Washington, D.C. 20585, USA
Phone 202-586-8302   Fax 202-586-1605

United States Export Bank
811 Vermont Avenue N.W.,
Washington, D.C. 20571, USA
Phone 202-566-8802
A US government agency that facilitates the export financing of US goods and services.

International Fund for Renewable Energy and Energy Efficiency (IFREE)
Suite 805, 777 North Capitol Street,
NE Washington, D.C. 20002, USA
Phone 202-408-7916   Fax 202-371-5115
IFREE fosters environmentally sound energy projects in developing countries. IFREE was
established in 1992 by the US Expert Council for Renewable Energy, in cooperation with the
USAID, US Department of Energy, US Environmental Protection Agency and the Rockefeller
Foundation.

Canadian International Development Agency (CIDA)
Energy Sector
200 Promenade du Portage
Hull, Quebec, Canada K1A 0G4
Phone 819-997-1492   Fax 819-997-1491

German Agency for Technical Cooperation (Deutsche Gesellschaft fur Technische
Zusammenarbeit – GTZ)
Postfach 5180
D-6236 Eschborn I Germany
Phone 49-6196-790   Fax 49-6196-791115

Japan International Cooperation Agency (JICA)
Shinjuku Mitsui Bldg, 2-1-1, Nishi-shinjuku
Shinjuku-ku, Japan
Phone 03-3346-5311-5314

A government-sponsored agency which implements a wide range of programmes which
contribute to the economic and social progress of the development world. JICA specializes in
technical training, consultation and supplying equipment for technical cooperation internationally.

Swedish International Development Agency (SIDA)
S-10525 Stockholm,
Sweden
Phone 46-8-728-5100   Fax 46-8-673-2141

Renewable Energy For Africa Development (REFAD)
122 C St., N.W., 4th Floor
Washington, D.C. 20001
Phone 202-383-2550 Fax 202-383-2555
United States of America
Source: Shepperd and Richards,1993.

Appendix 5
Incentives for RET dissemination and promotion in the region

The following table is a compilation of incentives granted to RET promotion, based
mainly on the existing national policies and programmes. These include subsidies, long-
term policy-oriented programmes, development of requisite institutional infrastructure, financing schemes, research and development, resource assessment studies
and training programmes.

On the basis of the compilation, an attempt is made to rank selected countries in the
region. Those countries, such as Botswana, Kenya and Zimbabwe, that have provided
maximum support to RETs and created a conducive environment for their exploitation and development have been awarded higher points.

This ranking is inconclusive, however, since it is based on the limited data and
information at our disposal. Some gaps that can be filled appear evidently in the table.
For instance, South Africa has more incentives than the ones presented. Nevertheless
the table represents an important landmark and threshold in quantifying the
experiences, promotion status and challenges facing RETs in most of the countries in
the region.

Country	Period and % included in energy plan	Institutional incentives	Financial incentives	Organization, management and maintenance	Human resource development and retention	Rank
BOTSWANA	1991–7	Government undertaking research and projects that mainly deal with renewables	45% duty on PV equipment removed by government in June 1986	Code of practice for domestic solar water heating systems	Technician course on PV theory instruction and maintenance by BTC and Botswana Polytechnic	114
		Renewables in the National Development plan VI I ((1991-7)	VAT and duty exemption on all PV imported by donors	One year guarantee on all RIIC windpumps. It covers materials and workmanship		
		Resource assessment studies by the University of Botswana Meteorology Department	1.3 million set aside for renewables in the National development plan VII	Group of consultants studied the potential of windpumps under a government scheme		
			Grant schemes for the purchase of windpumps. 71.5% of windpumps acquired through these.			
BURUNDI	1990–2000. SHP included in 5 year plans	Resource assessment studies by UNDP and GTZ for SHP development	US$1.9 million investment for SHP development by the Department of Water and Rural Electrification	Maintenance of SHP plants as part of Government policy		110
			US$40, 000 is yearly allocated to NRSE R&D by government. Funds are also provided by EEC.			

Country	Period and % included in energy plan	Institutional incentives	Financial incentives	Organization, management and maintenance	Human resource development and retention	Rank
BURUNDI cont.			Biogas digesters are built at government's expense and the cost is recovered from the beneficiary (with subsidies) on instalment. Funds are provided by GTZ.			
DJIBOUTI			A project funded by government and GEF (through UNDP) on production and commercialization of mechanical windpumps slotted for February 1996.			101
ETHIOPIA	94%, 1990–2000	Collection of relevant radiation data to enable planning of solar energy development	Under the UNDP/Ethiopia Development Programme, 12 hydro sites were studied at a cost of US$1,313,500 for the foreign currency component and US$1,492,570 tor the local component			103
KENYA	1994 –9	A gasohol zone was created where no pure gasoline was to be sold, thus facilitating market for gasohol	Donor and technical assistance for the Maendeleo stove project by GTZ	Adoption of a semi-commercial approach in the Maendeleo stove project whereby the commercial production centres produced the		112

Country	Period and % included in energy plan	Institutional incentives	Financial incentives	Organization, management and maintenance	Human resource development and retention	Rank
KENYA cont.				liners while various organizations with extension programme at grassroots level disseminated them. Close collaboration between donors government, universities, NGOs and other interested parties in the KCJ project.		
		Policy on SHP development was under discussion in 1983	The KREDP was supported by a US$4.8 million grant plus US$17 million provided by the government	Set of standards by the Kenya Bureau of Standards tor solar batteries	Training of Maendeo stove producers in the manufacture, business management and marketing of the stove	
		National masterplan covering all activities in hydro power	Removal of 45% duty on PV equipment by the government in 1986.	Kenya Energy Laboratory tests energy systems	Inclusion of solar energy in the national educational syllabus in the late 1980s	
		Improved stove R&D through funding by USAID under the Ministry of Energy	Exemption of VAT and duty for all PVs imported by donors	After sales service provided by the two producers of windpumps, Bob Harnies Engineering Ltd (BHEL) & Pwani Fabricators	Training of windpump end users by BHEL at no cost save for accommodation expenses	

Country	Period and % included in energy plan	Institutional incentives	Financial incentives	Organization, management and maintenance	Human resource development and retention	Rank
KENYA cont.		Installation of a hybrid wind generator system by the Ministry of Energy and KPLC in collaboration with the Belgian Development Cooperation (550kw).	17% sales tax exemption for Kijito windpump fabricators for all windpumps sold to projects and NGOs.	One year guarantee on all windpumps sold in the country	Ministry of Energy's Special Energy Programme launched training courses for biogas plant builders with instructions provided by GTZ.	
LESOTHO	80%, 2010 At least 5 main programmes implemented since 1978.	A 1981 study by a French company that identified 9 sites for SHP devdopment	Funding of two SHP plants by the Norwegian government		Training of LEC staff on SHP	
	Appropriate Technology Section established in 1978.	Annual total budget of the Division of Renewable energy is US$51,000		Renewable Energy for African Devdopment (REFAD) training programme in USA. Government sends people to be trained there.		
		Government's Village Water Supply (VWS) has installed about 43 water-pumping windmills	SADC to establish a revolving fund for PV rural electrification project		More than 40 technicians and science graduates trained under UNESCO/ FAO biogas projects	
MADAGASCAR	Provision of 83.5%, 2010	Government hydrological data by the National Meteorology Agency and the electric utility for the evaluation of SHP potential.	provided a US$407, 000 investment for a SHP project.			104

Country	Period and % included in energy plan	Institutional incentives	Financial incentives	Organization, management and maintenance	Human resource development and retention	Rank
MADAGASCAR cont		National energy policy recognizes SHP as an option for power generation.				
MALAWI	95%, 1988–97	Construction of a biogas digester in 1994 by ETHCO capable of producing 60 cubic metres of gas per day. An ethanol gasoline blend of 15:85 in 1963. Biogas demonstration units are being established by the Ministry of Women and Children's Affairs and Community Services in training institutions		ETHCO in collaboration with polytechnic Chancellor University and Halls garage involved in R&D on optional funding and development ot 100% ethanol engines and stoves.	Department of Energy has been carrying out several NRSE workshops	105
MAURITIUS	40%, 1992–4	The St Antoine sugar factory (plus other sugar factories) was allowed to sell excess electricity to the grid by the Central Electricity Board.	The Mauritius Research Council provided financial assistance for co-generation	Information and literature on co-generation was provided by the on-line computer centre at the University of Mauritius.		109

Country	Period and % included in energy plan	Institutional incentives	Financial incentives	Organization, management and maintenance	Human resource development and retention	Rank
SEYCHELLES	1990-4	The Ministry of Community Development has incorporated solar water heaters in housing schemes.	Exemption from tax on imported solar water heaters.	Solar companies offer after-sales service for systems installed.	TSSD with the assistance of two French experts organized a regional training programme on biomass gasification principles and operation of gasifiers on one island.	108
SOMALIA		Faculty of Engineering planning to undertake theoretical and experimental studies in solar energy.				
SUDAN	1%, 1992–2003	USAID study on the SHP potential The Sudanese Islamic Bank has expressed interest in future participation in new briquette production plants. In March 1988, the Rahad Corporation, in collaboration with Tenant Union, decided to establish a company to develop cotton stalk carbonization and briquetting into a commercial enterprise.		The Energy Research Council and Biomass Technology Group provide technical, management, and marketing assistance for briquette production		105

Country	Period and % included in energy plan	Institutional incentives	Financial incentives	Organization, management and maintenance	Human resource development and retention	Rank
SWAZILAND	45%, 1994-7			Village Technology Unit Centre demonstrations for solar devices.		103
TANZANIA	90%	Study by TANESCO on SHP plants	Government financial support for development of biogas production.	Biogas demonstration units.	Personnel are being trained in subjects related to biogas at the Applied Microbiology Unit at the University of Dar es Salaam.	108
		The government established CAMARTEC to implement a large-scale national biogas project.	Government partly funded and supported gasification projects to help sawmills meet the high investment costs.			
		The ministry allowed TAKAGAS biogas plant to sell electricity to the grid through TANESCO at market prices.	Government hoping for funding from the UN's Technical Cooperation Development Unit for methane gas project.			
		The use and development of biogas technology has been emphasized in the country's energy policy.				
		Research, development and field testing of a number of solar devices.				

Country	Period and % included in energy plan	Institutional incentives	Financial incentives	Organization, management and maintenance	Human resource development and retention	Rank
UGANDA		UEB is involved in development of SHP schemes of capacity 500KW and above.	Donor-funded scheme by, e.g. the World Harvest Mission	Technical assistance for SHP plants in church missions.	JEEP, IUCN and YWCA are carrying out awareness programmes to teach end-users how to produce their own stoves.	106
		Liberation of the power sub-sector will SHP development for sale of power to the grid.	Government policy on tax imported RETs components, devices and systems.	Rehabilitation of SHP plants in disuse as part of Rehabilitation Programme by the Ministry of Energy e.g. Kikagati SHP scheme.		
		Government has implemented two donor-supported biogas projects.	A loan of £59,000 in aid of a biogas pilot project was provided by China under an agreement for economic and technical cooperation.			
		A National Biomass Study (NBS) has been concluded				
		The Department of NRSE is encouraging local artisans to make burners fitted with biogas units The department plans to buy all the burners that are produced.	The World Bank provided a loan of US$103 million for a Department of NRSE project.			

Country	Period and % included in energy plan	Institutional incentives	Financial incentives	Organization, management and maintenance	Human resource development and retention	Rank
UGANDA cont		The Department of Environment Protection is involved in the dissemination of improved stoves for rural households.	Government increased taxes on petroleum imports to discourage their wasteful use. This has led to their substitution by other sources of energy, e.g. biomass, as a source of heat energy in industries.			
ZAMBIA	Third National Development Plan (1979–83) outlined policy proposals to develop alternative forms of energy	Standards and codes of practice for SHP systems.	Government intends to offer additional fiscal incentives such as guarantees to banks willing to lend to NRSE projects.	NCSR has demonstrated use of biogas in their pilot project. It made a local adaptation of designs of floating dome digester, gas stoves and lanterns.	In the Zambia charcoal project, artisans were trained in the making of improved stoves. Women's groups were also trained on how to use improved stoves properly.	110
		Feasibility study of the German government on hydro sites.	The Department of Energy had an initial budget allocation of K40 million to install photovoltaics.	Department of Energy has prepared a manual on charcoal production		
		The Department of Energy through the improved charcoal stove project has been disseminating the improved cookstove.	In 1984 government provided a fiscal incentive on photosensitive devices by issuing Statutory Instrument No 114 that led to removal of duty and sales tax on such systems.			

Country	Period and % included in energy plan	Institutional incentives	Financial incentives	Organization, management and maintenance	Human resource development and retention	Rank
ZAMBIA cont.		Government created NEC to carry out R&D programmes on RETs in 1980 and DOE in 1983.				
ZIMBABWE		It is mandatory for all the gasoline used in the country to be blended with ethanol	GEF is funding a solar electric systems' project with the aim of installing 9,000 units in rural households.	Solar PV system awareness promotion campaign	Government has incorporated renewable energy as part of the education curricula from primary school upwards.	III
		There is a policy on NRSE	Government grants donor funds under bilateral/multilateral agreement for NRSE. Soft loans for end users who are envisaged under the GEF and local financial institutions.	Establishment of solar systems manufacturers		
		Establishment of codes of practice and conduct for PV manufacturers to install and provide guarantees	PV and biogas technologies are subsidised by Government. Plan to reduce/remove taxes, duties and levies on other NRSE components especially on imported ones. RAD section under the Department of Energy budget is allocated funds for NRSE promotion.			

Country	Period and % included in energy plan	Institutional incentives	Financial incentives	Organization, management and maintenance	Human resource development and retention	Rank
SOUTH AFRICA		Opened a factory sponsored by the US government in Johannesburg to begin producing PV panels to electrify 10,000 rural schools, clinics etc., per year under a restructuring programme. ESKOM has a PV rural electrification programme.	The Foundation for Research Development provided financial aid for research into energy from landfill gas and sewage.			105

Notes on the ranking procedure

The ranking of the countries in all the tables is obviously subjective. The maximum number of points each country can score is 120. Each column in the appendix represents 4 points, while each incentive in the previous ranking tables is awarded 2 points. Those countries which have included RETs in their energy plans for a given period of time automatically get 2 points. Those countries in which RETs have a higher percentage in their energy plans and more programmes get higher points. Countries that have policies supporting a cross-section of technologies rather than just one technology get higher points. It is worth noting, however, that in this case potential is taken as the yardstick. Some of the incentives (for example, policy exemptions, liberalized power sector and resource assessment) which are considered crucial in implementing RET programmes in the region are also awarded higher points. For instance, the policy of the Zimbabwean government, which makes it mandatory for all gasoline used in the country to be blended with ethanol, or the selling of power to the national grid by the sugar industries in Mauritius, are awarded 3 points rather than 2.

The sum total of all the points awarded gives the rank of the country. Since none of the countries are operating in a policy vacuum and there are at least resources set aside and formulated policies (no matter how weak), each country gets a grace of 100 points above the total. For instance, the total for Botswana is 14 points but the ranking is 114.

Index

Yamba, Professor 55
Young Women's Christian
  Association (YWCA) 73, 199

Zaire 11, 196
Zambezi river 9, 124
Zambia 11-13, 22-3, 34, 38, 50, 55, 80,
  82, 85, 90, 97, 101, 126, 128, 136,
  139-40, 149, 156, 158, 161, 164-6,
  169-70, 176, 178, 180, 182, 187,
  189, 196, 199, 203-4, 206
Zambian Electricity Supply
  Commission (ZESCO) 129, 140

Zambian Environment Education
  Programme (ZEEP) 180
Zimbabwe 4, 9, 11-12, 16, 22-3, 25,
  27-9, 31, 34, 38, 41, 45, 61-2, 70-
  1, 73, 80, 82, 89-90, 101, 130, 141,
  148, 164, 166-7, 168, 170, 178,
  183, 185, 187, 190, 196, 199, 202-
  3, 209
Zimbabwe Electricity Supply
  Authority (ZESA) 216